NLS 15.95

O9-ABI-975

THE MONSTERS AND THE CRITICS
AND OTHER ESSAYS

J. R. R. TOLKIEN

THE MONSTERS AND THE CRITICS
and Other Essays

Edited by Christopher Tolkien

GLEN COVE PUBLIC LIBRARY
GLEN COVE AVENUE
GLEN COVE, NEW YORK 11542

Houghton Mifflin Company
Boston
1984

C.1

Copyright © 1983 by Frank Richard Williamson and Christopher Reuel Tolkien
as Executors of the Estate of J. R. R. Tolkien

All rights reserved. No part of this work may be reproduced
or transmitted in any form or by any means, electronic or
mechanical, including photocopying and recording, or by
any information storage or retrieval system, except as
may be expressly permitted by the 1976 Copyright Act or in
writing from the publisher. Requests for permission should be
addressed in writing to Houghton Mifflin Company,
2 Park Street, Boston, Massachusetts 02108.

Library of Congress Cataloging in Publication Data

Tolkien, J. R. R. (John Ronald Reuel), 1892-1973.
The monsters and the critics, and other essays.

Includes bibliographical references.
1. English philology—Addresses, essays, lectures.
2. Beowulf—Addresses, essays, lectures. I. Tolkien,
Christopher. II. Title.

| PE27.T65 | 1984 | 410 | 83-18400 |

ISBN 0-395-35635-0

Printed in the United States of America

Q   10   9   8   7   6   5   4   3   2   1

CONTENTS

THE MONSTERS AND THE CRITICS
AND OTHER ESSAYS

FOREWORD

With one exception, all the 'essays' by J. R. R. Tolkien collected together in this book were in fact lectures, delivered on special occasions; and while all were on specific topics, literary or linguistic, the whole audience on those occasions could in no case (save perhaps that of the *Valedictory Address*) be presumed to have more than a general knowledge of or interest in the subject* – and the one piece in this collection that was not a lecture, *On Translating Beowulf*, was not addressed to experts in the study of the poem. It is this common quality that is the basis of this book (other published writings of my father's deriving from his studies in early English were articles, not lectures, and were written with a specialized readership in mind); but indeed I think it will be found that all seven papers, though covering a period of nearly thirty years, and on quite different subjects, nonetheless constitute a unity.

In addition to the five pieces that have been previously published I have ventured to include two that have not, though both were publicly delivered. One of these, *Sir Gawain and the Green Knight*, was my father's principal pronouncement on the poem to which he devoted so much thought and study. The other, *A Secret Vice*, is unique, in that only on this one occasion, as it seems, did the 'invented world' appear publicly and in its own right in the 'academic world' – and that was some six years before the publication of *The Hobbit* and nearly a quarter of a century before that of *The Lord of the Rings*. It is of great interest in the history of the invented languages, and this seems a good opportunity and a suitable context for its publication: for it touches on themes developed in later essays in this book.

The first piece in this collection, *Beowulf: The Monsters and the Critics*, was the Sir Israel Gollancz Memorial Lecture to the British Academy, read on 25 November 1936, and was published

---

* *English and Welsh* has passages of a technical nature; it was addressed to those of 'philological learning' (p. 186).

in volume XXII of the *Proceedings* of the Academy (from which copies of the lecture are available). I acknowledge with thanks the permission of the British Academy, owners of the copyright, to reprint it here; and also permission to use the title of the lecture in the title of this book.

On Translating Beowulf was contributed, as 'Prefatory Remarks on Prose Translation of "Beowulf" ', to a new edition (1940) by Professor C. L. Wrenn of *Beowulf and the Finnesburg Fragment, A Translation into Modern English Prose*, by John R. Clark Hall (1911).

Sir Gawain and the Green Knight was the W. P. Ker Memorial Lecture in the University of Glasgow, delivered on 15 April 1953. Of this there seems to exist now only one text, a typescript made after the delivery of the lecture (which possibly suggests an intention to publish it), as appears from the statement (p. 84) 'Here the temptation-scenes were read aloud in translation.' My father's translation of *Sir Gawain* into alliterative verse in modern English had then been very recently completed. This translation was broadcast in dramatized form by the BBC in December 1953 (repeated in the following year), and the introduction to the poem which I included in the volume of translations (*Sir Gawain and the Green Knight, Pearl, and Sir Orfeo*, 1975) was taken from the radio talk which followed the broadcasts: this, though very brief, is closely related to the lecture printed here.

There are some minor matters concerning its presentation which must be mentioned. Despite my father's statement (p. 74) that 'where quotation is essential I will use a translation which I have just completed', he did not in fact do so throughout, several substantial quotations being given in the original. There does not seem to be any significance in this, however, and I have therefore substituted the translation in such cases. Moreover the translation at that time differed in many details of wording from the revised form published in 1975; and in all such differences I have substituted the latter. I have not inserted the 'temptation scenes' at the point where my father recited them when delivering the lecture, because if these are given in full they run to some 350 lines, and there is no indication in the text of how he reduced them. And lastly, since some readers may wish to refer to the translation rather than to the original poem (edited by J. R. R. Tolkien and

E. V. Gordon, second edition revised by N. Davis, Oxford 1967), but the former gives only stanza-numbers and the latter only line-numbers, I have given both: thus 40.970 means that line 970 is found in the 40th stanza.

The fourth essay, *On Fairy-Stories*, was originally an Andrew Lang lecture given at the University of St Andrews on 8 March 1939.* It was first published in the memorial volume *Essays Presented to Charles Williams* (Oxford 1947), and reissued (first in 1964) together with the story *Leaf by Niggle* under the title *Tree and Leaf*. For this some minor alterations were made, and it is this later text that is given here (with the correction of some errors that go back to the 1964 reprinting).

English and Welsh was an O'Donnell Lecture given at Oxford on 21 October 1955 (the day after the publication of *The Return of the King*, as noted by Humphrey Carpenter in his *Biography*, p. 223). These lectures were established in the Universities of Oxford, Edinburgh, and Wales to treat of 'the British or Celtic element in the English language and the dialects of English Counties and the special terms and words used in agriculture or handicrafts and the British or Celtic element in the existing population of England'; and *English and Welsh* was the opening lecture of a series given at Oxford. It was published in a collection entitled *Angles and Britons: O'Donnell Lectures* (University of Wales Press 1963); the copyright is owned by the University of Oxford, whose permission to publish it in this book I acknowledge with thanks.

A Secret Vice exists in a single manuscript without date or indication of the occasion of its delivery; but that the audience was a philological society is evident, and the Esperanto Congress in Oxford, referred to at the beginning of the essay as having taken place 'a year or more ago', was held in July 1930. Thus the date can be fixed as 1931. The manuscript was later hurriedly revised here and there, apparently for a second delivery of the paper long after – the words 'more than 20 years' (p. 203) were changed to 'almost 40 years'; and I have adopted some of these revisions in the text printed. The ironic title in the manuscript itself is *A Hobby for the Home* (with a later note: 'In other words: home-made or invented

---

* My father first gave the date as 1940 and then as 1938, which latter appears still in the Introductory Note to *Tree and Leaf*. Humphrey Carpenter has established the date given here (*Biography*, p. 191).

languages'), but my father referred to it in 1967 by a different title: 'The amusement of making up languages is very common among children (I once wrote a paper on it, called *A Secret Vice*)' (*The Letters of J. R. R. Tolkien*, p. 374). The words 'a secret vice' occur in the essay; and I have adopted this title. At the end I have given a much later version of one of the 'Elvish' poems included in the text, since it is one of the major pieces of Quenya (and incidentally upholds the now well-established tradition that all my father's writings have appendices).

The last piece in the book is the *Valedictory Address* delivered in Oxford on 5 June 1959, at the end of my father's last term as Merton Professor of English Language and Literature. This has been previously published in *J. R. R. Tolkien, Scholar and Storyteller*, edited by Mary Salu and Robert T. Farrell, Cornell University Press 1979; but there are many copies of this lecture, and since I made available the text for that volume I have come upon another to which my father made a good many alterations (without in any way changing the argument); these changes are incorporated in the text printed here. Whether they were made before or after the *Valedictory Address* was delivered I cannot say.

Only in the case of the previously unpublished pieces is this book in any sense an 'edition'; to those previously published I have added no annotation of any kind, save for a few explanations of detail in the *Valedictory Address*. The unpublished pieces, being derived from the author's own texts which are not in altogether final form, are on a different footing, but here also my notes are kept to a minimum and largely restricted to references and textual details.

I wish to thank Rayner Unwin for much help and advice in the planning of the book.

CHRISTOPHER TOLKIEN

BEOWULF: THE MONSTERS AND THE CRITICS

In 1864 the Reverend Oswald Cockayne wrote of the Reverend Doctor Joseph Bosworth, Rawlinsonian Professor of Anglo-Saxon: 'I have tried to lend to others the conviction I have long entertained that Dr Bosworth is not a man so diligent in his special walk as duly to read the books . . . which have been printed in our old English, or so-called Anglosaxon tongue. He may do very well for a professor.'[1] These words were inspired by dissatisfaction with Bosworth's dictionary, and were doubtless unfair. If Bosworth were still alive, a modern Cockayne would probably accuse him of not reading the 'literature' of his subject, the books written about the books in the so-called Anglo-Saxon tongue. The original books are nearly buried.

Of none is this so true as of *The Beowulf*, as it used to be called. I have, of course, read *The Beowulf*, as have most (but not all) of those who have criticized it. But I fear that, unworthy successor and beneficiary of Joseph Bosworth, I have not been a man so diligent in my special walk as duly to read all that has been printed on, or touching on, this poem. But I have read enough, I think, to venture the opinion that *Beowulfiana* is, while rich in many departments, specially poor in one. It is poor in criticism, criticism that is directed to the understanding of a poem as a poem. It has been said of *Beowulf* itself that its weakness lies in placing the unimportant things at the centre and the important on the outer edges. This is one of the opinions that I wish specially to consider. I think it profoundly untrue of the poem, but strikingly true of the literature about it. *Beowulf* has been used as a quarry of fact and fancy far more assiduously than it has been studied as a work of art.

It is of *Beowulf*, then, as a poem that I wish to speak; and though it may seem presumption that I should try with *swich a lewed mannes wit to pace the wisdom of an heep of lerned men*, in this department there is at least more chance for the *lewed man*. But there is so much that might still be said even under these limitations that I shall confine myself mainly to the *monsters* – Grendel and the Dragon, as they appear in what seems to me the best and most authoritative general criticism in English – and to certain considerations of the structure and conduct of the poem that arise from this theme.

There is an historical explanation of the state of *Beowulfiana* that I have referred to. And that explanation is important, if one would venture to criticize the critics. A sketch of the history of the subject is required. But I will here only attempt, for brevity's sake, to present my view of it allegorically. As it set out upon its adventures among the modern scholars, *Beowulf* was christened by Wanley Poesis – *Poeseos Anglo-Saxonicæ egregium exemplum*. But the fairy godmother later invited to superintend its fortunes was Historia. And she brought with her Philologia, Mythologia, Archaeologia, and Laographia.[2] Excellent ladies. But where was the child's name-sake? Poesis was usually forgotten; occasionally admitted by a side-door; sometimes dismissed upon the door-step. '*The Beowulf*', they said, 'is hardly an affair of yours, and not in any case a protégé that you could be proud of. It is an historical document. Only as such does it interest the superior culture of to-day.' And it is as an historical document that it has mainly been examined and dissected. Though ideas as to the nature and quality of the history and information embedded in it have changed much since Thorkelin called it *De Danorum Rebus Gestis*, this has remained steadily true. In still recent pronouncements this view is explicit. In 1925 Professor Archibald Strong translated *Beowulf* into verse;[3] but in 1921 he had declared: '*Beowulf* is the picture of a whole civilization, of the Germania which Tacitus describes. The main interest which the poem has for us is thus not a purely literary interest. *Beowulf* is an important historical document.'[4]

I make this preliminary point, because it seems to me that the air has been clouded not only for Strong, but for other more authoritative critics, by the dust of the quarrying researchers. It may well be asked: why should we approach this, or indeed any other poem, mainly as an historical document? Such an attitude is defensible: firstly, if one is not concerned with poetry at all, but seeking information wherever it may be found; secondly, if the so-called poem contains in fact no poetry. I am not concerned with the first case. The historian's search is, of course, perfectly legitimate, even if it does not assist criticism in general at all (for that is not its object), so long as it is not mistaken for criticism. To Professor Birger Nerman as an historian of Swedish origins *Beowulf* is doubtless an important document, but he is not writing a history of English poetry. Of the second case it may be said that to rate a poem, a thing at the least in metrical form, as mainly of historical interest should *in a literary survey* be equivalent to saying that it has no literary merits, and little more need in such a survey then be said about it. But such a judgement on *Beowulf* is false. So far from being a poem so poor that only its accidental historical interest can still recommend it, *Beowulf* is in fact so interesting as poetry, in places poetry so powerful, that this quite overshadows the historical content, and is largely independent even of the most important facts (such as the date and identity of Hygelac) that research has discovered. It is indeed a curious fact that it is one of the peculiar poetic virtues of *Beowulf* that has contributed to its own critical misfortunes. The illusion of historical truth and perspective, that has made *Beowulf* seem such an attractive quarry, is largely a product of art. The author has used an instinctive historical sense – a part indeed of the ancient English temper (and not unconnected with its reputed melancholy), of which *Beowulf* is a supreme expression; but he has used it with a poetical and not an historical object. The lovers of poetry can safely study the art, but the seekers after history must beware lest the glamour of Poesis overcome them.

Nearly all the censure, and most of the praise, that has been bestowed on *The Beowulf* has been due either to the belief that it was something that it was *not* – for example, primitive, pagan, Teutonic, an allegory (political or mythical), or most often, an epic; or to disappointment at the discovery that it was itself and not something that the scholar would have liked better – for example, a heathen heroic lay, a history of Sweden, a manual of Germanic antiquities, or a Nordic *Summa Theologica*.

I would express the whole industry in yet another allegory. A man inherited a field in which was an accumulation of old stone, part of an older hall. Of the old stone some had already been used in building the house in which he actually lived, not far from the old house of his fathers. Of the rest he took some and built a tower. But his friends coming perceived at once (without troubling to climb the steps) that these stones had formerly belonged to a more ancient building. So they pushed the tower over, with no little labour, in order to look for hidden carvings and inscriptions, or to discover whence the man's distant forefathers had obtained their building material. Some suspecting a deposit of coal under the soil began to dig for it, and forgot even the stones. They all said: 'This tower is most interesting.' But they also said (after pushing it over): 'What a muddle it is in!' And even the man's own descendants, who might have been expected to consider what he had been about, were heard to murmur: 'He is such an odd fellow! Imagine his using these old stones just to build a nonsensical tower! Why did not he restore the old house? He had no sense of proportion.' But from the top of that tower the man had been able to look out upon the sea.

I hope I shall show that that allegory is just – even when we consider the more recent and more perceptive critics (whose concern is in intention with literature). To reach these we must pass in rapid flight over the heads of many decades of critics. As we do so a conflicting babel mounts up to us, which I can report as something after this fashion.[5] '*Beowulf* is a half-baked native epic the development of which was killed by Latin learning; it was inspired by emulation of Virgil, and is a product of the education that came in with Christianity; it is feeble and incompetent as a narrative; the rules of narrative are cleverly observed in the manner of the learned epic; it is the confused product of a committee of muddle-headed and probably beer-bemused Anglo-Saxons (this is a Gallic voice); it is a string of pagan lays edited by monks; it is the work of a learned but inaccurate Christian antiquarian; it is a work of genius, rare and surprising in the period, though the genius seems to have been shown principally in doing something much better left undone (this is a very recent voice); it is a wild folk-tale (general chorus); it is a poem of an aristocratic and courtly tradition (same voices); it is a hotch-potch; it is a sociological, anthropological, archaeological document; it is a mythical allegory (very old voices these and generally shouted down, but not so far out as some of the newer cries); it is rude and rough; it is a masterpiece of metrical art; it has no shape at all; it is singularly weak in construction; it is a clever allegory of contemporary politics (old John Earle with some slight support from Mr Girvan, only they look to different periods); its architecture is solid; it is thin and cheap (a solemn voice); it is undeniably weighty (the same voice); it is a national epic; it is a translation from the Danish; it was imported by Frisian traders; it is a burden to English syllabuses; and (final universal chorus of all voices) it is worth studying.'

It is not surprising that it should now be felt that a view, a decision, a conviction are imperatively needed. But it is plainly only in the consideration of *Beowulf* as a poem, with an inherent poetic significance, that any view or conviction can be reached or steadily held. For it is of their nature that the jabberwocks of historical and antiquarian research burble in the tulgy wood of conjecture, flitting from one tum-tum tree to another. Noble animals, whose burbling is on occasion good to hear; but though their eyes of flame may sometimes prove searchlights, their range is short.

None the less, paths of a sort have been opened in the wood. Slowly with the rolling years the obvious (so often the last revelation of analytic study) has been discovered: that we have to deal with a poem by an Englishman using afresh ancient and largely traditional material. At last then, after inquiring so long whence this material came, and what its original or aboriginal nature was (questions that cannot ever be decisively answered), we might also now again inquire what the poet did with it. If we ask that question, then there is still, perhaps, something lacking even in the major critics, the learned and revered masters from whom we humbly derive.

The chief points with which I feel dissatisfied I will now approach by way of W. P. Ker, whose name and memory I honour. He would deserve reverence, of course, even if he still lived and had not *ellor gehworfen on Frean wære* upon a high mountain in the heart of that Europe which he loved: a great scholar, as illuminating himself as a critic, as he was often biting as a critic of the critics. None the less I cannot help feeling that in approaching *Beowulf* he was hampered by the almost inevitable weakness of his greatness: stories and plots must sometimes have seemed triter to him, the much-read, than they did to the old poets and their audiences. The dwarf on the spot sometimes sees things missed by the travelling giant ranging many countries. In considering a period when literature was narrower in range and men possessed a less diversified stock of ideas and themes, one must seek to recapture and esteem the deep pondering and profound feeling that they gave to such as they possessed.

In any case Ker has been potent. For his criticism is masterly, expressed always in words both pungent and weighty, and not least so when it is (as I occasionally venture to think) itself open to criticism. His words and judgements are often quoted, or reappear in various modifications, digested, their source probably sometimes forgotten. It is impossible to avoid quotation of the well-known passage in his *Dark Ages*:

> A reasonable view of the merit of *Beowulf* is not impossible, though rash enthusiasm may have made too much of it, while a correct and sober taste may have too contemptuously refused to attend to Grendel or the Fire-drake. The fault of *Beowulf* is that there is nothing much in the story. The hero is occupied in killing monsters, like Hercules or Theseus. But there are other things in the lives of Hercules and Theseus besides the killing of the Hydra or of Procrustes. Beowulf has nothing else to do, when he has killed Grendel and Grendel's mother in Denmark: he goes home to his own Gautland, until at last the rolling years bring the Fire-drake and his last adventure. It is too simple. Yet the three chief episodes are well wrought and well diversified; they are not repetitions, exactly; there is a change of temper between the wrestling with Grendel in the night at Heorot and the descent under water to encounter Grendel's mother; while the sentiment of the Dragon is different again. But the great beauty, the real value, of *Beowulf* is in its dignity of style. In construction it is curiously weak, in a sense preposterous; for while the main story is simplicity itself, the merest commonplace of heroic legend, all about it, in the historic allusions, there are revelations of a whole world of tragedy, plots different in import from that of *Beowulf*, more like the tragic

themes of Iceland. Yet with this radical defect, a disproportion that puts the irrelevances in the centre and the serious things on the outer edges, the poem of *Beowulf* is undeniably weighty. The thing itself is cheap; the moral and the spirit of it can only be matched among the noblest authors.[6]

This passage was written more than thirty years ago, but has hardly been surpassed. It remains, in this country at any rate, a potent influence. Yet its primary effect is to state a paradox which one feels has always strained the belief, even of those who accepted it, and has given to *Beowulf* the character of an 'enigmatic poem'. The chief virtue of the passage (not the one for which it is usually esteemed) is that it does accord some attention to the monsters, despite correct and sober taste. But the contrast made between the radical defect of theme and structure, and at the same time the dignity, loftiness in converse, and well-wrought finish, has become a commonplace even of the best criticism, a paradox the strangeness of which has almost been forgotten in the process of swallowing it upon authority.[7] We may compare Professor Chambers in his *Widsith*, p. 79, where he is studying the story of Ingeld, son of Froda, and his feud with the great Scylding house of Denmark, a story introduced in *Beowulf* merely as an allusion.

Nothing [Chambers says] could better show the disproportion of *Beowulf* which 'puts the irrelevances in the centre and the serious things on the outer edges', than this passing allusion to the story of Ingeld. For in this conflict between plighted troth and the duty of revenge we have a situation which the old heroic poets loved, and would not have sold for a wilderness of dragons.

I pass over the fact that the allusion has a dramatic purpose in *Beowulf* that is a sufficient defence both of its presence and of its manner. The author of *Beowulf* cannot be held responsible for the fact that we now have only his poem and not others dealing primarily with Ingeld. He was not selling one thing for another, but giving something new. But let us return to the dragon. 'A wilderness of dragons.' There is a sting in this Shylockian plural, the sharper for coming from a critic, who deserves the title of the poet's best friend. It is in the tradition of the Book of St Albans, from which the poet might retort upon his critics: 'Yea, a desserte of lapwyngs, a shrewednes of apes, a raffull of knaues, and a gagle of gees.'

As for the poem, one dragon, however hot, does not make a summer, or a host; and a man might well exchange for one good dragon what he would not sell for a wilderness. And dragons, real dragons, essential both to the machinery and the ideas of a poem or tale, are actually rare. In northern literature there are only *two* that are significant. If we omit from consideration the vast and vague Encircler of the World, Miðgarðsormr, the doom of the great gods and no matter for heroes, we have but the dragon of the Völsungs, Fáfnir, and Beowulf's bane. It is true that both of these are in *Beowulf*, one in the main story, and the other spoken of by a minstrel praising Beowulf himself. But this is not a wilderness of dragons. Indeed the allusion to the more renowned worm killed by the Wælsing is sufficient indication that the poet selected a dragon of well-founded purpose (or saw its significance in the plot as it had reached him), even as he was careful to compare his hero, Beowulf son of Ecgtheow, to the prince of the heroes of the North, the dragon-slaying Wælsing. He esteemed dragons, as rare as they are dire, as some do still. He liked them – as a poet, not as a sober zoologist; and he had good reason.

But we meet this kind of criticism again. In Chambers's *Beowulf and the Heroic Age* – the most significant single essay on the poem that I know – it is still present. The riddle is still unsolved. The folk-tale motive stands still like the spectre of old research, dead but unquiet in its grave. We are told again that the main story of *Beowulf* is a *wild folk-tale*. Quite true, of course. It is true of the main story of *King Lear*, unless in that case you would prefer to substitute *silly* for *wild*. But more: we are told that the same sort of stuff is found in Homer, yet there it is kept in its proper place. 'The folk-tale is a good servant', Chambers says, and does not perhaps realize the importance of the admission, made to save the face of Homer and Virgil; for he continues: 'but a bad master: it has been allowed in *Beowulf* to usurp the place of honour, and to drive into episodes and digressions the things which should be the main stuff of a well-conducted epic.'[8] It is not clear to me why good *conduct* must depend on the main *stuff*. But I will for the moment remark only that, if it is so, *Beowulf* is evidently not a well-conducted epic. It may turn out to be no epic at all. But the puzzle still continues. In the most recent discourse upon this theme it still appears, toned down almost to a melancholy question-mark, as if this paradox had at last begun to afflict with weariness the thought that endeavours to support it. In the final peroration of his notable lecture on *Folk-tale and History in Beowulf*, given last year, Mr Girvan said:

> Confessedly there is matter for wonder and scope for doubt, but we might be able to answer with complete satisfaction some of the questionings which rise in men's minds over the poet's presentment of his hero, if we could also answer with certainty the question why he chose just this subject, when to our modern judgment there were at hand so many greater, charged with the splendour and tragedy of humanity, and in all respects worthier of a genius as astonishing as it was rare in Anglo-Saxon England.

There is something irritatingly odd about all this. One even dares to wonder if something has not gone wrong with 'our modern judgement', supposing that it is justly represented. Higher praise than is found in the learned critics, whose scholarship enables them to appreciate these things, could hardly be given to the detail, the tone, the style, and indeed to the total effect of *Beowulf*. Yet this poetic talent, we are to understand, has all been squandered on an unprofitable theme: as if Milton had recounted the story of Jack and the Beanstalk in noble verse. Even if Milton had done this (and he might have done worse), we should perhaps pause to consider whether his poetic handling had not had some effect upon the trivial theme; what alchemy had been performed upon the base metal; whether indeed it remained base or trivial when he had finished with it. The high tone, the sense of dignity, alone is evidence in *Beowulf* of the presence of a mind lofty and thoughtful. It is, one would have said, improbable that such a man would write more than three thousand lines (wrought to a high finish) on matter that is really not worth serious attention; that remains thin and cheap when he has finished with it. Or that he should in the selection of his material, in the choice of what to put forward, what to keep subordinate 'upon the outer edges', have shown a puerile simplicity much below the level of the characters he himself draws in his own poem. Any theory that will at least allow us to believe that what he did was of design, and that for that design there is a defence that may still have force, would seem more probable.

It has been too little observed that all the machinery of 'dignity' is to be found elsewhere. Cynewulf, or the author of *Andreas*, or of *Guthlac* (most notably), have a command of dignified verse. In them there is well-wrought language, weighty words, lofty sentiment, precisely that which we are told is the real beauty of *Beowulf*. Yet it cannot, I think, be disputed, that *Beowulf* is more beautiful, that each line there is more significant (even when, as sometimes happens, it is the same line) than in the other long Old English poems. Where then resides the special virtue of *Beowulf*, if the common element (which belongs largely to the language itself, and to a literary tradition) is deducted? It resides, one might guess, in the theme, and the spirit this has infused into the whole. For, in fact, if there were a real discrepancy between theme and style, that style would not be felt as beautiful but as incongruous or false. And that incongruity is present in some measure in all the long Old English poems, save one – *Beowulf*. The paradoxical contrast that has been drawn between matter and manner in *Beowulf* has thus an inherent *literary* improbability.

Why then have the great critics thought otherwise? I must pass rather hastily over the answers to this question. The reasons are various, I think, and would take long to examine. I believe that one reason is that the shadow of research has lain upon criticism. The habit, for instance, of pondering a summarized plot of *Beowulf*, denuded of all that gives it particular force or individual life, has encouraged the notion that its main story is wild, or trivial, or typical, *even after treatment*. Yet all stories, great and small, are one or more of these three things in such nakedness. The comparison of skeleton 'plots' is simply not a critical literary process at all. It has been favoured by research in comparative folk-lore, the objects of which are primarily historical or scientific.[9] Another reason is, I think, that the allusions have attracted curiosity (anti-quarian rather than critical) to their elucidation; and this needs so much study and research that attention has been diverted from the poem as a whole, and from the function of the allusions, as shaped and placed, in the poetic economy of *Beowulf* as it is. Yet actually the appreciation of this function is largely inde-pendent of such investigations.

But there is also, I suppose, a real question of taste involved: a judgement that the heroic or tragic story on a strictly human plane is by nature superior. Doom is held less literary than ἁμαρτία. The proposition seems to have been passed as self-evident. I dissent, even at the risk of being held incorrect or not sober. But I will not here enter into debate, nor attempt at length a defence of the mythical mode of imagination, and the disen-tanglement of the confusion between myth and folk-tale into which these judgements appear to have fallen. The myth has other forms than the (now discredited) mythical allegory of nature: the sun, the seasons, the sea, and such things. The term 'folk-tale' is mis-leading; its very tone of depreciation begs the question. Folk-tales in being, as told – for the 'typical folk-tale', of course, is merely an abstract conception of research nowhere existing – do often contain elements that are thin and cheap, with little even potential virtue; but they also contain much that is far more powerful, and that cannot be sharply separated from myth, being derived from it, or capable in poetic hands of turning into it: that is of becoming largely significant – as a whole, accepted unanalysed. The significance of a myth is not easily to be pinned on paper by analytical reasoning. It is at its best when it is presented by a poet who feels rather than makes explicit what his theme portends; who presents it incarnate in the world of history and geography, as our poet has done. Its defender is thus at a disadvantage: unless he is careful, and speaks in parables, he will kill what he is studying by vivisection, and he will be left with a formal or mechanical allegory, and, what is more, probably with one that will not work. For myth is alive at once and in all its parts, and dies before it can be dissected. It is possible, I think, to be moved by the power of myth and yet to misunderstand the sensation, to ascribe it wholly to something else that is also present: to metrical art, style, or verbal skill. Correct and sober taste may refuse to admit that there can be an interest for *us* – the proud *we* that includes all intelligent living people – in ogres and dragons; we then perceive its puzzlement in face of the odd fact that it has derived great pleasure from a poem that is actually about these unfashionable creatures. Even though it attributes 'genius', as does Mr Girvan, to the author, it cannot admit that the monsters are anything but a sad mistake.

It does not seem plain that ancient taste supports the modern as much as it has been represented to do. I have the author of *Beowulf*, at any rate, on my side: a greater man than most of us. And I cannot myself perceive a period in the North when one kind alone was esteemed: there was room for myth and heroic legend, and for blends of these. As for the dragon: as far as we know anything about these old poets, we know this: the prince of the heroes of the North, supremely memorable – *hans nafn mun uppi meðan veröldin stendr* – was a dragon-slayer. And his most renowned deed, from which in Norse he derived his title Fáfnisbani, was the slaying of the prince of legendary worms. Although there is plainly considerable difference between the later Norse and the ancient English form of the story alluded to in *Beowulf*, already there it had these two primary features: the dragon, and the slaying of him as the chief deed of the greatest of heroes – *he wæs wreccena wide mærost*. A dragon is no idle fancy. Whatever may be his origins, in fact or invention, the dragon in legend is a potent creation of men's imagination, richer in significance than his barrow is in gold. Even to-day (despite the critics) you may find men not ignorant of tragic legend and history, who have heard of heroes and indeed seen them, who yet have been caught by the fascination of the worm. More than one poem in recent years (since *Beowulf* escaped somewhat from the dominion of the students of origins to the students of poetry) has been inspired by the dragon of *Beowulf*, but none that I know of by Ingeld son of Froda. Indeed, I do not think Chambers very happy in his particular choice. He gives battle on dubious ground. In so far as we can now grasp its detail and atmosphere the story of Ingeld the thrice faithless and easily persuaded is chiefly interesting as an episode in a larger theme, as part of a tradition that had acquired legendary, and so dramatically personalized, form concerning moving events in history: the arising of Denmark, and wars in the islands of the North. In itself it is not a supremely potent story. But, of course, as with all tales of any sort, its literary power must have depended mainly upon how it was handled. A poet may have made a great thing of it. Upon this chance must be founded the popularity of Ingeld's legend in England, for which there is some evidence.[10] There is no inherent magical virtue about heroic-tragic stories as such, and apart from the merits of individual treatments. The same heroic plot can yield good and bad poems, and good and bad sagas. The recipe for the central situations of such stories, studied in the abstract, is after all as 'simple' and as 'typical' as that of folk-tales. There are in any case many heroes but very few good dragons.

Beowulf's dragon, if one wishes really to criticize, is not to be blamed for being a dragon, but rather for not being dragon enough, plain pure fairy-story dragon. There are in the poem some vivid touches of the right kind – as *þa se wyrm onwoc, wroht wæs geniwad; stonc æfter stane*, 2285 – in which this dragon is real worm, with a bestial life and thought of his own, but the conception, none the less, approaches *draconitas* rather than *draco*: a personification of malice, greed, destruction (the evil side of heroic life), and of the undiscriminating cruelty of fortune that distinguishes not good or bad (the evil aspect of all life). But for *Beowulf*, the poem, that is as it should be. In this poem the balance is nice, but it is preserved. The large symbolism is near the surface, but it does not break through, nor become allegory. Something more significant than a standard hero, a man faced with a foe more evil than any human enemy of house or realm, is before us, and yet incarnate in time, walking in heroic history, and treading the named lands of the North. And this, we are told, is the radical defect of *Beowulf*, that its author, coming in a time rich in the legends of heroic men, has used them afresh in an original fashion, giving us not just one more, but something akin yet different: a measure and interpretation of them all.

We do not deny the worth of the hero by accepting Grendel and the dragon. Let us by all means esteem the old heroes: men caught in the chains of circumstance or of their own character, torn between duties equally sacred, dying with their backs to the wall. But *Beowulf*, I fancy, plays a larger part than is recognized in helping us to esteem them. Heroic lays may have dealt in their own way – we have little enough to judge by – a way more brief and vigorous, perhaps, though perhaps also more harsh and noisy (and less thoughtful), with the actions of heroes caught in circumstances that conformed more or less to the varied but fundamentally simple recipe for an heroic situation. In these (if we had them) we could see the exaltation of undefeated will, which receives doctrinal expression in the words of Byrhtwold at the battle of Maldon.[11] But though with sympathy and patience we might gather, from a line here or a tone there, the background of imagination which gives to this indomitability, this paradox of defeat inevitable yet unacknowledged, its full significance, it is in *Beowulf* that a poet has devoted a whole poem to the theme, and has drawn the struggle in different proportions, so that we may see man at war with the hostile world, and his inevitable overthrow in Time.[12] The particular is on the outer edge, the essential in the centre.

Of course, I do not assert that the poet, if questioned, would have replied in the Anglo-Saxon equivalents of these terms. Had the matter been so explicit to him, his poem would certainly have been the worse. None the less we may still, against his great scene, hung with tapestries woven of ancient tales of ruin, see the *hæleð* walk. When we have read his poem, as a poem, rather than as a collection of episodes, we perceive that he who wrote *hæleð under heofenum* may have meant in dictionary terms 'heroes under heaven', or 'mighty men upon earth', but he and his hearers were thinking of the *eormengrund*, the great earth, ringed with *garsecg*, the shoreless sea, beneath the sky's inaccessible roof; whereon, as in a little circle of light about their halls, men with courage as their stay went forward to that battle with the hostile world and the offspring of the dark which ends for all, even the kings and champions, in defeat. That even this 'geography', once held as a material fact, could now be classed as a mere folk-tale affects its value very little. It transcends astronomy. Not that astronomy has done anything to make the island seem more secure or the outer seas less formidable.

Beowulf is not, then, the hero of an heroic lay, precisely. He has no enmeshed loyalties, nor hapless love. *He is a man, and that for him and many is sufficient tragedy.* It is not an irritating accident that the tone of the poem is so high and its theme so low. It is the theme in its deadly seriousness that begets the dignity of tone: *lif is læne: eal scæceð leoht and lif somod.* So deadly and ineluctable is the underlying thought, that those who in the circle of light, within the besieged hall, are absorbed in work or talk and do not look to the battlements, either do not regard it or recoil. Death comes to the feast, and they say He gibbers: He has no sense of proportion.

I would suggest, then, that the monsters are not an inexplicable blunder of taste; they are essential, fundamentally allied to the underlying ideas of the poem, which give it its lofty tone and high seriousness. The key to the fusion-point of imagination that produced this poem lies, therefore, in those very references to Cain which have often been used as a stick to beat an ass – taken as an evident sign (were any needed) of the muddled heads of early Anglo-Saxons. They could not, it was said, keep Scandinavian bogies and the Scriptures separate in their puzzled brains. The New Testament was beyond their comprehension. I am not, as I have confessed, a man so diligent as duly to read all the books about *Beowulf*, but as far as I am aware the most suggestive approach to this point appears in the essay *Beowulf and the Heroic Age* to which I have already referred.[13] I will quote a small part of it.

> In the epoch of *Beowulf* a Heroic Age more wild and primitive than that of Greece is brought into touch with Christendom, with the Sermon on the Mount, with Catholic theology and ideas of Heaven and Hell. We see the difference, if we compare the wilder things – the folktale element – in *Beowulf* with the wilder things of Homer. Take for example the tale of Odysseus and the Cyclops – the No-man trick. Odysseus is struggling with a monstrous and wicked foe, but he is not exactly thought of as struggling with the powers of darkness. Polyphemus, by devouring his guests, acts in a way which is hateful to Zeus and the other gods: yet the Cyclops is himself god-begotten and under divine protection, and the fact that Odysseus has maimed him is a wrong which Poseidon is slow to forgive. But the gigantic foes whom Beowulf has to meet are identified with the foes of God. Grendel and the dragon are constantly referred to in

language which is meant to recall the powers of darkness with which Christian men felt themselves to be encompassed. They[14] are the 'inmates of Hell', 'adversaries of God', 'offspring of Cain', 'enemies of mankind'. Consequently, the matter of the main story of *Beowulf*, monstrous as it is, is not so far removed from common mediaeval experience as it seems to us to be from our own. . . . Grendel hardly differs[15] from the fiends of the pit who were always in ambush to waylay a righteous man. And so Beowulf, for all that he moves in the world of the primitive Heroic Age of the Germans, nevertheless is almost a Christian knight.[16]

There are some hints here which are, I think, worth pursuing further. Most important is it to consider how and why the monsters become 'adversaries of God', and so begin to symbolize (and ultimately to become identified with) the powers of evil, even while they remain, as they do still remain in *Beowulf*, mortal denizens of the material world, in it and of it. I accept without argument throughout the attribution of *Beowulf* to the 'age of Bede' – one of the firmer conclusions of a department of research most clearly serviceable to criticism: inquiry into the probable date of the effective composition of the poem as we have it. So regarded *Beowulf* is, of course, an historical document of the first order for the study of the mood and thought of the period and one perhaps too little used for the purpose by professed historians.[17] But it is the mood of the author, the essential cast of his imaginative apprehension of the world, that is my concern, not history for its own sake; I am interested in that time of fusion only as it may help us to understand the poem. And in the poem I think we may observe not confusion, a half-hearted or a muddled business, but a fusion that has occurred *at a given point* of contact between old and new, a product of thought and deep emotion.

One of the most potent elements in that fusion is the Northern courage: the theory of courage, which is the great contribution of early Northern literature. This is not a military judgement. I am not asserting that, if the Trojans could have employed a Northern king and his companions, they would have driven Agamemnon and Achilles into the sea, more decisively than the Greek hexameter routs the alliterative line – though it is not improbable. I refer rather to the central position the creed of unyielding will holds in the North. With due reserve we may turn to the tradition of pagan imagination as it survived in Icelandic. Of English pre-Christian mythology we know practically nothing. But the fundamentally similar heroic temper of ancient England and Scandinavia cannot have been founded on (or perhaps rather, cannot have generated) mythologies divergent on this essential point. 'The Northern Gods', Ker said, 'have an exultant extravagance in their warfare which makes them more like Titans than Olympians; *only they are on the right side, though it is not the side that wins. The winning side is Chaos and Unreason*' – mythologically, the monsters – '*but the gods, who are defeated, think that defeat no refutation*'.[18] And in their war men are their chosen allies, able when heroic to share in this 'absolute resistance, perfect because without hope'. At least in this vision of the final defeat of the humane (and of the divine made in its image), and in the essential hostility of the gods and heroes on the one hand and the monsters on the other, we may suppose that pagan English and Norse imagination agreed.

But in England this imagination was brought into touch with Christendom, and with the Scriptures. The process of 'conversion' was a long one, but some of its effects were doubtless immediate: an alchemy of change (producing ultimately the mediaeval) was at once at work. One does not have to wait until all the native traditions of the older world have been replaced or forgotten; for the minds which still retain them are changed, and the memories viewed in a different perspective: *at once they become more ancient and remote, and in a sense darker*. It is through such a blending that there was available to a poet who set out to *write* a poem – and in the case of *Beowulf* we may probably use this very word – on a scale and plan unlike a minstrel's lay, both new faith and new learning (or education), and also a body of native tradition (itself requiring to be learned) for the changed mind to contemplate together.[19] The native 'learning' cannot be denied in the case of *Beowulf*. Its display has grievously perturbed the critics, for the author draws upon tradition at will for his own purposes, as a poet of later times might draw upon history or the classics and expect his allusions to be understood (within a certain class of hearers). He was in fact, like Virgil, learned enough in the vernacular department to have an historical perspective, even an antiquarian curiosity. He cast his time into the long-ago, because already the long-ago had a special poetical attraction. He knew much about old days, and though his knowledge – of such things as sea-burial and the funeral pyre, for instance – was rich and poetical rather than accurate with the accuracy of modern archaeology (such as that is), one thing he knew clearly: those days were heathen – heathen, noble, and hopeless.

But if the specifically Christian was suppressed,[20] so also were the old gods. Partly because they had not really existed, and had been always, in the Christian view, only delusions or lies fabricated by the evil one, the *gastbona*, to whom the hopeless turned especially in times of need. Partly because their old names (certainly not forgotten) had been potent, and were connected in memory still, not only with mythology or such fairy-tale matter as we find, say, in *Gylfaginning*, but with active heathendom, religion and *wigweorþung*. Most of all because they were not actually essential to the theme.

The monsters had been the foes of the gods, the captains of men, and within Time the monsters would win. In the heroic siege and last defeat men and gods alike had been imagined in the same host. Now the heroic figures, the men of old, *hæleð under heofenum*, remained and still fought on until defeat. For the monsters do not depart, whether the gods go or come. A Christian was (and is) still like his forefathers a mortal hemmed in a hostile world. The monsters remained the enemies of mankind, the infantry of the old war, and became inevitably the enemies of the one God, *ece Dryhten*, the eternal Captain of the new. Even so the vision of the war changes. For it begins to dissolve, even as the contest on the fields of Time thus takes on its largest aspect. The tragedy of the great temporal defeat remains for a while poignant, but ceases to be finally important. It is no defeat, for the end of the world is part of the design of Metod, the Arbiter who is above the mortal world. Beyond there appears a possibility of eternal victory (or eternal defeat), and the real battle is between the soul and its adversaries. So the old monsters became images of the evil spirit or spirits, or rather the evil spirits entered into the monsters and took visible shape in the hideous bodies of the *þyrsas* and *sigelhearwan* of heathen imagination.

But that shift is not complete in *Beowulf* – whatever may have been true of its period in general. Its author is still concerned primarily with *man on earth*, rehandling in a new perspective an ancient theme: that man, each man and all men, and all their works shall die. A theme no Christian need despise. Yet this theme plainly would not be so treated, but for the nearness of a pagan time. The shadow of its despair, if only as a mood, as an intense emotion of regret, is still there. The worth of defeated valour in this world is deeply felt. As the poet looks back into the past, surveying the history of kings and warriors in the old traditions, he sees that all glory (or as we might say 'culture' or 'civilization') ends in night. The solution of that tragedy is not treated – it does not arise out of the material. We get in fact a poem from a pregnant moment of poise, looking back into the pit, by a man learned in old tales who was struggling, as it were, to get a general view of them all, perceiving their common tragedy of inevitable ruin, and yet feeling this more *poetically* because he was himself removed from the direct pressure of its despair. He could view from without, but still feel immediately and from within, the old dogma: despair of the event, combined with faith in the value of doomed resistance. He was still dealing with the great temporal tragedy, and not yet writing an allegorical homily in verse. Grendel inhabits the visible world and eats the flesh and blood of men; he enters their houses by the doors. The dragon wields a physical fire, and covets gold not souls; he is slain with iron in his belly. Beowulf's *byrne* was made by Weland, and the iron shield he bore against the serpent by his own smiths: it was not yet the breastplate of righteousness, nor the shield of faith for the quenching of all the fiery darts of the wicked.

Almost we might say that this poem was (in one direction) inspired by the debate that had long been held and continued after, and that it was one of the chief contributions to the controversy: shall we or shall we not consign the heathen ancestors to perdition? What good will it do posterity to read the battles of Hector? *Quid Hinieldus cum Christo?* The author of *Beowulf* showed forth the permanent value of that *pietas* which treasures the memory of man's struggles in the dark past, man fallen and not yet saved, disgraced but not dethroned. It would seem to have been part of the English temper in its strong sense of tradition, dependent doubtless on dynasties, noble houses, and their code of honour, and strengthened, it may be, by the more inquisitive and less severe Celtic learning, that it should, at least in some quarters and despite grave and Gallic voices, preserve much from the northern past to blend with southern learning, and new faith.

It has been thought that the influence of Latin epic, especially of the *Aeneid*, is perceptible in *Beowulf*, and a necessary explanation, if only in the exciting of emulation, of the development of the long and studied poem in early England. There is, of course, a likeness in places between these greater and lesser things, the *Aeneid* and *Beowulf*, if they are read in conjunction. But the smaller points in which imitation or reminiscence might be perceived are inconclusive, while the real likeness is deeper and due to certain qualities in the authors independent of the question whether the Anglo-Saxon had read Virgil or not. It is this deeper likeness which makes things, that are either the inevitabilities of human poetry or the accidental congruences of all tales, ring alike. We have the great pagan on the threshold of the change of the world; and the great (if lesser) Christian just over the threshold of the great change in his time and place: the backward view: *multa putans sortemque animo miseratus iniquam.*[21]

But we will now return once more to the monsters, and consider especially the difference of their status in the northern and southern mythologies. Of Grendel it is said: *Godes yrre bær*. But the Cyclops is god-begotten and his maiming is an offence against his begetter, the god Poseidon. This radical difference in mythological status is only brought out more sharply by the very closeness of the similarity in conception (in all save mere size) that is seen, if we compare *Beowulf*, 740 ff., with the description of the Cyclops devouring men in *Odyssey*, ix – or still more in *Aeneid*, iii. 622 ff. In Virgil, whatever may be true of the fairy-tale world of the Odyssey, the Cyclops walks veritably in the historic world. He is seen by Aeneas in Sicily, *monstrum horrendum, informe, ingens*, as much a perilous fact as Grendel was in Denmark, *earmsceapen on weres wæstmum . . . næfne he wæs mara þonne ænig man oðer*; as real as Acestes or Hrothgar.[22]

At this point in particular we may regret that we do not know more about pre-Christian English mythology. Yet it is, as I have said, legitimate to suppose that in the matter of the position of the monsters in regard to men and gods the view was fundamentally the same as in later Icelandic. Thus, though all such generalizations are naturally imperfect in detail (since they deal with matter of various origins, constantly reworked, and never even at most more than partially systematized), we may with some truth contrast the 'inhumanness' of the Greek gods, however anthropomorphic, with the 'humanness' of the Northern, however titanic. In the southern myths there is also rumour of wars with giants and great powers not Olympian, the *Titania pubes fulmine deiecti*, rolling like Satan and his satellites in the nethermost Abyss. But this war is differently conceived. It lies in a chaotic past. The ruling gods are not besieged, not in ever-present peril or under future doom.[23] Their offspring on earth may be heroes or fair women; it may also be the other creatures hostile to men. The gods are not the allies of men in their war against these or other monsters. The interest of the gods is in this or that man as part of their individual schemes, not as part of a great strategy that includes all good men, as the infantry of battle. In Norse, at any rate, the gods are within Time, doomed with their allies to death. Their battle is with the monsters and the outer darkness. They gather heroes for the last defence. Already before euhemerism saved them by embalming them, and they dwindled in antiquarian fancy to the mighty ancestors of northern kings (English and Scandinavian), they had become in their very being the enlarged shadows of great men and warriors upon the walls of the world. When Baldr is slain and goes to Hel he cannot escape thence any more than mortal man.

This may make the southern gods more godlike – more lofty, dread, and inscrutable. They are timeless and do not fear death. Such a mythology may hold the promise of a profounder thought. In any case it was a virtue of the southern mythology that it could not stop where it was. It must go forward to philosophy or relapse into anarchy. For in a sense it had shirked the problem precisely by not having the monsters in the centre – as they are in *Beowulf* to the astonishment of the critics. But such horrors cannot be left permanently unexplained, lurking on the outer edges and under suspicion of being connected with the Government. It is the strength of the northern mythological imagination that it faced this problem, put the monsters in the centre, gave them victory but no honour, and found a potent but terrible solution in naked will and courage. 'As a working theory absolutely impregnable.' So potent is it, that while the older southern imagination has faded for ever into literary ornament, the northern has power, as it were, to revive its spirit even in our own times. It can work, even as it did work with the *goðlauss* viking, without gods: martial heroism as its own end. But we may remember that the poet of *Beowulf* saw clearly: the wages of heroism is death.

For these reasons I think that the passages in *Beowulf* concerning the giants and their war with God, together with the two mentions of Cain (as the ancestor of the giants in general and Grendel in particular) are specially important.

They are directly connected with Scripture, yet they cannot be dissociated from the creatures of northern myth, the ever-watchful foes of the gods (and men). The undoubtedly scriptural Cain is connected with *eotenas* and *ylfe*, which are the *jötnar* and *álfar* of Norse. But this is not due to mere confusion – it is rather an indication of the precise point at which an imagination, pondering old and new, was kindled. At this point new Scripture and old tradition touched and ignited. It is for this reason that these elements of Scripture alone appear in a poem dealing of design with the noble pagan of old days. For they are precisely the elements which bear upon this theme. Man alien in a hostile world, engaged in a struggle which he cannot win while the world lasts, is assured that his foes are the foes also of Dryhten, that his courage noble in itself is also the highest loyalty: so said thyle and clerk.

In *Beowulf* we have, then, an historical poem about the pagan past, or an attempt at one – literal historical fidelity founded on modern research was, of course, not attempted. It is a poem by a learned man writing of old times, who looking back on the heroism and sorrow feels in them something permanent and something symbolical. So far from being a confused semi-pagan – historically unlikely for a man of this sort in the period – he brought probably *first* to his task a knowledge of Christian poetry, especially that of the Cædmon school, and especially *Genesis*.[24] He makes his minstrel sing in Heorot of the Creation of the earth and the lights of Heaven. So excellent is this choice as the theme of the harp that maddened Grendel lurking joyless in the dark without that it matters little whether this is anachronistic or not.[25] *Secondly*, to his task the poet brought a considerable learning in native lays and traditions: only by learning and training could such things be acquired, they were no more born naturally into an Englishman of the seventh or eighth centuries, by simple virtue of being an 'Anglo-Saxon', than ready-made knowledge of poetry and history is inherited at birth by modern children.

It would seem that, in his attempt to depict ancient pre-Christian days, intending to emphasize their nobility, and the desire of the good for truth, he turned naturally when delineating the great King of Heorot to the Old Testament. In the *folces hyrde* of the Danes we have much of the shepherd patriarchs and kings of Israel, servants of the one God, who attribute to His mercy all the good things that come to them in this life. We have in fact a Christian English conception of the noble chief before Christianity, who could lapse (as could Israel) in times of temptation into idolatry.[26] On the other hand, the traditional matter in English, not to mention the living survival of the heroic code and temper among the noble households of ancient England, enabled him to draw differently, and in some respects much closer to the actual heathen *hæleð*, the character of Beowulf, especially as a young knight, who used his great gift of *mægen* to earn *dom* and *lof* among men and posterity.

Beowulf is not an actual picture of historic Denmark or Geatland or Sweden about A.D. 500. But it is (if with certain minor defects) on a general view a self-consistent picture, a construction bearing clearly the marks of design and thought. The whole must have succeeded admirably in creating in the minds of the poet's contemporaries the illusion of surveying a past, pagan but noble and fraught with a deep significance – a past that itself had depth and reached backward into a dark antiquity of sorrow. This impression of depth is an effect and a justification of the use of episodes and allusions to old tales, mostly darker, more pagan, and desperate than the foreground.

To a similar antiquarian temper, and a similar use of vernacular learning, is probably due the similar effect of antiquity (and melancholy) in the *Aeneid* – especially felt as soon as Aeneas reaches Italy and the *Saturni gentem . . . sponte sua veterisque dei se more tenentem. Ic þa leode wat ge wið feond ge wið freond fæste worhte, æghwæs untæle ealde wisan*. Alas for the lost lore, the annals and old poets that Virgil knew, and only used in the making of a new thing! The criticism that the important matters are put on the outer edges misses this point of artistry, and indeed fails to see why the old things have in *Beowulf* such an appeal: it is the poet himself who made antiquity so appealing. His poem has more value in consequence, and is a greater contribution to early mediaeval thought than the harsh and intolerant view that consigned all the heroes to the devil. We may be thankful that the product of so noble a temper has been preserved by chance (if such it be) from the dragon of destruction.

The general structure of the poem, so viewed, is not really difficult to perceive, if we look to the main points, the strategy, and neglect the many points of minor tactics. We must dismiss, of course, from mind the notion that *Beowulf* is a 'narrative poem', that it tells a tale or intends to tell a tale sequentially. The poem 'lacks steady advance': so Klaeber heads a critical section in his edition.[27] But the poem was not meant to advance, steadily or unsteadily. It is essentially a balance, an opposition of ends and beginnings. In its simplest terms it is a contrasted description of two moments in a great life, rising and setting; an elaboration of the ancient and intensely moving contrast between youth and age, first achievement and final death. It is divided in consequence into two opposed portions, different in matter, manner, and length: A from 1 to 2199 (including an exordium of 52 lines); B from 2200 to 3182 (the end). There is no reason to cavil at this proportion; in any case, for the purpose and the production of the required effect, it proves in practice to be right.

This simple and *static* structure, solid and strong, is in each part much diversified, and capable of enduring this treatment. In the conduct of the presentation of Beowulf's rise to fame on the one hand, and of his kingship and death on the other, criticism can find things to question, especially if it is captious, but also much to praise, if it is attentive. But the only serious weakness, or apparent weakness, is the long recapitulation: the report of Beowulf to Hygelac. This recapitulation is well done. Without serious discrepancy[28] it retells rapidly the events in Heorot, and retouches the account; and it serves to illustrate, since he himself describes his own deeds, yet more vividly the character of a young man, singled out by destiny, as he steps suddenly forth in his full powers. Yet this

is perhaps not quite sufficient to justify the repetition. The explanation, if not complete justification, is probably to be sought in
different directions.

For one thing, the old tale was not first told or invented by this
poet. So much is clear from investigation of the folk-tale analogues.
Even the legendary association of the Scylding court with a
marauding monster, and with the arrival from abroad of a champion and deliverer was probably already old. The plot was not the
poet's; and though he has infused feeling and significance into its
crude material, that plot was not a perfect vehicle of the theme or
themes that came to hidden life in the poet's mind as he worked
upon it. Not an unusual event in literature. For the contrast –
youth and death – it would probably have been better, if we had
no journeying. If the single nation of the *Geatas* had been the scene,
we should have felt the stage not narrower, but symbolically
wider. More plainly should we have perceived in one people and
their hero all mankind and its heroes. This at any rate I have
always myself felt in reading *Beowulf*; but I have also felt that this
defect is rectified by the bringing of the tale of Grendel to Geatland.
As Beowulf stands in Hygelac's hall and tells his story, he sets his
feet firm again in the land of his own people, and is no longer
in danger of appearing a mere *wrecca*, an errant adventurer and
slayer of bogies that do not concern him.

There is in fact a double division in the poem: the fundamental
one already referred to, and a secondary but important division
at line 1887. After that the essentials of the previous part are taken
up and compacted, so that all the tragedy of Beowulf is contained
between 1888 and the end.[29] But, of course, without the first half
we should miss much incidental illustration; we should miss also
the dark background of the court of Heorot that loomed as large
in glory and doom in ancient northern imagination as the court
of Arthur: no vision of the past was complete without it. And
(most important) we should lose the direct contrast of youth and
age in the persons of Beowulf and Hrothgar which is one of the
chief purposes of this section: it ends with the pregnant words
oþ þæt hine yldo benam mægenes wynnum, se þe oft manegum scod.

In any case we must not view this poem as in intention an
exciting narrative or a romantic tale. The very nature of Old
English metre is often misjudged. In it there is no single rhythmic

pattern progressing from the beginning of a line to the end, and repeated with variation in other lines. The lines do not go according to a tune. They are founded on a balance; an opposition between two halves of roughly equivalent[30] phonetic weight, and significant content, which are more often rhythmically contrasted than similar. They are more like masonry than music. In this fundamental fact of poetic expression I think there is a parallel to the total structure of *Beowulf*. *Beowulf* is indeed the most successful Old English poem because in it the elements, language, metre, theme, structure, are all most nearly in harmony. Judgement of the verse has often gone astray through listening for an accentual rhythm and pattern: and it seems to halt and stumble. Judgement of the theme goes astray through considering it as the narrative handling of a plot: and it seems to halt and stumble. Language and verse, of course, differ from stone or wood or paint, and can be only heard or read in a time-sequence; so that in any poem that deals at all with characters and events some narrative element must be present. We have none the less in *Beowulf* a method and structure that within the limits of the verse-kind approaches rather to sculpture or painting. It is a composition not a tune.

This is clear in the second half. In the struggle with Grendel one can as a reader dismiss the certainty of literary experience that the hero will not in fact perish, and allow oneself to share the hopes and fears of the Geats upon the shore. In the second part the author has no desire whatever that the issue should remain open, even according to literary convention. There is no need to hasten like the messenger, who rode to bear the lamentable news to the waiting people (2892 ff.). They may have hoped, but we are not supposed to. By now we are supposed to have grasped the plan. Disaster is foreboded. Defeat is the theme. Triumph over the foes of man's precarious fortress is over, and we approach slowly and reluctantly the inevitable victory of death.[31]

'In structure', it was said of *Beowulf*, 'it is curiously weak, in a sense preposterous,' though great merits of detail were allowed. In structure actually it is curiously strong, in a sense inevitable, though there are defects of detail. The general design of the poet is not only defensible, it is, I think, admirable. There may have previously existed stirring verse dealing in straightforward manner and even in natural sequence with Beowulf's deeds, or with the fall of Hygelac; or again with the fluctuations of the feud between the houses of Hrethel the Geat and Ongentheow the Swede; or with the tragedy of the Heathobards, and the treason that destroyed the Scylding dynasty. Indeed this must be admitted to be practically certain: it was the existence of such connected legends – connected in the mind, not necessarily dealt with in chronicle fashion or in long semi-historical poems – that permitted the peculiar use of them in *Beowulf*. This poem cannot be criticized or comprehended, if its original audience is imagined in like case to ourselves, possessing only *Beowulf* in splendid isolation. For *Beowulf* was not designed to tell the tale of Hygelac's fall, or for that matter to give the whole biography of Beowulf, still less to write the history of the Geatish kingdom and its downfall. But it used knowledge of these things for its own purpose – to give that sense of perspective, of antiquity with a greater and yet darker antiquity behind. These things are mainly on the outer edges or in the background because they belong there, if they are to function in this way. But in the centre we have an heroic figure of enlarged proportions.

Beowulf is not an 'epic', not even a magnified 'lay'. No terms borrowed from Greek or other literatures exactly fit: there is no reason why they should. Though if we must have a term, we should choose rather 'elegy'. It is an heroic-elegiac poem; and in a sense all its first 3,136 lines are the prelude to a dirge: *him þa gegiredan Geata leode ad ofer eorðan unwaclicne*: one of the most moving ever written. But for the universal significance which is given to the fortunes of its hero it is an enhancement and not a detraction, in fact it is necessary, that his final foe should be not some Swedish prince, or treacherous friend, but a dragon: a thing made by imagination for just such a purpose. Nowhere does a dragon come in so precisely where he should. But if the hero falls before a dragon, then certainly he should achieve his early glory by vanquishing a foe of similar order.

There is, I think, no criticism more beside the mark than that which some have made, complaining that it is monsters in both halves that is so disgusting; one they could have stomached more easily. That is nonsense. I can see the point of asking for *no* monsters. I can also see the point of the situation in *Beowulf*. But no point at all in mere reduction of numbers. It would really have been preposterous, if the poet had recounted Beowulf's rise to fame in a 'typical' or 'commonplace' war in Frisia, and then ended him with a dragon. Or if he had told of his cleansing of Heorot, and then brought him to defeat and death in a 'wild' or 'trivial' Swedish invasion! If the dragon is the right end for Beowulf, and I agree with the author that it is, then Grendel is an eminently suitable beginning. They are creatures, *feond mancynnes*, of a similar order and kindred significance. Triumph over the lesser and more nearly human is cancelled by defeat before the older and more elemental. And the conquest of the ogres comes at the right moment: not in earliest youth, though the nicors are referred to in Beowulf's *geogoðfeore* as a presage of the kind of hero we have to deal with; and not during the later period of recognized ability and prowess;[32] but in that first moment, which often comes in great lives, when men look up in surprise and see that a hero has unawares leaped forth. The placing of the dragon is inevitable: a man can but die upon his death-day.

I will conclude by drawing an imaginary contrast. Let us suppose that our poet had chosen a theme more consonant with 'our modern judgement'; the life and death of St Oswald. He might then have made a poem, and told first of Heavenfield, when Oswald as a young prince against all hope won a great victory with a remnant of brave men; and then have passed at once to the lamentable defeat of Oswestry, which seemed to destroy the hope of Christian Northumbria; while all the rest of Oswald's life, and the traditions of the royal house and its feud with that of Deira might be introduced allusively or omitted. To any one but an historian in search of facts and chronology this would have been a fine thing, an heroic-elegiac poem greater than history. It would be much better than a plain narrative, in verse or prose, however steadily advancing. This mere arrangement would at once give it more significance than a straightforward account of one king's life: the contrast of rising and setting, achievement and death. But even so it would fall far short of *Beowulf*. Poetically it would be greatly enhanced if the poet had taken violent liberties with history and much enlarged the reign of Oswald, making him old and full of years of care and glory when he went forth heavy with foreboding to face the heathen Penda: the contrast of youth and age would add enormously to the original theme, and give it a more universal meaning. But even so it would still fall short of *Beowulf*. To match his theme with the rise and fall of poor 'folk-tale' Beowulf the poet would have been obliged to turn Cadwallon and Penda into giants and demons. It is just because the main foes in *Beowulf* are inhuman that the story is larger and more significant than this imaginary poem of a great king's fall. It glimpses the cosmic and moves with the thought of all men concerning the fate of human life and efforts; it stands amid but above the petty wars of princes, and surpasses the dates and limits of historical periods, however important. At the beginning, and during its process, and most of all at the end, we look down as if from a visionary height upon the house of man in the valley of the world. A light starts – *lixte se leoma ofer landa fela* – and there is a sound of music; but the outer darkness and its hostile offspring lie ever in wait for the torches to fail and the voices to cease. Grendel is maddened by the sound of harps.

And one last point, which those will feel who to-day preserve the ancient *pietas* towards the past: *Beowulf* is not a 'primitive' poem; it is a late one, using the materials (then still plentiful) preserved from a day already changing and passing, a time that has now for ever vanished, swallowed in oblivion; using them for a new purpose, with a wider sweep of imagination, if with a less bitter and concentrated force. When new *Beowulf* was already antiquarian, in a good sense, and it now produces a singular effect. For it is now to us itself ancient; and yet its maker was telling of things already old and weighted with regret, and he expended his art in making keen that touch upon the heart which sorrows have that are both poignant and remote. If the funeral of Beowulf moved once like the echo of an ancient dirge, far-off and hopeless, it is to us as a memory brought over the hills, an echo of an echo. There is not much poetry in the world like this; and though *Beowulf* may not be among the very greatest poems of our western world and its tradition, it has its own individual character, and peculiar solemnity; it would still have power had it been written in some time or place unknown and without posterity, if it contained no name that could now be recognized or identified by research. Yet it is in fact written in a language that after many centuries has still essential kinship with our own, it was made in this land, and moves in our northern world beneath our northern sky, and for those who are native to that tongue and land, it must ever call with a profound appeal – until the dragon comes.

APPENDIX

(a) Grendel's Titles

The changes which produced (before A.D. 1066) the mediaeval devil are not complete in *Beowulf*, but in Grendel change and blending are, of course, already apparent. Such things do not admit of clear classifications and distinctions. Doubtless ancient pre-Christian imagination vaguely recognized differences of 'materiality' between the solidly physical monsters, conceived as made of the earth and rock (to which the light of the sun might return them), and elves, and ghosts or bogies. Monsters of more or less human shape were naturally liable to development on contact with Christian ideas of sin and spirits of evil. Their parody of human form (*earmsceapen on weres wæstmum*) becomes symbolical, explicitly, of sin, or rather this mythical element, already present implicit and unresolved, is emphasized: this we see already in *Beowulf*, strengthened by the theory of descent from Cain (and so from Adam), and of the curse of God. So Grendel is not only under this inherited curse, but also himself sinful: *manscaða, synscaða, synnum beswenced*; he is *fyrena hyrde*. The same notion (combined with others) appears also when he is called (by the author, not by the characters in the poem) *hæþen*, 852, 986, and *helle hæfton, feond on helle*. As an image of man estranged from God he is called not only by all names applicable to ordinary men, as *wer, rinc, guma, maga*, but he is conceived as having a spirit, other than his body, that will be punished. Thus *alegde hæpene sawle: þær him hel onfeng*, 852; while Beowulf himself says *ðær abidan sceal miclan domes, hu him scir Metod scrifan wille*, 978.

But this view is blended or confused with another. Because of his ceaseless hostility to men, and hatred of their joy, his super-human size and strength, and his love of the dark, he approaches to a *devil*, though he is not yet a true devil in purpose. Real devilish qualities (deception and destruction of the soul), other than those which are undeveloped symbols, such as his hideousness and habitation in dark forsaken places, are hardly present. But he and his mother are actually called *deofla*, 1680; and Grendel is said when fleeing to hiding to make for *deofla gedræg*. It should be noted that *feond* cannot be used in this question: it still means 'enemy' in *Beowulf*, and is for instance applicable to Beowulf and Wiglaf in relation to the dragon. Even *feond on helle*, 101, is not so clear as it seems (see below); though we may add *wergan gastes*, 133, an expression for 'devil' later extremely common, and actually applied in line 1747 to the Devil and tempter himself. Apart, however, from this expression little can be made of the use of *gast*, *gæst*. For one thing it is under grave suspicion in many places (both applied to Grendel and otherwise) of being a corruption of *gæst*, *gest* 'stranger'; compare Grendel's title *cwealmcuma*, 792 = *wælgæst*, 1331, 1995. In any case it cannot be translated either by the modern *ghost* or *spirit*. *Creature* is probably the nearest we can now get. Where it is genuine it applies to Grendel probably in virtue of his relationship or similarity to bogies (*scinnum ond scuccum*), physical enough in form and power, but vaguely felt as belonging to a different order of being, one allied to the malevolent 'ghosts' of the dead. Fire is conceived as a *gæst* (1123).

This approximation of Grendel to a devil does not mean that there is any confusion as to his habitation. Grendel was a fleshly denizen of this world (until physically slain). *On helle* and *helle* (as in *helle gast* 1274) mean 'hellish', and are actually equivalent to the first elements in the compounds *deapscua*, *sceadugengea*, *helruna*. (Thus the original genitive *helle* developed into the Middle English adjective *helle*, *hellene* 'hellish', applicable to ordinary men, such as usurers; and even *feond on helle* could be so used. Wyclif applies *fend on helle* to the friar walking in England as Grendel in Denmark.) But the symbolism of darkness is so fundamental that it is vain to look for any distinction between the *þystru* outside Hrothgar's hall in which Grendel lurked, and the shadow of Death, or of hell after (or in) Death.

Thus in spite of shifting, actually in process (intricate, and as difficult as it is interesting and important to follow), Grendel remains primarily an ogre, a physical monster, whose main function is hostility to humanity (and its frail efforts at order and art upon earth). He is of the *fifelcyn*, a *þyrs* or *eoten*; in fact the *eoten*, for this ancient word is actually preserved in Old English only as applied to him. He is most frequently called simply a foe: *feond*, *lað*, *sceaða*, *feorhgeniðla*, *laðgeteona*, all words applicable to enemies of any kind. And though he, as ogre, has kinship with devils, and is doomed when slain to be numbered among the evil spirits, he is not when wrestling with Beowulf a materialized apparition of soul-destroying evil. It is thus true to say that Grendel is not yet a real mediaeval devil – except in so far as mediaeval bogies themselves had failed (as was often the case) to become real devils. But the distinction between a devilish ogre, and a devil revealing himself in ogre-form – between a monster, devouring the body and bringing temporal death,

that is inhabited by an accursed spirit, and a spirit of evil aiming ultimately at the soul and bringing eternal death (even though he takes a
form of visible horror, that may bring and suffer physical pain) –
is a real and important one, even if both kinds are to be found before
and after 1066. In *Beowulf* the weight is on the physical side: Grendel
does not vanish into the pit when grappled. He must be slain by plain
prowess, and thus is a real counterpart to the dragon in Beowulf's history.

(Grendel's mother is naturally described, when separately treated,
in precisely similar terms: she is *wif, ides, aglæc wif*; and rising to the
inhuman: *merewif, brimwylf, grundwyrgen*. Grendel's title *Godes andsaca*
has been studied in the text. Some titles have been omitted: for instance
those referring to his *outlawry*, which are applicable in themselves to him
by nature, but are of course also fitting either to a descendant of Cain,
or to a devil: thus *heorowearh, dædhata, mearcstapa, angengea*.)

(b) 'Lof' and 'Dom'; 'Hell' and 'Heofon'

Of pagan 'belief' we have little or nothing left in English. But the
spirit survived. Thus the author of *Beowulf* grasped fully the idea of
lof or *dom*, the noble pagan's desire for the *merited praise* of the noble.
For if this limited 'immortality' of renown naturally exists as a strong
motive together with actual heathen practice and belief, it can also
long outlive them. It is the natural residuum when the gods are
destroyed, whether unbelief comes from within or from without. The
prominence of the motive of *lof* in *Beowulf* – long ago pointed out by
Earle – may be interpreted, then, as a sign that a pagan time was not
far away from the poet, and perhaps also that the end of English paganism (at least among the noble classes for whom and by whom such
traditions were preserved) was marked by a twilight period, similar
to that observable later in Scandinavia. The gods faded or receded, and
man was left to carry on his war unaided. His trust was in his own power
and will, and his reward was the praise of his peers during his life and
after his death.

At the beginning of the poem, at the end of the first section of the
exordium, the note is struck: *lofdædum sceal in mægþa gehwære man geþeon*.
The last word of the poem is *lofgeornost*, the summit of the praise of the
dead hero: that was indeed *lastworda betst*. For Beowulf had lived
according to his own philosophy, which he explicitly avowed: *ure
æghwylc sceal ende gebidan worolde lifes; wyrce se ðe mote domes ær deaþe: þæt
bið dryhtguman æfter selest*, 1386 ff. The poet as commentator recurs again
to this: *swa sceal man don, þonne he æt guðe gegan þenceð longsumne lof:
na ymb his lif cearað*, 1534 ff.

Lof is ultimately and etymologically *value, valuation*, and so *praise*, as we say (itself derived from *pretium*). *Dom* is *judgement, assessment*, and in one branch *just esteem, merited renown*. The difference between these two is not in most passages important. Thus at the end of *Widsith*, which refers to the minstrel's part in achieving for the noble and their deeds the prolonged life of fame, both are combined: it is said of the generous patron, *lof se gewyrceð, hafað under heofonum heahfæstne dom*. But the difference has an importance. For the words were not actually synonymous, nor entirely commensurable. In the Christian period the one, *lof*, flowed rather into the ideas of heaven and the heavenly choirs; the other, *dom*, into the ideas of the judgement of God, the particular and general judgements of the dead.

The change that occurs can be plainly observed in *The Seafarer*, especially if lines 66–80 of that poem are compared with Hrothgar's *giedd* or sermon in *Beowulf* from 1755 onwards. There is a close resemblance between *Seafarer* 66–71 and Hrothgar's words 1761–8, a part of his discourse that may certainly be ascribed to the original author of *Beowulf*, whatever revision or expansion the speech may otherwise have suffered. The Seafarer says:

> *ic gelyfe no*
> *þæt him eorðwelan ece stondað.*
> *Simle þreora sum þinga gehwylce*
> *ær his tid[d]ege to tweon weorþeð:*
> *adl oþþe yldo oþþe ecghete*
> *fægum fromweardum feorh oðþringeð.*

Hrothgar says:

> *oft sona bið*
> *þæt þec adl oððe ecg eafoþes getwæfeð,*
> *oððe fyres feng, oððe flodes wylm,*
> *oððe gripe meces, oððe gares fliht,*
> *oððe atol yldo; oððe eagena bearhtm*
> *forsiteð ond forsworceð. Semninga bið*
> *þæt þec, dryhtguma, deað oferswyðeð.*

Hrothgar expands *þreora sum* on lines found elsewhere, either in great elaboration as in the *Fates of Men*, or in brief allusion to this well-known theme as in *The Wanderer* 80 ff. But the Seafarer, after thus proclaiming that all men shall die, goes on: 'Therefore it is for all noble men *lastworda betst* (the best memorial), and praise (*lof*) of the living who commemorate him after death, that ere he must go hence, he should merit and achieve on earth by heroic deeds against the malice of enemies (*feonda*), opposing the devil, that the children of men may praise him afterwards, and his *lof* may live with the angels for ever and ever, the glory of eternal life, rejoicing among the hosts.'

This is a passage which from its syntax alone may with unusual certainty be held to have suffered revision and expansion. It could easily be simplified. But in any case it shows a modification of heathen *lof* in two directions: first in making the deeds which win *lof* resistance to spiritual foes – the sense of the ambiguous *feonda* is, in the poem as pre-served, so defined by *deofle togeanes*; secondly, in enlarging *lof* to include the angels and the bliss of heaven. *lofsong, loftsong* are in Middle English especially used of the heavenly choirs.

But we do not find anything like this definite alteration in *Beowulf*. There *lof* remains pagan *lof*, the praise of one's peers, at best vaguely prolonged among their descendants *awa to ealdre*. (On *soðfæstra dom*, 2820, see below.) In *Beowulf* there is *hell*: justly the poet said of the people he depicted *helle gemundon on modsefan*. But there is practically no clear reference to *heaven* as its opposite, to heaven, that is, as a place or state of reward, of eternal bliss in the presence of God. Of course *heofon*, singular and plural, and its synonyms, such as *rodor*, are frequent; but they refer usually either to the particular landscape or to the sky under which all men dwell. Even when these words are used with the words for God, who is Lord of the heavens, such expressions are primarily parallels to others describing His general governance of nature (e.g. 1609 ff.), and His realm which includes land and sea and sky.

Of course it is not here maintained – very much the contrary – that the *poet* was ignorant of theological heaven, or of the Christian use of *heofon* as the equivalent of *caelum* in Scripture: only that this use was of intention (if not in practice quite rigidly) excluded from a poem dealing with the pagan past. There is one clear exception in lines 186 ff: *wel bið þæm þe mot æfter deaðdæge Drihten secean, ond to Fæder fæþmum freoðo wilnian.* If this, and the passage in which it occurs, is genuine – descends, that is, without addition or alteration from the poet who wrote *Beowulf* as a whole – and is not, as, I believe, a later expansion, then the point is not destroyed. For the passage remains still definitely an aside, an exclamation of the Christian author, who knew about heaven, and expressly denied such knowledge to the Danes. The characters within the poem do not understand heaven, or have hope of it. They refer to *hell* – an originally pagan word.[33] *Beowulf* predicts it as the destiny of Unferth and Grendel. Even the noble monotheist Hrothgar – so he is drawn, quite apart from the question of the genuineness of the bulk of his sermon from 1724-60 – refers to no heavenly bliss. The reward of virtue which he foretells for Beowulf is that his *dom* shall live *awa to ealdre*, a fortune also bestowed upon Sigurd in Norse (that his name *æ mun uppi*). This idea of lasting *dom* is, as we have seen, capable of being christianized; but in *Beowulf* it is not christianized, probably deliberately, when the characters are speaking in their proper persons, or their actual thoughts are reported.

The author, it is true, says of Beowulf that *him of hreðre gewat sawol secean soðfæstra dom*. What precise theological view he held concerning the souls of the just heathen we need not here inquire. He does not tell us, saying simply that Beowulf's spirit departed to whatever judgement awaits such just men, though we may take it that this comment implies that it was not destined to the fiery hell of punishment, being reckoned among the good. There is in any case here no doubt of the transmutation of words originally pagan. *soðfæstra dom* could by itself have meant simply the 'esteem of the true-judging', that *dom* which Beowulf as a young man had declared to be the prime motive of noble conduct; but here combined with *gewat secean* it must mean either the glory that belongs (in eternity) to the just, or the judgement of God upon the just. Yet Beowulf himself, expressing his own opinion, though troubled by dark doubts, and later declaring his conscience clear, thinks at the end only of his barrow and memorial among men, of his childlessness, and of Wiglaf the sole survivor of his kindred, to whom be bequeaths his arms. His funeral is not Christian, and his reward is the recognized virtue of his kingship and the hopeless sorrow of his people.

The relation of the Christian and heathen thought and diction in *Beowulf* has often been misconceived. So far from being a man so simple or so confused that he muddled Christianity with Germanic paganism, the author probably drew or attempted to draw distinctions, and to represent moods and attitudes of characters conceived dramatically as living in a noble but heathen past. Though there are one or two special problems concerning the tradition of the poem and the possibility that it has here and there suffered later unauthentic retouching,[34] we cannot speak in general either of confusion (in one poet's mind or in the mind of a whole period), or of patch-work revision producing confusion. More sense can be made of the poem, if we start rather with the hypothesis, not in itself unlikely, that the poet tried to do something definite and difficult, which had some reason and thought behind it, though his execution may not have been entirely successful.

The strongest argument that the actual language of the poem is not in general the product either of stupidity or accident is to be found in the fact that we can observe *differentiation*. We can, that is, in this matter of philosophy and religious sentiment distinguish, for instance: (*a*) the poet as narrator and commentator; (*b*) Beowulf; and (*c*) Hrothgar. Such differentiation would not be achieved by a man himself confused in mind, and still less by later random editing. The kind of thing that accident contrives is illustrated by *drihten wereda*, 'lord of hosts', a familiar Christian expression, which appears in line 2186, plainly as an alteration of *drihten Wedera* 'lord of the Geats'. This alteration is obviously due to some man, the actual scribe of the line or some predecessor, more familiar with *Dominus Deus Sabaoth* than with Hrethel and the Weder-Geatish house. But no one, I think, has ventured to ascribe this confusion to the author.

That such differentiation does occur, I do not attempt here to prove by analysis of all the relevant lines of the poem. I leave the matter to those who care to go through the text, only insisting that it is essential to pay closer attention than has usually been paid to the *circumstances* in which the references to religion, Fate, or mythological matters each appear, and to distinguish in particular those things which are said in *oratio recta* by one of the characters, or are reported as being said or thought by them. It will then be seen that the narrating and commenting poet obviously stands apart. But the two characters who do most of the speaking, Beowulf and Hrothgar, are also quite distinct. Hrothgar is consistently portrayed as a wise and noble monotheist, modelled largely it has been suggested in the text on the Old Testament patriarchs and kings; he refers all things to the favour of God, and never omits explicit thanks for mercies. Beowulf refers sparingly to God, except as the arbiter of critical events, and then principally as *Metod*, in which the idea of God approaches nearest to the old Fate. We have in Beowulf's language little differentiation of God and Fate. For instance, he says *gæð a wyrd swa hio scel* and immediately continues that *dryhten* holds the balance in his combat (441); or again he definitely equates *wyrd* and *metod* (2526 f.).[35] It is Beowulf who says *wyrd oft nereð unfægne eorl, þonne his ellen deah* (immediately after calling the sun *beacen Godes*), which contrasts with the poet's own comment on the man who escaped the dragon (2291): *swa mæg unfæge eaðe gedigean wean ond wræcsið, se ðe Wealdendes hyldo gehealdeþ*. Beowulf only twice explicitly thanks God or acknowledges His help: in lines 1658–61, where he acknowledges God's protection and the favour of *ylda Waldend* in his combat under the water; in his last speech, where he thanks *Frean Wuldurcyninge . . . ecum Dryhtne* for all the treasure, and for helping him to win it for his people. Usually he makes no such references. He ascribes his conquest of the nicors to luck – *hwæþre me gesælde*, 570 ff. (compare the similar words used of Sigemund, 890). In his account to

Hygelac his only explanation of his preservation in the water-den is *næs ic fæge þa gyt* (2141). He does not allude to God at all in this report.

Beowulf knows, of course, of hell and judgement: he speaks of it to Unferth; he declares that Grendel shall abide *miclan domes* and the judgement of *scir metod*; and finally in his last examination of conscience he says that *Waldend fira* cannot accuse him of *morðorbealo maga*. But the crimes which he claims to have avoided are closely paralleled in the heathen *Völuspá*, where the grim hall, *Náströndu á*, contains especially *menn meinsvara ok morðvarga* (perjurers and murderers).

Other references he makes are casual and formal, such as *beorht beacen Godes*, of the sun (571). An exceptional case is *Godes leoht geceas* 2469, describing the death of Hrethel, Beowulf's grandfather. This would appear to refer to heaven. Both these expressions have, as it were, inadvertently escaped from Christian poetry. The first, *beacen Godes*, is perhaps passable even for a heathen in this particular poem, in which the theory throughout is that good pagans, when not tempted or deluded by the devil, knew of the one God. But the second, especially since Beowulf himself is formally the speaker, is an item of unsuitable diction – which cannot be dismissed as a later alteration. A didactic reviser would hardly have added this detail to the description of the heathen king's death: he would rather have removed the heathen, or else sent him to hell. The whole story alluded to is pagan and hopeless, and turns on blood-feud and the motive that when a son kills his brother the father's sorrow is intensified because no vengeance can be exacted. The explanation of such occasional faults is not to be sought in Christian revision, but in the fact that before *Beowulf* was written Christian poetry was already established, and was known to the author. The language of *Beowulf* is in fact partly 're-paganized' by the author with a special purpose, rather than christianized (by him or later) without consistent purpose. Throughout the poem the language becomes more intelligible, if we assume that the diction of poetry was already christianized and familiar with Old and New Testament themes and motives. There is a gap, important and effective poetically whatever was its length in time, between Cædmon and the poet of *Beowulf*. We have thus in Old English not only the old heroic language often strained or misused in applica-tion to Christian legend (as in *Andreas* or *Elene*), but in *Beowulf* language of Christian tone occasionally (if actually seldom) put inadvertently in the mouth of a character conceived as heathen. All is not perfect to the last detail in *Beowulf*. But with regard to *Godes leoht geceas*, the chief defect of this kind, it may be observed that in the very long speech of Beowulf from 2425–2515 the poet has hardly attempted to keep up the pretence of *oratio recta* throughout. Just before the end he reminds us and himself that Beowulf is supposed to be speaking by a renewed *Beowulf maðelode* (2510). From 2444 to 2489 we have not really a monologue in character at all, and the words *Godes leoht geceas* go rather with *gewat secean soðfæstra dom* as evidence of the author's own view of the destiny of the just pagan.

When we have made allowance for imperfections of execution, and even for some intentional modification of character in old age (when Beowulf becomes not unnaturally much more like Hrothgar), it is plain that the characters and sentiments of the two chief actors in the poem are differently conceived and drawn. Where Beowulf's thoughts are revealed by the poet we can observe that his real trust was in *his own might*. That the possession of this might was a 'favour of God' is actually a comment of the poet's, similar to the comment of Scandinavian Christians upon their heathen heroes. Thus in line 665 we have *georne truwode modgan mægenes, metodes hyldo*. No *and* is possible metrically in the original; none should appear in translation: the favour of God *was* the possession of *mægen*. Compare 1272–3: *gemunde mægenes strenge, gimfæste gife ðe him God sealde*.[36] Whether they knew it or not, *cupon* (or *ne cupon*) *heofena Helm herian*, the supreme quality of the old heroes, their valour, was their special endowment by God, and as such could be admired and praised.

Concerning Beowulf the poet tells us finally that when the dragon's ruinous assault was reported, he was filled with doubt and dismay, and *wende se wisa þæt he Wealdende ofer ealde riht ecean Dryhtne bitre gebulge*. It has been said that *ofer ealde riht*, 'contrary to ancient law', is here given a Christian interpretation; but this hardly seems to be the case. This is a heathen and unchristian fear – of an inscrutable power, a *Metod* that can be offended inadvertently: indeed the sorrow of a man who, though he knew of God, and was eager for justice, was yet far estranged, and 'had hell in his heart'.

(c) Lines 175–88

These lines are important and present certain difficulties. We can with confidence accept as original and genuine these words as far as *helle gemundon on modsefan* – which is strikingly true, in a sense, of all the characters depicted or alluded to in the poem, even if it is here actually applied only to those deliberately turning from God to the Devil. The rest requires, and has often received, attention. If it is original, the poet must have intended a distinction between the wise Hrothgar, who certainly knew of and often thanked God, and a certain party of the pagan Danes – heathen priests, for instance, and those that had recourse to them under the temptation of calamity – specially deluded by the *gastbona*, the destroyer of souls.[37] Of these, particularly those permanently in the service of idols (*swylce wæs þeaw hyra*), which in Christian theory and in fact did not include all the community, it is perhaps possible to say that they did not know (*ne cupon*), nor even know of (*ne wiston*), the one God, nor know how to worship him. At any rate the hell (of fire) is only predicted for those showing malice (*sliðne nið*), and it is not plain that the *freoðo* of the Father is ultimately obtainable by none of these men of old. It is probable that the contrast between 92–8 and 175–88 is intentional: the song of the minstrel in the days of untroubled joy, before the assault of Grendel, telling of the Almighty and His fair creation, and the loss of knowledge and praise, and the fire awaiting such malice, in the time of temptation and despair.

But it is open to doubt whether lines 181–88 are original, or at any rate unaltered. Not of course because of the apparent discrepancy – though it is a matter vital to the whole poem: we cannot dismiss lines simply because they offer difficulty of such a kind. But because, unless my ear and judgement are wholly at fault, they have a ring and measure unlike their context, and indeed unlike that of the poem as a whole. The place is one that offers at once special temptation to enlargement or alteration and special facilities for doing either without grave dislocation.[38] I suspect that the second half of line 180 has been altered, while what follows has remodelled or replaced a probably shorter passage, making the comment (one would say, guided by the poem as a whole) that they *forsook* God under tribulation, and incurred the danger of hell-fire. This in itself would be a comment of the *Beowulf* poet, who was probably provided by his original material with a reference to *wigweorpung* in the sacred site of Heorot at this juncture in the story.

In any case the *unleugbare Inkonsequenz* (Hoops) of this passage is felt chiefly by those who assume that by references to the Almighty the legendary Danes and the Scylding court are depicted as 'Christian'. If that is so, the mention of heathen *þeaw* is, of course, odd; but it offers only one (if a marked) example of a confusion of thought fundamental to the poem, and does not then merit long consideration. Of all the attempts to deal with this *Inkonsequenz* perhaps the least satisfactory is the most recent: that of Hoops,[39] who supposes that the poet had to represent the Danish prayers as addressed to the Devil for the protection of the honour of the *Christengott*, since the prayers were not answered. But this attributes to the poet a confusion (and insincerity) of thought that an 'Anglo-Saxon' was hardly modern or advanced enough to achieve. It is difficult to believe that he could have been so singularly ill instructed in the nature of Christian prayer. And the pretence that *all* prayers to the *Christengott* are answered, and swiftly, would scarcely have deceived the stupidest member of his audience. Had he embarked on such bad theology, he would have had many other difficulties to face: the long time of woe before God relieved the distress of these Christian Danes by sending Scyld (13); and indeed His permission of the assaults of Grendel at all upon such a Christian people, who do not seem depicted as having perpetrated any crime punishable by calamity. But in fact God did provide a cure for Grendel – Beowulf, and this is recognized by the poet in the mouth of Hrothgar himself (381 ff.). We may acquit the maker of *Beowulf* of the suggested motive, whatever we may think of the *Inkonsequenz*. He could hardly have been less aware than we that in history (in England and in other lands), and in Scripture, people could depart from the one God to other service in time of trial – precisely because that God has never guaranteed to His servants immunity from temporal calamity, before or after prayer. It is to idols that men turned (and turn) for quick and literal answers.

NOTES

1   *The Shrine*, p. 4.

2   Thus in Professor Chambers's great bibliography (in his *Beowulf: An Introduction*) we find a section, §8. Questions of Literary History, Date, and Authorship; Beowulf in the Light of History, Archaeology, Heroic Legend, Mythology, and Folklore. It is impressive, but there is no section that names Poetry. As certain of the items included show, such consideration as Poetry is accorded at all is buried unnamed in §8.

3   *Beowulf translated into modern English rhyming verse*, Constable, 1925.

4   *A Short History of English Literature*, Oxford Univ. Press, 1921, pp. 2–3. I choose this example, because it is precisely to general literary histories that we must usually turn for literary judgements on *Beowulf*. The experts in *Beowulfiana* are seldom concerned with such judgements. And it is in the highly compressed histories, such as this, that we discover what the process of digestion makes of the special 'literature' of the experts. Here is the distilled product of Research. This compendium, moreover, is competent, and written by a man who had (unlike some other authors of similar things) read the poem itself with attention.

5   I include nothing that has not somewhere been said by some one, if not in my exact words; but I do not, of course, attempt to represent all the *dicta*, wise or otherwise, that have been uttered.

6   *The Dark Ages*, pp. 252-3.

7   None the less Ker modified it in an important particular in *English Literature, Mediæval*, pp. 29–34. In general, though in different words, vaguer and less incisive, he repeats himself. We are still told that 'the story is commonplace and the plan is feeble', or that 'the story is thin and poor'. But we learn also at the end of his notice that: 'Those distracting allusions to things apart from the chief story make up for their want of proportion. They give the impression of reality and weight; the story is not in the air . . . it is part of the solid world.' By the admission of so grave an artistic reason for the procedure of the poem Ker himself began the undermining of his own criticism of its structure. But this line of thought does not seem to have been further pursued. Possibly it was this very thought, working in his mind, that made Ker's notice of *Beowulf* in the small later book, his 'shilling shocker', more vague and hesitant in tone, and so of less influence.

8   *Foreword* to Strong's translation, p. xxvi: see note 3.
9   It has also been favoured by the rise of 'English schools', in whose syllabuses *Beowulf* has inevitably some place, and the consequent production of compendious literary histories. For these cater (in fact, if not in intention) for those seeking knowledge about, and ready-made judgements upon, works which they have not the time, or (often enough) the desire, to know at first hand. The small literary value of such summaries is sometimes recognized in the act of giving them. Thus Strong (op. cit.) gives a fairly complete one, but remarks that 'the short summary does scant justice to the poem'. Ker in *E. Lit.* (*Med.*) says: 'So told, in abstract, it is not a particularly interesting story.' He evidently perceived what might be the retort, for he attempts to justify the procedure in this case, adding: 'Told in this way the story of Theseus or Hercules would still have much more in it.' I dissent. But it does not matter, for the comparison of two plots 'told in this way' is no guide whatever to the merits of literary versions told in quite different ways. It is not necessarily the best poem that loses least in précis.
10 Namely the use of it in *Beowulf*, both dramatically in depicting the sagacity of Beowulf the hero, and as an essential part of the traditions concerning the Scylding court, which is the legendary background against which the rise of the hero is set – as a later age would have chosen the court of Arthur. Also the probable allusion in Alcuin's letter to Speratus: see Chambers's *Widsith*, p. 78.
11 This expression may well have been actually used by the *eald geneat*, but none the less (or perhaps rather precisely on that account) is probably to be regarded not as new-minted, but as an ancient and honoured *gnome* of long descent.
12 For the words *hige sceal þe heardra, heorte þe cenre, mod sceal þe mare þe ure mægen lytlað* are not, of course, an exhortation to simple courage. They are not reminders that fortune favours the brave, or that victory may be snatched from defeat by the stubborn. (Such thoughts were familiar, but otherwise expressed: *wyrd oft nereð unfægne eorl, þonne his ellen deah.*) The words of Byrhtwold were made for a man's last and hopeless day.
13 *Foreword* to Strong's translation, p. xxviii. See note 3.
14 This is not strictly true. The dragon is not referred to in such terms, which are applied to Grendel and to the primeval giants.
15 He differs in important points, referred to later.
16 I should prefer to say that he moves in a northern heroic age imagined by a Christian, and therefore has a noble and gentle quality, though conceived to be a pagan.
17 It is, for instance, dismissed cursorily, and somewhat contemptuously in the recent (somewhat contemptuous) essay of Dr Watson, *The Age of Bede* in *Bede, His Life, Times, and Writings*, ed. A. Hamilton Thompson, 1935.
18 *The Dark Ages*, p. 57.
19 If we consider the period as a whole. It is not, of course, necessarily true of individuals. These doubtless from the beginning showed many degrees from deep instruction and understanding to disjointed superstition, or blank ignorance.
20 Avoidance of obvious anachronisms (such as are found in *Judith*, for instance, where the heroine refers in her own speeches to Christ and the Trinity), and the absence of all definitely *Christian* names and terms, is natural and plainly intentional. It must be observed that there is a difference between the comments of the author and the things said in reported speech by his characters. The two chief of these, Hrothgar and Beowulf, are again differentiated. Thus the only definitely Scriptural references, to Abel (108) and to Cain (108, 1261), occur where the poet is speaking as commentator. The theory of Grendel's origin is not known to the actors: Hrothgar denies all knowledge of the ancestry of Grendel (1355). The giants (1688 ff.) are, it is true, represented pictorially, and in Scriptural terms. But this suggests rather that the author identified native and Scriptural accounts, and gave his picture Scriptural colour, since of the two accounts Scripture was the truer. And if so it would be closer to that told in remote antiquity when the

sword was made, more especially since the *wundorsmiþas* who wrought it were actually giants (1558, 1562, 1679): they would know the true tale. See note 25.

21 In fact the real resemblance of the *Aeneid* and *Beowulf* lies in the constant presence of a sense of many-storied antiquity, together with its natural accompaniment, stern and noble melancholy. In this they are really akin and together differ from Homer's flatter, if more glittering, surface.

22 I use this illustration following Chambers, because of the close resemblance between Grendel and the Cyclops in kind. But other examples could be adduced: Cacus, for instance, the offspring of Vulcan. One might ponder the contrast between the legends of the torture of Prometheus and of Loki: the one for assisting men, the other for assisting the powers of darkness.

23 There is actually no final principle in the legendary hostilities contained in classical mythology. For the present purpose that is all that matters: we are not here concerned with remoter mythological origins, in the North or South. The gods, Cronian or Olympian, the Titans, and other great natural powers, and various monsters, even minor local horrors, are not clearly distinguished in origin or ancestry. There could be no permanent policy of war, led by Olympus, to which human courage might be dedicated, among mythological races so promiscuous. Of course, nowhere can absolute rigidity of distinction be expected, because in a sense the foe is always both within and without; the fortress must fall through treachery as well as by assault. Thus Grendel has a perverted human shape, and the giants or *jötnar*, even when (like the Titans) they are of super-divine stature, are parodies of the human-divine form. Even in Norse, where the distinction is most rigid, Loki dwells in Asgarðr, though he is an evil and lying spirit, and fatal monsters come of him. For it is true of man, maker of myths, that Grendel and the Dragon, in their lust, greed, and malice, have a part in him. But mythically conceived the gods do not recognize any bond with *Fenris úlfr*, any more than men with Grendel or the serpent.

24 The *Genesis* which is preserved for us is a late copy of a damaged original, but is still certainly in its older parts a poem whose composition must be referred to the early period. That *Genesis A* is actually older than *Beowulf* is generally recognized as the most probable reading of such evidence as there is.

25 Actually the poet may have known, what we can guess, that such creation-themes were also ancient in the North. *Völuspá* describes Chaos and the making of the sun and moon, and very similar language occurs in the Old High German fragment known as the *Wessobrunner Gebet*. The song of the minstrel Iopas, who had his knowledge from Atlas, at the end of the first book of the *Aeneid* is also in part a song of origins: *hic canit errantem lunam solisque labores, unde hominum genus et pecudes, unde imber et ignes*. In any case the Anglo-Saxon poet's view throughout was plainly that true, or truer, knowledge was possessed in ancient days (when men were not deceived by the Devil); at least they knew of the one God and Creator, though not of heaven, for that was lost. See note 20.

26 It is of Old Testament lapses rather than of any events in England (of which he is not speaking) that the poet is thinking in lines 175 ff., and this colours his manner of allusion to knowledge which he may have derived from native traditions concerning the Danes and the special heathen religious significance of the site of Heorot (*Hleiðrar, æt hærgtrafum*, the tabernacles) – it was possibly a matter that embittered the feud of Danes and Heathobeards. If so, this is another point where old and new have blended. On the special importance and difficulty for criticism of the passage 175–88 see the Appendix.

27 Though only explicitly referred to here and in disagreement, this edition is, of course, of great authority, and all who have used it have learned much from it.

28 I am not concerned with minor discrepancies at any point in the poem. They are no proof of composite authorship, nor even of incompetent authorship. It is very difficult, even in a newly invented tale of any length, to avoid such defects; more so still in rehandling old and oft-told tales. The points that are seized in the study,

with a copy that can be indexed and turned to and fro (even if never read straight through as it was meant to be), are usually such as may easily escape an author and still more easily his natural audience. Virgil certainly does not escape such faults, even within the limits of a single book. Modern printed tales, that have presumably had the advantage of proof-correction, can even be observed to hesitate in the heroine's Christian name.

29   The least satisfactory arrangement possible is thus to read only lines 1–1887 and not the remainder. This procedure has none the less been, from time to time, directed or encouraged by more than one 'English syllabus'.

30   Equivalent, but not necessarily *equal*, certainly not as such things may be measured by machines.

31   That the particular bearer of enmity, the Dragon, also dies is important chiefly to Beowulf himself. He was a great man. Not many even in dying can achieve the death of a single worm, or the temporary salvation of their kindred. Within the limits of human life Beowulf neither lived nor died in vain – brave men might say. But there is no hint, indeed there are many to the contrary, that it was a war to end war, or a dragon-fight to end dragons. It is the end of Beowulf, and of the hope of his people.

32   We do, however, learn incidentally much of this period: it is not strictly true, even of our poem as it is, to say that after the deeds in Heorot Beowulf 'has nothing else to do'. Great heroes, like great saints, should show themselves capable of dealing also with the ordinary things of life, even though they may do so with a strength more than ordinary. We may wish to be assured of this (and the poet has assured us), without demanding that he should put such things in the centre, when they are not the centre of his thought.

33   Free as far as we know from definite physical location. Details of the original northern conception, equated and blended with the Scriptural, are possibly sometimes to be seen colouring the references to Christian hell. A celebrated example is the reference in *Judith* to the death of Holofernes, which recalls remarkably certain features in *Völuspá*. Cf. *Judith* 115: *wyrmum bewunden*, and 119: *of ðam wyrmsele* with *Vǫl.* 36 *sá's undinn salr orma hryggjum*: which translated into O.E. would be *se is wunden sele wyrma hrycgum*.

34   Such as 168–9, probably a clumsily intruded couplet, of which the only certain thing that can be said is that it interrupts (even if its sense were plain) the natural connexion between 165–7 and 170; the question of the expansion (in this case at any rate skilful and not inapt) of Hrothgar's *giedd*, 1724–60; and most notably lines 175–88.

35   Of course the use of words more or less equivalent to 'fate' continued throughout the ages. The most Christian poets refer to *wyrd*, usually of unfortunate events; but sometimes of good, as in *Elene* 1047, where the conversion of Judas is ascribed to *wyrd*. There remains always the main mass of the workings of Providence (*Metod*) which are inscrutable, and for practical purposes dealt with as 'fate' or 'luck'. *Metod* is in Old English the word that is most nearly allied to 'fate', although employed as a synonym of *god*. That it could be so employed is due probably to its having anciently in English an agental significance (as well as an abstract sense), as in Old Norse where *mjǫtuðr* has the senses 'dispenser, ruler' and 'doom, fate, death'. But in Old English *metodsceaft* means 'doom' or 'death'. Cf. 2814 f. where *wyrd* is more active than *metodsceaft*. In Old Saxon *metod* is similarly used, leaning also to the side of the inscrutable (and even hostile) aspects of the world's working. Gabriel in the *Héliand* says of John the Baptist that he will not touch wine: *so habed im* uurdgiscapu, metod *gimarcod endi maht godes* (128); it is said of Anna when her husband died: *that sie thiu mikila maht* metodes *todelda, uured* uurdigiscapu (511). In Old Saxon *metod(o)giscapu* and *metodigisceft*, equal Fate, as O.E. *metodsceaft*.

36   Compare, for instance, the intrusive commentary in *Fóstbrœðra saga* which observes in a description of a grim pagan character: *ekki var hjarta hans sem fóarn í fugli, ekki*

var þat blóðfult, svá at þat skylfi af hræðslu, heldr var þat hert af enum hæsta höfuðsmið í öllum hvatleik (ch. 2); and again *Almáttigr er sá sem svá snart hjarta ok óhrætt lét í brjóst Þorgeiri; ok ekki var hans hugpryði af mönnum ger né honum í brjóst borin, heldr af enum hæsta höfuðsmið* (ib.). Here the notion is explicitly (if unseasonably and absurdly) expressed.

37 It is not strictly true to say, as is said, for instance, by Hoops, that he is 'identified' with their heathen god. The Christian theory was that such gods did not exist, and were inventions of the Devil, and that the power of idols was due to the fact that he, or one of his emissaries, often actually inhabited them, and could be seen in their real hideousness if the veil of illusion was removed. Compare Aelfric's homilies on St Bartholomew, and St Matthew, where by the power of an angel or saint the devil residing in idols was revealed as a black *silhearwa*.

38 Similarly it is the very marked character already by the poet given to Hrothgar which has induced and made possible without serious damage the probable revision and expansion of his sermon. Well done as the passage in itself is, the poem would be better with the excision of approximately lines 1740–60; and these lines are on quite independent grounds under the strongest suspicion of being due to later revision and addition. The actual joints have, nevertheless, if that is so, been made with a technical competence as good as that which I here assume for the earlier passage.

39 *Kommentar zum Beowulf*, p. 39.

ON TRANSLATING BEOWULF

I

ON TRANSLATION AND WORDS

No defence is usually offered for translating *Beowulf*. Yet the making, or at any rate the publishing, of a modern English rendering needs defence: especially the presentation of a translation into plain prose of what is in fact a poem, a work of skilled and close-wrought metre (to say no more). The process has its dangers. Too many people are willing to form, and even to print, opinions of this greatest of the surviving works of ancient English poetic art after reading only such a translation, or indeed after reading only a bare 'argument', such as appears in the present book. On the strength of a nodding acquaintance of this sort (it may be supposed), one famous critic informed his public that *Beowulf* was 'only small beer'. Yet if beer at all, it is a drink dark and bitter: a solemn funeral-ale with the taste of death. But this is an age of potted criticism and pre-digested literary opinion; and in the making of these cheap substitutes for food translations unfortunately are too often used.

To use a prose translation for this purpose is, none the less, an abuse. *Beowulf* is not merely in verse, it is a great poem; and the plain fact that no attempt can be made to represent its metre, while little of its other specially poetic qualities can be caught in such a medium, should be enough to show that 'Clark Hall', revised or unrevised, is not offered as a means of judging the original, or as a substitute for reading the poem itself. The proper purpose of a prose translation is to provide an aid to study.

If you are not concerned with poetry, but with other matters, such as references to heroic names now nearly faded into oblivion, or the mention of ancient customs and beliefs, you may find in this competent translation all that you require for comparison with other sources. Or nearly all – for the use of 'Anglo-Saxon' evidence is never, of course, entirely safe without a knowledge of the language. No translation that aims at being readable in itself can, without elaborate annotation, proper to an edition of the original, indicate all the possibilities or hints afforded by the text. It is not possible, for instance, in translation always to represent a recurring word in the original by one given modern word. Yet the recurrence may be important.

Thus 'stalwart' in 198, 'broad' in 1621, 'huge' in 1663, 'mighty' in 2140 are renderings of the one word *eacen*; while the related *eacencræftig*, applied to the dragon's hoard, is in 2280 and 3051 rendered 'mighty'. These equivalents fit the contexts and the modern English sentences in which they stand, and are generally recognized as correct. But an enquirer into ancient beliefs, with the loss of *eacen* will lose the hint that in poetry this word preserved a special connotation. Originally it means not 'large' but 'enlarged', and in all instances may imply not merely size and strength, but an *addition* of power, beyond the natural, whether it is applied to the superhuman thirtyfold strength possessed by Beowulf (in this Christian poem it is his special gift from God), or to the mysterious magical powers of the giant's sword and the dragon's hoard imposed by runes and curses. Even the *eacne eardas* (1621) where the monsters dwelt may have been regarded as possessing, while these lived, an added power beyond the natural peril. This is only a casual example of the kind of difficulty and interest revealed by the language of Old English verse (and of *Beowulf* in particular), to which no literary translation can be expected to provide a complete index. For many Old English poetical words there are (naturally) no precise modern equivalents of the same scope and tone: they come down to us bearing echoes of ancient days beyond the shadowy borders of Northern history. Yet the compactness of the original idiom, inevitably weakened even in prose by transference to our looser modern language, does not tolerate long explanatory phrases. For no study of the fragmentary Anglo-Saxon documents is translation a complete substitute.

But you may be engaged in the more laudable labour of trying actually to read the original poem. In that case the use of this translation need not be disdained. It need not become a 'crib'. For a good translation is a good companion of honest labour, while a 'crib' is a (vain) substitute for the essential work with grammar and glossary, by which alone can be won genuine appreciation of a noble idiom and a lofty art.

Old English (or Anglo-Saxon) is not a very difficult language, though it is neglected by many of those concerned with the long period of our history during which it was spoken and written. But the idiom and diction of Old English verse is not easy. Its manner and conventions, and its metre, are unlike those of modern English verse. Also it is preserved fragmentarily and by chance, and has only in recent times been redeciphered and interpreted, without the aid of any tradition or gloss: for in England, unlike Iceland, the old Northern poetic tradition was at length completely broken and buried. As a result many words and phrases are met rarely or only once. There are many words only found in *Beowulf*. An example is *eoten* 'giant' 112, etc. This word, we may believe on other evidence, was well known, though actually it is only recorded in its Anglo-Saxon form in *Beowulf*, because this poem alone has survived of the oral and written matter dealing with such legends. But the word rendered 'retinue' in 924 is *hose*, and though philologists may with confidence define this as the dative of a feminine noun *hōs* (the Anglo-Saxon equivalent of Old High German and Gothic *hansa*), it is in fact found in this line of *Beowulf* alone; and how far it was not only 'poetical', but already archaic and rare in the time of the poet, we do not know. Yet we need to know, if a translation strictly true in verbal effect is to be devised. Such lexical niceties may not trouble many students, but none can help finding that the learning of new words that will seldom or never again be useful is one of the (accidental) difficulties presented by Old English verse. Another is presented by the poetical devices, especially the descriptive compounds, which, if they are seldom in fact 'unnatural', are generally foreign to our present literary and linguistic habits. Their precise meaning and full significance (for a contemporary) is not always easy to define, and their translation is a problem for the translator over which he often must hesitate. A simple example is *sundwudu*, literally 'flood-timber' or 'swimming-timber'. This is 'ship' in 208 (the riddle's bare solution, and often the best available, though quite an inadequate, rendering), and 'wave-borne timbers' in 1906 (an attempt to unfold, at the risk of dissipating it, the briefly flashed picture). Similar is *swan-rad*, rendered 'swan's-road' in 200:

the bare solution 'sea' would lose too much. On the other hand, a full elucidation would take far too long. Literally it means 'swan-riding': that is, the region which is to the swimming swan as the plain is to the running horse or wain. Old English *rad* is as a rule used for the act of riding or sailing, not as its modern descendant 'road', for a beaten track. More difficult are such cases as *onband beadurune* in 502, used of the sinister counsellor, Unferth, and rendered 'gave vent to secret thoughts of strife'. Literally it means 'unbound a battle-rune (*or* battle-runes)'. What exactly is implied is not clear. The expression has an antique air, as if it had descended from an older time to our poet: a suggestion lingers of the spells by which men of wizardry could stir up storms in a clear sky.

These compounds, especially when they are used not with but instead of such ordinary words as *scip* 'ship', or *sæ* 'sea' (already twelve hundred years ago the terms of daily life), give to Old English verse, while it is still unfamiliar, something of the air of a conundrum. So the early scholars of the seventeenth and eighteenth centuries thought: to them, even when they understood Ælfred or Ælfric well enough, 'Saxon poetry' often seemed a tissue of riddles and hard words woven deliberately by lovers of enigma. This view is not, of course, just: it is a beginner's misapprehension. The riddle element is present, but Old English verse was not generally dark or difficult, and was not meant to be. Even among the actual verse-riddles extant in Anglo-Saxon, many are to be found of which the object is a cameo of recognizable description rather than a puzzle. The primary poetic object of the use of compounds was compression, the force of brevity, the packing of the pictorial and emotional colour tight within a slow sonorous metre made of short balanced word-groups. But familiarity with this manner does not come all at once. In the early stages – as some to whom this old verse now seems natural enough can doubtless well remember – one's nose is ground close to the text: both story and poetry may be hard to see for the words. The grinding process is good for the noses of scholars, of any age or degree; but the aid of a translation may be a welcome relief. As a general guide, not only in those hard places which remain the cruces of the expert, this translation can be recommended.

The older version of Dr Clark Hall did good service; but it must be admitted that it was often a faulty guide in diction – not only as representing the original (which is difficult or impossible fully to achieve), but as offering an harmonious choice of modern English words. It did not often rival the once famous oddities of Earle's *Deeds of Beowulf*,[1] though the 'ten timorous trothbreakers together' in 2846 (reminiscent of the 'two tired toads that tried to trot to Tutbury'), and the 'song of non-success' in 787 (for *sigeleasne sang* – 'a song void of triumph') are of a similar vintage. But it fell too often into unnecessary colloquialisms, such as 'lots of feuds' 2028 (now 'many'), quite alien to the tone of the original in its own day. Too often notables, visitors and subalterns appeared instead of the more fitting, and indeed more literally accurate, counsellors, strangers, and young knights. The fire-dragon appeared as a reptile and a salamander (2689); the jewels of his hoard were called 'bright artistic gems'.

The revision has as far as possible emended these things. Though hampered naturally by the fact that it is a revision, not a translation afresh, it is now a better guide in these respects. But no translation, whatever its objects – a student's companion (the main purpose of this book), or a verse-rendering that seeks to transplant what can be transplanted of the old poetry – should be used or followed slavishly, in detail or general principle, by those who have access to the original text. Perhaps the most important function of any translation used by a student is to provide not a model for imitation, but an exercise for correction. The publisher of a translation cannot often hedge, or show all the variations that have occurred to him; but the presentation of one solution should suggest other and (perhaps) better ones. The effort to translate, or to improve a translation, is valuable, not so much for the version it produces, as for the understanding of the original which it awakes. If writing in (one's own) books is ever proper or useful, the emendation or refinement of a translation used in close comparison with a well-studied text is a good case for the use of a careful pencil. The making of notes of this sort is at any rate more profitable than the process more popular (especially with those reading for examinations): the inter-linear glosses in the text itself,

---

[1] Several are to be found on p. 25 of that book: notably the renowned 'boss of horrors' for *fyrena hyrde* 750, here rendered 'master of crimes'; and 'genial saloon' for *winsele* 771, here rendered 'winehall'. The suggestion of Grand Guignol and less reputable 'pubs' is wholly false to the original.

which as a rule only disfigure the page without aiding the diffident memory.

A warning against colloquialism and false modernity has already been given by implication above. Personally you may not like an archaic vocabulary, and word-order, artificially maintained as an elevated and literary language. You may prefer the brand new, the lively and the snappy. But whatever may be the case with other poets of past ages (with Homer, for instance) the author of *Beowulf* did not share this preference. If you wish to translate, not re-write, *Beowulf*, your language must be literary and traditional: not because it is now a long while since the poem was made, or because it speaks of things that have since become ancient; but because the diction of *Beowulf* was poetical, archaic, artificial (if you will), in the day that the poem was made. Many words used by the ancient English poets had, even in the eighth century, already passed out of colloquial use for anything from a lifetime to hundreds of years.[2] They were familiar to those who were taught to use and hear the language of verse, as familiar as *thou* or *thy* are to-day; but they were literary, elevated, recognized as old (and esteemed on that account). Some words had never, in the senses given to them by the poets, been used in ordinary language at all. This does not apply solely to poetic devices such as *swan-rad*; it is true also of some simple and much used words, such as *beorn* 211, etc., and *freca* 1563. Both meant 'warrior', or in heroic poetry 'man'. Or rather both were used for 'warrior' by poets, while *beorn* was still a form of the word 'bear',[3] and *freca* a name of the wolf,[4] and they were still used in verse when the original senses were forgotten. To use *beorn* and *freca* became a sign that your language was 'poetical', and these words survived, when much else of the ancient diction had perished, as the special property of the writers of alliterative verse in the Middle Ages. As *bern* and *freik* they survived indeed in Northern English (especially in Scotland) down to modern times; and yet never in their long his-

---

[2] Those who have access to texts and editions will easily find many examples. Nouns, such as *guma* 'man', are the largest class, but other words of other kind are also frequent, such as *ongeador* 1595 'together'; *gamol* 58, etc. 'old'; *sin* 1236, etc. 'his'. In these four cases the ancestors of the normal modern words *mann, togædere, ald, his* were already the current words in the poet's day.

[3] O.E. *bera*; O.N. *biörn* 'bear'.

[4] Literally 'greedy one'; O.N. *freki*, wolf.

tory of use in this sense, over a thousand years, were they ever part of the colloquial speech.

This sort of thing – the building up of a poetic language out of words and forms archaic and dialectal or used in special senses – may be regretted or disliked. There is nonetheless a case for it: the development of a form of language familiar in meaning and yet freed from trivial associations, and filled with the memory of good and evil, is an achievement, and its possessors are richer than those who have no such tradition. It is an achievement possible to people of relatively small material wealth and power (such as the ancient English as compared with their descendants); but it is not necessarily to be despised on that account. But, whether you regret it or not, you will misrepresent the first and most salient characteristic of the style and flavour of the author, if in translating *Beowulf*, you deliberately eschew the traditional literary and poetic diction which we now possess in favour of the current and trivial. In any case a self-conscious, and often silly, laughter comes too easily to us to be tempted in this way. The things we are here dealing with are serious, moving, and full of 'high sentence' – if we have the patience and solidity to endure them for a while. We are being at once wisely aware of our own frivolity and just to the solemn temper of the original, if we avoid *hitting* and *whacking* and prefer 'striking' and 'smiting'; *talk* and *chat* and prefer 'speech' and 'discourse'; *exquisite* and *artistic* and prefer the 'cunning craft' and 'skill' of ancient smiths; *visitors* (suggesting umbrellas, afternoon tea, and all too familiar faces) and prefer 'guests' with a truer note of real hospitality, long and arduous travel, and strange voices bearing unfamiliar news; *well-bred, brilliant,* or *polite noblemen* (visions of snobbery columns in the press, and fat men on the Riviera) and prefer the 'worthy brave and courteous men' of long ago.

But the opposite fault, once more common, should be equally avoided. Words should not be used merely because they are 'old' or obsolete. The words chosen, however remote they may be from colloquial speech or ephemeral suggestions, must be words that remain in literary use, especially in the use of verse, among educated people. (To such *Beowulf* was addressed, into whatever hands it may since have fallen.) They must need no gloss. The fact that a word was still used by Chaucer, or by Shakespeare, or even later, gives it no claim, if it has in our time perished from literary use. Still less is translation of *Beowulf* a fitting occasion for the exhumation of dead words from Saxon or Norse graves. Antiquarian sentiment and philological knowingness are wholly out of place. To render *leode* 'freemen, people' by *leeds* (favoured by William Morris) fails both to translate the Old English and to recall *leeds* to life. The words used by the Old English poets, however honoured by long use and weighted with the associations of old verse, were emphatically those which had survived, not those which might have survived, or in antiquarian sentiment ought to have survived.

Different, though related, is the etymological fallacy. A large number of words used in *Beowulf* have descended to our own day. But etymological descent is of all guides to a fit choice of words the most untrustworthy: *wann* is not 'wan' but 'dark'; *mod* is not 'mood' but 'spirit' or 'pride'; *burg* is not a 'borough' but a 'strong place'; an *ealdor* is not an 'alderman' but a 'prince'. The vocabulary of Old English verse may have philological interests but it had no philological objects.[5]

The difficulties of translators are not, however, ended with the choice of a general style of diction. They have still to find word for word: to deal with the so-called 'synonyms' of Old English verse and with the compounds. Translation of the individual simple words means, or should mean, more than just indicating the general scope of their sense: for instance, contenting oneself with 'shield' alone to render Old English *bord*, *lind*, *rand* and *scyld*. The variation, the *sound* of different words, is a feature of the style that should to some degree be represented, even if the differences of original meaning are neglected by the poet or no longer remembered – events which in early Old English poetry probably occurred far less often than is sometimes supposed. But in cases where

---

[5] It is a habit of many glossaries to Old English texts to record, in addition to a genuine translation, also that modern word which is (or is supposed to be) derived from the Old English word, and even to print this etymological intruder in special type so that it is impressed on the eye to the disadvantage of the correct rendering. The habit is pernicious. It may amuse the glossators, but it wastes space upon what is in the circumstances an irrelevance. It certainly does not assist the memory of students, who too often have to learn that the etymological gloss is worse than useless. Students should handle such glossaries with suspicion. The reading of *Beowulf* is an opportunity for learning the Old English language and mastering a form of poetic expression. Lessons in the later history of English were better reserved for other occasions.

Old English has built up a long list of synonyms, or partial equivalents, to denote things with which Northern heroic verse was specially concerned – such as the sea, and ships, and swords, and especially men (warriors and sailors), it will sometimes be found impossible to match its richness of variation even with the most indiscriminate collection of words. For *man* in *Beowulf* there appear at least ten virtual synonyms: *beorn, ceorl, freca, guma, hæleð* and *hæle, leod, mann* and *manna, rinc, secg,* and *wer.*[6] This list can be extended to at least twenty-five items by the inclusion of words whose sense remained in varying degrees more specific, though in heroic verse they could as a rule replace the simple *mann*: words implying noble birth such as *æðeling* and *eorl*; meaning youths or young men, such as *cniht, hyse, maga, mecg*; or denoting the various companions, followers, and servants of lords and kings, such as *gædeling, geneat, gesið, scealc, ðegn*; or explicitly signifying 'warrior', such as *cempa, oretta, wiga, wigend*. With this list not even a hotch-potch series such as *man, warrior, soldier, mortal, brave, noble, boy, lad, bachelor, knight, esquire, fighter, churl, hero, fellow, cove, wight, champion, guy, individual, bloke*, will compete: not even in length, certainly not in fitness. In such a case (the most extreme) we have to be content with less variation – the total effect is probably not much changed: our ears, unaccustomed to this kind of thing, may be as much impressed by less. There is, however, no need to increase our poverty by avoiding words of chivalry. In the matter of armour and weapons we cannot avoid them, since our only terms for such things, now vanished, have come down through the Middle Ages, or have survived from them. There is no reason for avoiding *knights, esquires, courts,* and *princes*. The men of these legends were conceived as kings of chivalrous courts, and members of societies of noble knights, real Round Tables. If there be any danger of calling up inappropriate pictures of the Arthurian world, it is a less one than the danger of too many warriors and chiefs begetting the far more inept picture of Zulus or Red Indians. The imagination of the author of *Beowulf* moved upon the threshold of Christian chivalry, if indeed it had not already passed within.

The translation of the compounds sets a different problem,

---

[6] Not all of these are strictly synonymous. *Ceorl, mann, wer,* were also current words with proper senses (freeman, human being, adult male or husband).

already glanced at above. A satisfactory solution will seldom be arrived at by translation of the elements separately and sticking them together again: for instance, by rendering the 'kenning' or descriptive compound *gleo-beam* 2263, denoting the harp, as 'glee-beam', or (avoiding the etymological fallacy) as 'mirth-wood'. Of *brimclifu* 222 an accurate and acceptable translation may be 'seacliffs', but this is a rare good fortune. A literal rendering of 81–5 *sele hlifade heah ond horngeap; heaðowylma bad laðan liges; ne wæs hit lenge ða gen ðæt se ecghete aðumsweoran æfter wælniðe wæcnan scolde* would be like this: 'hall towered high and *horn-spacious*; *war-surges* awaited of hostile flame; it was not at hand yet that the *blade-hate* of *son-father-in-law* after *slaughter-malice* should awake'. But this is certainly not modern English, even if it is intelligible.

It is plain that the translator dealing with these compounded words must hesitate between simply naming the thing denoted (so 'harp' 1065, for *gomen-wudu* 'play-wood'), and resolving the combination into a phrase. The former method retains the compactness of the original but loses its colour; the latter retains the colour, but even if it does not falsify or exaggerate it, it loosens and weakens the texture. Choice between the evils will vary with occasions. One may differ in detail from the present translation, but hardly (if one respects modern as well as ancient English) in general principle: a preference for resolution.

The compounds found in Old English verse are not, however, all of the same kind, and resolution is not in all cases equally desirable. Some are quite prosaic: made for the expression of ideas without poetic intention. Such words are found both in verse and prose, and their translation depends simply on their meaning as a whole. It is not necessary to 'resolve' *mundbora*,[7] since the simple words 'protector' or 'patron' get as near as we can to the meaning of this word.

A larger, intermediate, class is formed by those words in which composition is used as a natural and living device of the contemporary English language. The distinction between verse and prose or colloquial use here lies mainly in the fact that these compounds are more frequent in verse, and coined with greater freedom. In themselves – even those which are only used, or at least are only

---

[7] The 'bearer of *mund*', that is, one who has taken an inferior or friendless man under his *mund* or 'tutela'.

recorded, in verse – they would sound as natural in contemporary ears as would *tobacco-stall* or *tea-drinker* in ours. Of this class are *heals-beag* 'neck-ring', *bat-weard* 'boat-guard', and *hord-wela* 'hoard(ed) wealth' – three examples which (probably by mere chance) only occur in *Beowulf*. No 'Anglo-Saxon' who heard or read them would have been conscious that they were combinations never before used, even if he had in fact never met them before. Our language has not lost, though it has much limited, the compounding habit. Neither 'neck-ring' nor 'boat-guard' are recorded in the *Oxford Dictionary*,[8] but they are inoffensive, although 'hoard-wealth' is now unnatural. This class of compound is in general the one for which compound equivalents in modern English can with discretion most often be found or made.

But it shades off, as the intention becomes more fanciful or pictorial, and the object less to denote and more to describe or recall the vision of things, into the 'poetic class': the principal means by which colour was given to Old English verse. In this class, sometimes called by the Icelandic name 'kenning' (description), the compound offers a partial and often imaginative or fanciful description of a thing, and the poets may use it instead of the normal 'name'. In these cases, even where the 'kenning' is far from fresh and has become the common property of verse-makers, the substitution of the mere name in translation is obviously as a rule unjust. For the kenning flashes a picture before us, often the more clear and bright for its brevity, instead of unrolling it in a simile.

I have called this the poetic class, because there is a poetic intention in their making. But compounds of this kind are not confined to verse: not even those which are poetic and fanciful. We find 'kennings' in ordinary language, though they have then as a rule become trite in the process of becoming familiar. They may be no longer analysed, even when their form has not actually become obscured by wear. We need not be led astray in our valuation of the living compounds of poetry by such current 'kennings' as the prose *lichama* = body, or *hlafweard* = master. It is true that *lichama* the 'raiment of flesh', discardable, distinct from the *sawol* or 'soul' to which it was intricately fitted, became an ordinary

---

[8] *Boat-ward*, in the northern form *batward*, is recorded from Wyntoun's Chronicle of the fifteenth century – probably made afresh and not descended from Old English.

word for 'body', and in its later form *licuma* revealed the evaporation of feeling for its analysis and full meaning. It is true that *hlaf-weard* 'bread-keeper' is seldom found in this clear form, and usually appeared as *hlaford* (whence our wholly obscured *lord*), having become among the English the ordinary word for 'lord' or 'master', often with no reference to the bounty of the patriarch. But this emptying of significance is not true even of the most hackneyed of the 'kennings' of the poets. It is not true of *swanrad* 200, *beadoleoma* 1523, *woruldcandel* 1965, *goldwine* 1171, *banhus* 2508, and the host of similar devices in Old English verse.[9] If not fresh, in the sense of being struck out then and there where we first meet them, they are fresh and alive in preserving a significance and feeling as full, or nearly as full, as when they were first devised. Though *lic-hama* had faded into *licuma*, though there is now 'nothing new under the sun', we need not think that *ban-hus* meant merely 'body', or such a stock phrase as *hæleð under heofenum* 52 merely 'men'.

He who in those days said and who heard *flæschama* 'flesh-raiment', *ban-hus* 'bone-house', *hreðer-loca* 'heart-prison', thought of the soul shut in the body, as the frail body itself is trammelled in armour, or as a bird in a narrow cage, or steam pent in a cauldron. There it seethed and struggled in the *wylmas*, the boiling surges beloved of the old poets, until its passion was released and it fled away on *ellor-sið*, a journey to other places 'which none can report with truth, not lords in their halls nor mighty men beneath the sky' (50–52). The poet who spoke these words saw in his thought the brave men of old walking under the vault of heaven upon the island earth[10] beleaguered by the Shoreless Seas[11] and the outer darkness, enduring with stern courage the brief days of life,[12] until the hour of fate[13] when all things should perish, *leoht and lif samod*. But he did not say all this fully or explicitly. And therein lies the unrecapturable magic of ancient English verse for those who have ears to hear: profound feeling, and poignant vision, filled with the beauty and mortality of the world, are aroused by brief phrases, light touches, short words resounding like harpstrings sharply plucked.

---

[9] On *swanrad*, see above. *Beado-leoma* 'ray of light in battle' is a sword (drawn and glinting); *woruld-candel* 'candle of the world' is the sun; *goldwine* 'goldfriend', is a lord or king (generous in gifts of treasure to his kin and loyal knights); *ban-hus* 'the house whose timbers are bones' is the body.

[10] *middangeard*.   [11] *garsecg*.   [12] *læne lif* 2845.   [13] *metodsceaft* 1180, 2815.

II

ON METRE

These prefatory remarks have so far been addressed primarily to students of Old English; but many things have been touched on that they will know already, and will find better elsewhere (especially in the original poem itself). For other readers have not been forgotten: those who may be obliged or content to take this translation as a substitute for the original. Such readers may find the remarks of interest: an aid in estimating what they miss, and in what ways Old English poetry differs from any modern rendering.

The remarks have been limited to verbal detail, and nothing has been said about the matter of the poem. For we are here dealing with *translation*. Criticism of the content could not be treated, even with inadequate brevity, in a preface twice as long.[1] There remains, however, one subject of major importance in considering any translation of a poem: the *metre*. A brief account of this is, therefore, here given. To students of Old English fuller and more accurate accounts are available. But they may find this sketch of use, although its object is to convey a notion of the metre (and the relation of this to style and diction) even to those who have little knowledge of the original language. The account is based on modern English, a novel but defensible procedure; for it brings out the ancestral kinship of the two languages, as well as the differences between them, and illustrates the old unfamiliar forms by words of whose tones and accents the student has living knowledge.

Metre

The Old English line was composed of two opposed word-groups or 'halves'. Each half was an example, or variation, of one of six basic patterns.

The patterns were made of *strong* and *weak* elements, which may

---

[1] Reference must be made to the editions and other items in the short bibliography [i.e. that provided in 'Clark Hall']. To these may be added Professor R. W. Chambers's essay, '*Beowulf*' and the Heroic Age, prefaced to Strong's metrical translation (1925), reprinted in *Man's Unconquerable Mind* (1939).

be called 'lifts' and 'dips'. The standard lift was a *long stressed* syllable (usually with a relatively high tone). The standard dip was an *unstressed* syllable, long or short, with a low tone.

The following are examples in modern English of normal forms of the six patterns:

A   falling-falling   :   *kníghts in | ármour.*
                                                  4   1   4   1

B   rising-rising   :   *the róar|ing séa.*
                                                  1   4   1   4

C   clashing   :   *on hígh | móuntains.*
                                                1   4   4 or 3   1

                      ⎧ *a* falling by stages: *bríght | árchàngels.*
D   ⎨   4   3   2   1
                     ⎩ *b* broken fall   :   *bóld | brázenfàced.*
                                                4   3   1   2

E   fall and rise   :   *híghcrèsted | hélms.*
                                               4   2 1   4 or 3

A, B, C have equal feet, each containing a lift and dip. D and E have unequal feet: one consists of a single lift, the other has a subordinate stress (marked `) inserted.

These are the normal patterns of four elements into which Old English words naturally fell, and into which modern English words still fall. They can be found in any passage of prose, ancient or modern. Verse of this kind differs from prose, *not* in re-arranging words to fit a special rhythm, repeated or varied in successive lines, but in choosing the simpler and more compact word-patterns and clearing away extraneous matter, so that these patterns stand opposed to one another.

The selected patterns were all of approximately equal metrical *weight*:[2] the effect of loudness (combined with length and voice-pitch), as judged by the ear in conjunction with emotional and

---

[2] To a full *lift* a value 4 may be given. The *subordinate stresses* (reduced in force and lowered in tone) that appear in such compounds as *highcrested* may be given value 2. But reduction also occurs in other cases. For instance, the second of two clashing stresses in a sentence; or of two juxtaposed words (of equal significance when separate), such as nouns and adjectives, tends to be reduced to approximate value 3. Using these rough values we see that the normal total value of each pattern is 10; C tends to be slightly lighter, and E to be slightly heavier.

logical *significance*.[3] The line was thus essentially a *balance* of two equivalent blocks. These blocks might be, and usually were, of different pattern and rhythm. There was in consequence no common tune or rhythm shared by lines in virtue of being 'in the same metre'. The ear should not listen for any such thing, but should attend to the shape and balance of the halves. Thus *the róaring séa rólling lándward* is not metrical because it contains an 'iambic' or a 'trochaic' rhythm, but because it is a balance B + A.

Here is a free version of *Beowulf* 210–228 in this metre. The passage should be read slowly, but naturally: that is with the stresses and tones required solely by the sense. The lifts and dips utilized in this metre are those occurring in any given sequence of words in natural (if formal) speech, irrespective of whether the passage is regarded as verse or prose. The lines must not be strained to fit any familiar modern verse-rhythm. The reduced stresses (when their fall in force and tone approximates to value 2) are marked (`).

Beowulf and his Companions set sail

E	210	Tíme pàssed a|wáy. On the tíde | flóated	C
B		under bánk | their bóat. In her bóws | móunted	C
A+		bráve mèn | blíthely. Bréakers | túrning	A
A		spúrned the | shíngle. Spléndid | ármour	A
B		they bóre | abóard, in her bósom | píling	C
A	215	wéll-fòrged | wéapons, then awáy | thrúst her	C
C		to vóyage | gládly vàliant|-tìmbered.	A
A		She] wènt then over | wáve-tòps, wínd pur|súed her,	A
D*a*		fléet|, fóam-thròated like a flý|ing bírd;	B
B		and her cúrv|ing prów on its cóurse | wáded,	C
C	220	till in dúe | séason on the dáy | áfter	C
C		those séa|fàrers sáw be|fóre them	A
A+		shóre-cliffs | shímmering and shéer | móuntains,	C
E+		wíde cápes by the | wáves: to wát|er's énd	B
C		the shíp had | jóurneyed. Then ashóre | swíftly	C
B	225	they léaped | to lánd, lórds of | Góthland,	A
E+		bóund fást their | bóat. Their býrn|ies ráttled,	B
D*b*+		grím | géar of wár. Gód | thánked they thèn	D*b*
C		that their séa|-pàssage sáfe had | próven.	A

<hr>

[3] And so not purely phonetic, nor exactly measurable in figures (such as those used above) or by a machine.

VARIATIONS

There were many variations on the basic patterns, some of which appear above. The principal were these.

1. *The dips.* The standard form was monosyllabic. There was, however, no *metrical* limit to the number of syllables in a dip, as long as they were genuinely *weak* (altogether inferior to the neighbouring stresses). This imposes a practical limit, as more than three really weak syllables are seldom found consecutively. Polysyllabic dips are frequent at the beginning of B and C.

> A, C, D end always in a monosyllabic dip in Old English, because words of the form $-\!\!\!^{'} \times \times$ (like *hándily*, *ínstantly*) did not exist in the language. See p. 69)

2. *The lifts.* A subordinate or reduced stress could act as a lift in A, B, C. So *váliant-tìmbered* 216, *séafàrers* 221, *séa-pàssage* 228.

3. *Breaking.* A lift could be 'broken' into two syllables $^{'} \times$, a *short stressed* followed by a *weak* syllable. That is *vĕssel*, *mĕllow*, are metrical equivalents of *boat*, *ripe*. Examples are seen above: A 216, 222; B 226; C 214, 224.

Examples of Da would be *bright pàradises*, *hĕaven's archangels*; of Db *sàllow pastyfaced*; of E *fĕatherwingĕd shafts*. Both lifts could be broken: as *sĕven sàlamanders* (Da) or *fĕatherwingĕd àrrows* (E).

4. *Lightening.* The clash of long-stressed syllables, in a compound or in a sentence, could be relieved by substituting a *single short stressed* syllable for the second lift: for example, *gold-diggers* instead of *goldminers*. This is frequent in the clashing pattern C; *sea-pàssage* 228 is an example.

This can also occur in the subordinate stresses of Da and E. Examples would be *wide grassmĕadows* and *ill-written verse*.

5. *Overweighting* and *Extension* (marked +). These are a means of including certain common but slightly excessive patterns in the metre; also of adding weight to the line where required, and of packing much significant word-material into a small space.

Overweighting is most frequently seen in pattern A. It consists in replacing the dip by a long (subordinate) stress. This may affect either or both of the dips. Examples are seen in 212, 217, 222. An example with double overweight would be *wéllmàde wárgeàr*. The overweight or 'heavy dip' may be broken: thus *wellfàshioned wargear* or *wellmade wartrăppings*.

Lightly stressed words (such as familiar and more or less colourless finite verbs and adverbs) often appear as 'heavy dips'. They are frequent in the first dips of B and C: as B *càme wálk|ing hóme*; C *sàw stránge | vísions*. But these are not felt to be overweighted. The second dip of B, C and the dip of D, E may not be overweighted.

Overweighting of D and E takes the form of substituting a separate word for the subordinate stress. The half-line then contains three separate words, and the effect is heavier than the norm, unless one of these words is of a naturally weak class. An example of D*b* + is seen in 227, of E + in 223, 226.[4] An example of D*a* + would be *bríght bládes dráwing*.

Extension is seen in the addition of a dip to the monosyllabic foot of D*a*, and occasionally of D*b*: thus *árdent árchàngels*; *bóld and brázenfàced*. A similar extension of E (as *híghcrèsted hélmets*) is avoided.

The + patterns produced by overweighting and extension are excessive. They are usually confined to the first half of the line, and are regularly provided with *double* alliteration (see below). If the overweight in one foot is relieved by lightening in the other foot, then the total pattern is not excessive. Thus *wéllfòrged wěapons* 215 is an example of a frequent variety of A, with 'lightening' of the second lift after the long (subordinate) stress *-forged*. In *wènt then over wáve-tòps* 217 the overweight in *wave-tops* is compensated by the use of a lightly stressed unemphatic word as first lift. This special variety of A, with light beginning and heavy ending, is very frequently employed in lines marking (as here) a transition, or a new point in a narrative.

Syllables that did not fall inside a pattern were avoided – one of the reasons for the frequent asyndeton, and the love of short parallel sentences that mark the style. In good verse, such as *Beowulf*, the avoidance was strict in the second half-line, where

---

[4] But E in 210, and D*b* in 227 are not regarded as overweighted, since *pàssed*, *thèn* are not strong words.

such a sequence as *the rólling ócean* (dip + A, or B + dip) is practically never found. At the beginning of the line a prefixed dip, or 'anacrusis', is occasionally used, chiefly in pattern A. An example occurs in 217 where *she*] is prefixed – the original has a similar anacrusis at the same point (see below).

ALLITERATION

Old English verse is called 'alliterative'. This is a misnomer in two ways. Alliteration, though important, is not fundamental. Verse built on the plan described above, if written 'blank', would retain a similar metrical character. The so-called 'alliteration' depends not on *letters* but on *sounds*. 'Alliteration' or head-rhyme is, in comparison with end-rhyme, too brief, and too variable in its incidence, to allow mere letter-agreements or 'eye-alliterations'.

Alliteration in this metre is the agreement of the *stressed elements* in beginning with the *same consonant*,[5] or in beginning with *no* consonant.[5] All words beginning with a *stressed* vowel of any quality 'alliterate', as *old* with *eager*. The alliteration of dips is not observed or of metrical importance. The alliteration of subordinate stresses (in A +, D, E) was avoided.

Arrangement
This was governed by the following rules:

1. One full lift in each half-line must alliterate. The key-alliteration or 'head-stave' was borne by the *first lift* in the *second* half. Thus *tide* 210 shows the head-stave to be *t*. With this the strongest lift in the first half must agree: thus *time*.

2. In the second half the *first lift only* can alliterate; the second lift must *not* alliterate.

3. In the first half both the lifts may alliterate. The stronger lift *must* bear the alliteration, the weaker can agree or not; but double alliteration was necessary in certain cases (see below).

---

[5] Phonetically speaking: thus *ph* will alliterate with *f*, but *sh* will not alliterate with *s*; *yes* will alliterate with *use*. In Old English, *st*, *sp*, *sc* are regarded as 'consonantal diphthongs', each having an individual character. Each can only alliterate with itself, as *stone* with *stiff*, or *strong*. In other cases only the first of a group of initial consonants is compulsorily repeated.

A consequence of these rules is that the second half of the line must be so arranged that the stronger lift comes first. As a result the lines tend to end with the naturally inferior words (such as finite verbs), and so to fall away in *force* and *significance* together. There is normally an immediate rise of intensity at the beginning of the line, except in the case of light beginnings such as 217 (see above).

In all patterns the first lift is as a rule (for phonetic and syntactic reasons) the stronger. This is always the case in C, D*a* and *b*, and E. These patterns must bear the stave on the first lift or both (not only on the second lift).

> Dominance of the first lift distinguishes D*a* and D*b* from C and B respectively. Thus *sàw stránge vísions* is not D*a* but C with heavy first dip; *gàzed stónyfàced* is not D*b* but B with heavy first dip. Where, nonetheless, double alliteration occurs, as in *rùshed rédhànded* or *stàred stóny-fàced*, we have intermediate patterns of CD*a* and BD*b* respectively.

In pattern A dominance of the first lift was usual, but not compulsory. Not infrequently occur varieties with the second lift stronger. In these cases the second lift must alliterate, and the first need not. Thus in 217 *pàssed* could be substituted for *wènt*.

Function

The main *metrical* function of alliteration is to *link* the two separate and balanced patterns together into a complete line. For this reason it is placed as near the beginning of the second half as possible, and is never repeated on the last lift (rule 2 above). Delay would obscure this main linking function; repetition by separating off the last word-group and making it self-sufficient would have a similar effect.[6]

A subsidiary function is the quickening and relief of heavy, overweighted or extended, patterns. These (described above) all required *double alliteration*. Examples are seen above in 212, 222, 226, 227. Double alliteration is also frequent when both lifts approach equality as in *under bánk their bóat* 211. It is thus usually

---

[6] This can be plainly observed in the decadent alliterative verse of Middle English where this rule is often broken.

found when two strong words are co-ordinated (and joined with *and, or*): as *boats and barges*; *ferrets or foxes*.

Crossed alliteration is occasionally found in the forms *ab|ab* and *ab|ba*. But this is either accidental, or a gratuitous ornament, and not strictly metrical. The alliteration must still be regular according to the above rules, and the head-stave be borne by the first lift of the second half. An example of *s, f|s, f* occurs above in 221, and of *s, þ|s, þ* in 228.

Rhyme is employed in this verse only gratuitously, and for special effects. It may appear in the normal form or as 'consonantal rhyme', e.g. *und|and*. Both are found together in the original poem 212–13 *wundon||sund wið sande* where the special effect (breakers are beating on the shore) may be regarded as deliberate.

For further illustration the original of lines 210–228 is here given with metrical indications.

D*b* +	210	fýrst fórð gewàt.	flóta wæs on ýðum	A
A		bát under béorge.	béornas géarwe	A
C		on stéfn stìgon.	stréamas wúndon	A
A		súnd wið sánde.	sécgas bǽron	A
C		on béarm nàcan	béorhte frǽtwe	A
A+	215	gúð-sèaro géatolic.	gúman út scùfon	D*a*
A+		wéras on wíl-síð	wúdu búndènne.	D*a*
A		ge]wàt ða ofer wǽg-hòlm wínde gefýsed		A
D*b*		flóta fámig-hèals	fúgle gelícost,	A
A		òððæt ymb án-tìd	óðres dógres[7]	A
A	220	wúnden-stèfna	gewáden hæfde,	C
C		ðæt ða líðende	lánd gesáwon	A
A+		brím-clìfu blícan,	béorgas stéape,	A
D*a* +		síde sǽ-nèssas.	ðá wæs súnd-lìdan[8]	C
		éoletes[9] æt énde.	ðànon úp hràðe	C
A	225	Wédera léode	on wáng stìgon,	C
A+		sǽ-wùdu sǽldon.	sýrcan hrýsedon	A
A		gúð-gewǽdo.	góde ðáncèdon	D*a*
C		ðæsðe him ýð-làde	éaðe wúrdon.	A

The absence of B from this extract, and the predominance of A, are notable in comparison with the modern version.

[7] MS. *dōgores* a late form.
[8] MS. *sund liden*, emended by Crawford.
[9] Unknown or corrupt word, the metrical value of which is not determinable.

Owing (among other things) to inflexions, words of the
A-type, as *lándes*, were very frequent in Old English. These
have usually been replaced by monosyllables, as *land's*, or the
B-phrase *of land*. The placing of a subordinate stress on the
middle syllable of all trisyllables beginning with a long stress
as *búndènne*, *ðáncèdon*, *līðènde* (compared with modern *hándily*,
ínstantly) is another marked difference between the language
of the Beowulf period and that of the present.

A literal rendering of this passage, word by word and in the same
order, would run as follows. Words expressed in Old English by
inflexions are in brackets.

210	‖Time on departed.	**B** was on Ws
	B under hill.	**M** eager
	on prow strode.	Ws rolled
	S against sand.	**M** bore
	into bosom (of) **B**	bright trappings
215	war-gear <u>wellmade.</u>	**M** out thrust
	M on wish-journey	timber fastened.‖
	Departed men over W-**S**	(by) wind urged
	B foamy-neck	(to) bird likest,
	until after due-time	(of) second day
220	curved-prow [= B]	advanced had,
	that those voyagers	land saw
	S-cliffs gleaming,	hills steep,
	long S-capes.	then it was (for) <u>S-voyager</u> [= B]
	(of) ? <u>waterway</u> at end.	thence up quickly
225	(of) <u>Wederas</u> M	on plain strode,
	S-timber [= B] roped——shirts rattled
	<u>war-raiment</u>——God thanked
	that (for) them W-passage	easy proved.‖

The poetical words are <u>underlined</u>. In addition, the compounds
war-gear 215, *wish-journey* 216, *foamy-neck* 218, *curved-prow* 220,
sea-cliffs 222, *sea-capes* 223, *sea-timber* 226, *war-raiment* 227, *wave-
passage* 228, are poetical, whether the separate elements are so or not.
    Here B represents three words for *boat*, two poetical (*flota*,
naca), and one normal (*bāt*); in addition there are the 'kennings'

in 220, 223, 226. W represents three words for *wave*, one normal
(*wǣg*), one more literary and archaic but not confined to verse
(*ȳð*), and one (*strēam* 'current, stream') whose application to the
sea is mainly poetical. M represents five words for *men*, different in
each case, three poetical (*beornas, secgas, guman*), and two used in
prose (*weras* 'adult males, husbands'; *lēode* 'people'). S represents
four words for *sea*, three poetical (*sund*, in prose 'swimming';
holm, brim), and one normal (*sǣ*).

The letters B, W, M, S are here used simply to show the frequency of the poetical 'synonyms', and the way they are employed. It is not implied that the variations are pointless, or that
the poet is using different counters of precisely the same value but
different metrical colours – such different colour is in any case a
point of poetical value. Thus *flota* is literally 'floater', and is therefore in fact a simple kenning for *boat*; *sund* means 'swimming';
holm probably 'eminence' (the *high* sea); *brim* is properly 'breakers,
surf'. On *beornas* see above p. 54.

This literal version also illustrates other important points. It will
be noted that the stop comes normally in the middle of the line.
Sense-break and metrical break are usually opposed. This is not
so at the beginning, at line 216, and at the end of the passage.
That is because we have in this extract a 'verse-period', sub-
divided at 216. The previous 'period' ended at the end of 209.
We then have a transition-phrase, stopped off and occupying one
half-line, a not uncommon Old English device. The period describing the journey then proceeds, often in short sentences
straddling the line-endings. An exceptionally long passage without
a full stop is 217 *departed* – 223 *sea-capes*. There is an end-stop at
216 marking the end of the launching and the setting out; and an
end-stop marking the end of the period at 228. The next period
begins with 229, where the poet turns to the Danish coastguard.

The frequent fall in *significance*, which goes together with the
frequent metrical and phonetic fall in stress and pitch, can also be
noted at the end of lines. 212, 213, 215, 220, 221, 225, 226, 227,
228 end in finite verbs, 224 in an unemphatic adverb, and 223 in
the second element of a compound.

To these may be added *gelīcost* (subordinate to *fugle*) 218.
We thus have some 12 'falling' endings out of 19.

The force was renewed and the tone raised at the beginning of the line (as a rule[10]), and there the strongest and heaviest words were usually placed. The more significant elements in the preceding final half-line were frequently caught up and re-echoed or elaborated. Thus 210–11 *boat-boat*; 212–13 *waves-sea*; 214–15 *bright trappings – war-gear well-made*; 221 *land* is elaborated in 222–23 as cliffs by the breaking waves, steep hills, and capes jutting into the sea.

This 'parallelism' is characteristic of the style and structure of *Beowulf*. It both favours and is favoured by the metre. It is seen not only in these lesser verbal details, but in the arrangement of minor passages or periods (of narrative, description, or speech), and in the shape of the poem as a whole. Things, actions, or processes, are often depicted by separate strokes, juxtaposed, and frequently neither joined by an expressed link, nor subordinated. The 'separate strokes' may be single parallel words: there is no 'and' between *flota* 210, *bāt* 211; *strēamas* 212, *sund* 213; *guman* 215, *weras* 216; and similarly 221–23, 226–27. Or sentences: in 224–28 the landing of the men, who moored their ship, while their shirts of mail rang as they moved, is dealt with by separate verbs, unconnected but each with the subject *lēode*. Into this series is inserted, without any connecting word, the short sentence || 'shirts rattled, war-raiment'||.[11] On a larger scale: the strife of the Swedes and Geats in the later part of the poem is dealt with in separate passages, describing prominent incidents on both sides that are not worked into a narrative sequence. Finally, *Beowulf* itself is like a line of its own verse written large, a balance of two great blocks, A + B; or like two of its parallel sentences with a single subject but no expressed conjunction. Youth + Age; he rose – fell. It may not be, at large or in detail, fluid or musical, but it is strong to stand: tough builder's work of true stone.

---

[10] After end-stops, such as those in 216, 228, this was not always so. The next line at the head of a period or transition often began with a dip or weak stress and rose at the end. Thus after 216 we get *gewàt*, the highest point in 217 being *wǣg*. After 228 the next period begins with the comparatively rare rising B-pattern: thus 229 *ðā of wéalle geséah* 'then from cliff behéld'.

[11] In this case *hrysedon* is possibly transitive and the subject *lēode*. But the unconnected insertion is frequent in undoubted cases. For instance, in 402, where this translation has 'the warrior guiding them' (subordinating construction), the original has 'they hastened—man guided—under Heorot's roof'. Similarly in 405, where the translation reproduces the original unconnected insertion '——corslet shone——'.

SIR GAWAIN AND THE
GREEN KNIGHT

It is a great honour to be invited to lecture in this ancient university, and under the illustrious name of W. P. Ker. I was once
allowed to use for a time his copy of *Sir Gawain and the Green
Knight*. It showed clearly that he had – as usual, in spite of the
enormous range of his reading and experience of literature – read
this work with close attention.

It is indeed a poem that deserves close and detailed attention,
and after that (not before, according to a too common critical
procedure) careful consideration, and re-consideration. It is one
of the masterpieces of fourteenth-century art in England, and of
English Literature as a whole. It is one of those greater works
which not only bear the trampling of the Schools, endure becoming a *text*, indeed (severest test) a *set text*, but yield more and more
under this pressure. For it belongs to that literary kind which
has deep roots in the past, deeper even than its author was aware.
It is made of tales often told before and elsewhere, and of elements
that derive from remote times, beyond the vision or awareness of
the poet: like *Beowulf*, or some of Shakespeare's major plays, such
as *King Lear* or *Hamlet*.

It is an interesting question: what is this flavour, this atmosphere, this virtue that such *rooted* works have, and which compen-
sates for the inevitable flaws and imperfect adjustments that
must appear, when plots, motives, symbols, are rehandled and
pressed into the service of the changed minds of a later time,
used for the expression of ideas quite different from those which
produced them. But though *Sir Gawain* would be a very suitable
text on which to base a discussion of this question, that is not the
kind of thing about which I wish to speak today. I am not concerned at this moment with research into the origins of the tale or
its details, or into the question of precisely in what form these
reached the author of this poem, before he set to work on it. I wish

to speak about his handling of the matter, or one particular aspect of this: the movement of his mind, as he wrote and (I do not doubt) re-wrote the story, until it had the form that has come down to us. But the other question must not be forgotten. Antiquity like a many-figured back-cloth hangs ever behind the scene. Behind our poem stalk the figures of elder myth, and through the lines are heard the echoes of ancient cults, beliefs and symbols remote from the consciousness of an educated moralist (but also a poet) of the late fourteenth century. His story is not *about* those old things, but it receives part of its life, its vividness, its tension from them. That is the way with the greater fairy-stories – of which this is one. There is indeed no better medium for moral teaching than the good fairy-story (by which I mean a real deep-rooted tale, told as a tale, and not a thinly disguised moral allegory). As the author of *Sir Gawain*, it would seem, perceived; or felt instinctively, rather than consciously: for being a man of the fourteenth century, a serious, didactic, encyclopaedic, not to say pedantic century, he inherited 'faerie', rather than turned deliberately to it.

Out of all the many new things, then, upon which one might hope to say something new – even now, when this poem has become the subject of several editions, translations, discussions, and numerous articles – such as the Beheading Game, the Perilous Host, the Green Man, the Sunlike mythical figure that looms behind the courteous Gawain, nephew of King Arthur, as certainly if more remotely as the Bear-boy lurks behind the heroic Beowulf, nephew of King Hygelac; or such as the Irish influence on Britain, and the influence of both on France, and the French return; or coming down to our author's own time: the 'Alliterative Revival', and the contemporary debate about its use in narrative, almost lost now save for brief echoes in *Sir Gawain* and in Chaucer (who, I think, knew *Sir Gawain*, and probably the author also) – out of all these and other matters which the title *Sir Gawain and the Green Knight* might suggest I wish to turn to one, more neglected, and yet, I think, more fundamentally important: the kernel, the very nub of the poem as it was finally made, its great third 'fit', and within that the temptation of Sir Gawain and his confession.

In speaking of this matter, the temptation and confession of Gawain, I must rely, of course, on a knowledge of the poem as a whole, in itself or in a translation. Where quotation is essential, I will use a translation which I have just completed, since I have made it with two objects (to some extent, I hope, achieved): to preserve the original metre and alliteration, without which translation is of little value except as a crib; and to preserve, to exhibit in an intelligible modern idiom, the nobility and the courtesy of this poem, by a poet to whom 'courtesy' meant so much.

Since I am not speaking of the poem as a whole, or its admirable construction, I need only indicate one point in this, which is for my purpose significant. The poem is divided into four fits or cantos; but the third is much the largest, much more than a quarter of the whole (872 lines out of a total of 2530): a numerical pointer, as it were, to the real primary interest of the poet. And yet actually he has tried to conceal the numerical evidence by attaching, skilfully yet artificially, part of what really belongs to the situation of the Third Fit to the Second Fit. The temptation of Sir Gawain really begins as far back as the beginning of stanza 39 (line 928) (if not earlier) and lasts for more than a thousand lines. All else is by comparison, even when highly pictorial, perfunctory. The temptation was to this poet the raison d'être of his poem; all else was to him scenery, background, or else machinery: a device for getting Sir Gawain into the situation which he wished to study.

Of what lay before, therefore, I need only briefly remind you. We have the setting, with a brief sketch of the magnificence of the Arthurian court in the midst of the highest festival of the year (to the English), the feast of Christmas. At dinner on New Year's Day there rides into the hall a great Green Knight on a green horse, with a green axe, and issues his challenge: any man in the court that has the courage may take the axe and strike the Green Knight a single unopposed blow, on condition that he promises after a year and a day to allow the Green Knight to give him one unopposed blow in return.

In the event it is Sir Gawain that takes up the challenge. But of all this I wish only to point out one important aspect. From this very beginning we can already perceive the moral purpose of the poet at work, or we can do so at a re-reading, after consideration. It is necessary to the temptation that Gawain's actions should be capable of moral approbation; and amidst all the 'faerie' the poet is at pains to show that they were so. He takes up the challenge to rescue the king from the false position in which his rashness has placed him. Gawain's motive is not pride in his own prowess, not boastfulness, not even the light-hearted frivolity of knights making absurd bets and vows in the midst of the Christmas revels. His motive is a humble one: the protection of Arthur, his elder kinsman, of his king, of the head of the Round Table, from indignity and peril, and the risking instead of himself, the least of the knights (as he declares), and the one whose loss could most easily be endured. He is involved therefore in the business, as far as it was possible to make the fairy-story go, as a matter of duty and humility and self-sacrifice. And since the absurdity of the challenge could not wholly be got rid of – absurdity, that is, if the story is to be conducted on a serious moral plane, in which every action of the hero, Gawain, is to be scrutinized and morally assessed – the king himself is criticized, both by the author as narrator, and by the lords of the court.

One further point, to which we shall return later. From the beginning Gawain is tricked, or at least trapped. He accepts the challenge, to deal the blow *quat-so bifallez after* ('whatever the consequences') and in a year's time to present himself, without substitute or assistant, to receive a return blow with whatever weapon the Green Knight chooses. He is no sooner involved than he is informed that he must seek out the Green Knight himself, to get his 'wages' where he lives in some region unnamed. He accepts this onerous addition. But when he had delivered the stroke and beheaded the Knight, the trap is sprung; for the challenger is not slain, he picks up his own head, strides back onto his horse, and rides off, after the ugly severed head, held aloft in his hand, has warned Gawain to be true to his vow.

Now we, and no doubt many of our poet's audience, may not be surprised by this. If we are introduced to a green man, with green hair and face, on a green horse, at the court of King Arthur, we expect 'magic'; and Arthur and Gawain should have expected it also, we think. As indeed most of those present seem to have done: 'a phantom and fay-magic folk there thought it' (11.240). But this poet was as it were determined to take the story and its machinery for granted, and then examine the problems of conduct, especially as regards Sir Gawain, that arose. One of the things that he will be most concerned with is *lewté*, 'keeping faith'. It is there-

fore highly important from the outset to consider precisely the
relations of the Green Knight and Gawain, and the exact nature
of the contract between them, just as if we were dealing with a
normal and possible engagement between two 'gentlemen'. Thus
the poet is at pains, I think, to indicate that the 'magic', though
it might be feared as a possibility by the challenged, is concealed
by the challenger in the drawing up of the agreement. The king
takes the challenge at its face-value, a piece of folly: that is, asking
to be slain on the spot; and later, when Gawain is preparing his
blow:

'Take care, cousin,' quoth the king, 'one cut to address,
and if thou learnest him his lesson, I believe very well
that thou wilt bear any blow that he gives back later.'

(17.372–4)

And so, though Gawain's good faith is involved – by his own
words: *quat-so bifallez after* – his opponent has actually concealed
the fact that he could not be slain in this manner, being protected
by magic. And Gawain is now pledged to a perilous quest and
journey the only probable end of which will be his death. For he
has not (yet) any magic; and when the time comes he must set
forth, the deliverer of his king and kinsman, and the upholder of
the honour of his order, with unflinching courage and *lewté*,
alone and unprotected.

The time does come at last, and Sir Gawain prepares to depart
in search of the Green Knight and the Green Chapel where the
tryst has been set. And then at least the poet allows no room for
doubt, whatever you may think of my introduction of ethical
considerations into the First Fit, and the fairy-tale scene of the
Beheading. He describes the armour of Sir Gawain, and though we
now may be caught rather by the contrast of his glowing scarlet
and glittering gold with the green of the challenger, and ponder its
possible inherited significance, the poet's interest is not there. He
gives in fact all told only a few lines to all the gear and the
colour red (*red* and *goulez*) is only twice named. It is the shield
with which he is concerned. The shield of Gawain he uses indeed
to blazon forth his own mind and purpose, and to that he devotes
three whole stanzas. Upon the shield he imposes – and we may

deliberately use this word, for here beyond doubt we have an addition of his own – instead of the heraldic charges found in other romances, lion, eagle, or gryphon, the symbol of the pentangle. Now it does not greatly matter what significance or significances are elsewhere or earlier ascribed to this symbol.[1] Just as it does not matter greatly what other or older significances were attached to green or red, to holly or to axes. For the significance that the pentangle is to bear in this poem is made plain – plain enough, that is, in general purport[2]: it is to betoken 'perfection' indeed, but perfection in religion (the Christian faith), in piety and morality, and the 'courtesy' that flows therefrom into human relations; perfection in the details of each, and a perfect and unbroken bond between the higher and lower planes. It is with this sign upon his shield (and as we later learn embroidered also on his coat-armour), imposed there by our poet (for the reasons that he gives for the use of it are in themselves and in the style of their enumeration such as Sir Gawain himself could not possibly have had, still less openly asserted, for the adoption of this charge) – it is with this sign that Sir Gawain rides forth from Camelot.

His long and perilous journey in search of the Green Chapel is briefly, and in general adequately described. Adequately, that is, if in places perfunctory, and in others obscure to the commentators, for the purpose of the poet. He is anxious now to reach the castle of the temptation. We need not concern ourselves on this occasion with any further points until the castle comes in sight. And when it does, we shall be concerned with what the author has made of it, not with the materials, wholly different in purport, out of which he may be thought to have built it.

How does Gawain find the castle? *In answer to prayer.* He has been journeying since All Hallows. It is now Christmas Eve, and he is lost in a wild strange country of tangled forest; but his chief concern is that he should not miss Mass on Christmas morning. He was

troubled lest a truant at that time he should prove
from the service of the sweet Lord, who on that selfsame night
of a maid became man our mourning to conquer.
And therefore sighing he said: 'I beseech thee, O Lord,
and Mary who is the mildest mother most dear,

for some harbour where with honour I might hear the Mass
and thy Matins tomorrow. This meekly I ask,
and thereto promptly I pray with Pater and Ave and Creed.'

(32.750–8)

It is when he has so prayed, and made an act of contrition, and
blessed himself thrice with the sign of the cross, that he suddenly
catches sight through the trees of the beautiful white castle, and
rides on to a courteous welcome, and the answer to his prayer.

Out of whatever more ancient stones may have been built the
gleaming but solid magnificence of this castle, whatever turn the
story may take, whatever details may be discovered that the author
inherited and overlooked or failed to accommodate to his new
purpose, this much is clear: our poet is bringing Gawain to no
haunt of demons, enemies of human kind, but to a courteous and
Christian hall. There the Court of Arthur and the Round Table
are held in honour; and there the chapel-bells ring for Vespers,
and the kind air of Christendom blows.

On the morn when every man remembers the time
that our dear Lord for our doom to die was born,
in every home wakes happiness on earth for His sake.
So did it there on that day with the dearest delights.

(41.995–8)

There Gawain was to feel and be 'at home' for a short while, to
find himself unexpectedly in the midst of the life and society that
he most liked, and where his very skill and pleasure in courteous
converse would ensure him the highest honour.

Yet his temptation has begun. We shall not appreciate it at a
first reading perhaps, but any reconsideration will reveal it to us
that this strange tale, this *mayn meruayle* (whether we believe in it
or not), has been carefully re-drawn by a skilled hand directed by a
wise and noble mind. It is in the very setting to which Gawain is
used, and in which he has hitherto achieved the highest repute,
that he is to be tested, within Christendom and so as a Christian.
He himself and all that he stands for are to be assayed.

And if the pentangle with its touch of learned pedantry, at war
it seemed with the artistic instinct of a narrative poet,[3] may for

a moment have made us fear that we were going to lose Faerie only
to gain a formalized allegory, we are now swiftly reassured.
'Perfection' Gawain may have been given as a standard to strive for
(for with no less ideal could he achieve a near-perfection), but he
himself is not presented as a mathematical allegory, but as a man,
an individual human being. His very 'courtesy' proceeds not solely
from the ideals, or the fashions, of his imagined time, but from
his own character. He enjoys the sweet society of gentle ladies
intensely, and he is immediately moved deeply by beauty. This
is how his first meeting with the fair Lady of the Castle is described.
Gawain had attended Vespers in the chapel, and when they are
over the lady comes forth from her private pew.

> And from her closet she came with many comely maidens.
> She was fairer in face, in her flesh and her skin,
> her proportions, her complexion, and her port than all others,
> and more lovely than Guinevere to Gawain she looked.
> He came through the chancel to pay court to her grace . . .
>
> (39.942–6)

There follows a brief description of her beauty in contrast to the
old and wrinkled and ugly lady that was at her side:

> For if the younger was youthful, yellow was the elder;
> with rose-hue the one face was richly mantled,
> rough wrinkled cheeks rolled on the other;
> on the kerchiefs of the one many clear pearls were,
> her breast and bright throat were bare displayed,
> fairer than white snow that falls on the hills;
> the other was clad with a cloth that enclosed all her neck,
> enveloped was her black chin with chalk-white veils . . .
>
> (39.951–8)

> When Gawain glimpsed that gay lady that so gracious looked,
> with leave sought of the lord towards the ladies he went;
> the elder he saluted, low to her bowing,
> about the lovelier he laid then lightly his arms
> and kissed her in courtly wise with courtesy speaking.
>
> (40.970–4)

And the next day at the dinner on Christmas Day he is set on the dais beside her, and of all the mirth and splendour of the feast the author (as he says himself) is concerned only to depict their delight.

> Yet I ween that Wawain and that woman so fair
> in companionship took such pleasure together
> in sweet society soft words speaking,
> their courteous converse clean and clear of all evil,
> that with their pleasant pastime no prince's sport
>   compares.
>   Drums beat, and trumps men wind,
>   many pipers play their airs;
>   each man his needs did mind,
>   and they two minded theirs.   (41.1010–19)

This is the setting, but the situation is not yet fully prepared. Though Gawain takes his ease for a while, he does not forget his quest. For four days he enjoys the merrymaking, but in the evening of the fourth day when there are now but three left of the old year before the appointed New Year's Day, he begs leave to depart on the morrow. He tells no more of his errand than that he is obliged to try and find a place called the Green Chapel and reach it on New Year's morning. Then he is told by the lord that he can rest at ease three days longer and complete the cure of all the hardships of his journey, for the Green Chapel is not two miles away. A guide shall be found to lead him thither on the morning itself.

At this point the author makes one of his many skilful combinations of elements of older fairy-story with the character of Gawain (as he is depicting him) to provide the machinery of his own version. In what follows we glimpse the Perilous Host who must be obeyed in every command, however silly or outrageous it may seem; but we see also that warmth, almost we might say impetuous excess, of courtesy that characterizes Gawain. Just as when he rehearsed the compact with the Green Knight he said largely 'whatever may be the consequences' and so landed himself in more than he bargained for; so now in delight and gratitude he cries:

'Now I thank you a thousand times for this beyond all!

Now my quest is accomplished, as you crave it, I will
dwell a few days here, and else do what you order.'

(44.1080–2)

The lord immediately seizes on this, and holds him to his word:
Gawain is to lie late abed, and then spend the days with the lady,
while the lord goes off hunting. And then a seemingly absurd
compact is propounded.

'One thing more,' said the master, 'we'll make an agreement:
whatever I win in the wood at once shall be yours,
and whatever gain you may get you shall give in exchange.
Shall we swap thus, sweet man – come, say what you think! –
whether one's luck be light, or one's lot be better?'
'By God,' quoth good Gawain, 'I agree to it all,
and whatever play you propose seems pleasant to me.'
'Done! 'Tis a bargain! Who'll bring us the drink?'
So said the lord of that land. They laughed one and all;
they drank and they dallied, and they did as they pleased,
these lords and ladies, as long as they wished,
and then with customs of France and many courtly phrases
they stood in sweet debate and soft words bandied,
and lovingly they kissed, their leave taking.
With trusty attendants and torches gleaming
they were brought at the last to their beds so soft,
     one and all.
  Yet ere to bed they came,
  he the bargain did oft recall;
  he knew how to play a game
  the old governor of that hall.   (45.1105–25)

So ends the Second Fit and the great Third Fit begins, about
which I wish specially to speak. I will say little about its admirable
construction, since that has often been commented upon. Indeed
(once granted an interest in contemporary sport and its details, or
even without that concession) its excellence is obvious enough to
any attentive reader: the way in which the hunts are 'inter-
leaved' between the temptations; the significant diminuendo
from the herds of deer (of real economic value in winter) slain
in the first hunt to the 'foul fox-fell' of the last day, contrasting

with the increasing peril of the temptations; the dramatic purpose of the hunts, not only in timing, and in preserving a double
view with the three main actors kept all the while in sight, but also
in elongating and making most weighty the three vital days out of
the whole year of the general action: all this needs no elaboration. [4]
But the hunts have also another function, essential to the handling
of the tale in this version, that is more to my purpose. As I have
already indicated, any consideration of 'analogues', especially
the less courtly, or indeed any close examination of our text
without reference to others, will suggest that our poet has done
his best to turn the place of the temptation into a real chivalrous
castle, no mirage of enchantment or abode of fays, where the laws
of courtesy, hospitality, and morality run. The hunts play a significant place in this change of atmosphere. The lord behaves
as a real wealthy lord might be expected to behave in the season.
He must be out of the way, but he does not remain mysteriously
aloof, or just vanish. His absence and the lady's opportunity
are thus accounted for naturally; and this helps to make the
temptations also more natural, and so to set them on a normal
moral plane.

There would not, I think, and I am sure that the author
intended that there should not, be any more suspicion in the minds
of genuine first-time readers or hearers of his story[5] than in the
mind of Sir Gawain himself (as is clearly shown) that the temptations were all a 'put-up job', just part of the perils and trials that
he had been inveigled from Arthur's court to undergo and so be
destroyed or utterly disgraced. In fact it is possible to wonder
whether the author has not gone too far. Has not his contrivance
a grave weakness? All – apart perhaps from unusual but not
incredible magnificence – all is so normal in the castle that on
reflexion the question must soon arise: 'What would have happened, if Gawain had not passed the test?' For we learn in the
end that the lord and lady were conniving; yet the test was meant
to be real, to procure if possible Gawain's downfall and the
disgrace of his 'high order'. The lady was in fact his 'enemy keen'.
How then was she protected, if her lord was far away, hallooing
and hunting in the forest? It is no answer to this question to point
to ancient and barbaric customs or to tales in which memory of
them is still enshrined. For we are not in that world, and if indeed

the author knew anything about it he has wholly rejected it. But he has not wholly rejected 'magic'. And the answer may be that 'fairy-story', though concealed, or taken for granted as part of the machinery of events, is really as integral to this part of the narrative as to those where it is more obvious and unaltered, such as the incursion of the Green Knight. Only *fayryȝe* (240) will suffice to make the plot of the lord and lady intelligible and workable in the imagined world that the author has contrived. We must suppose that just as Sir Bertilak could go green again and change shape for the tryst at the Chapel, so the lady could have protected herself by some sudden change, or destroying power, to which Sir Gawain would have become exposed by falling to temptation, even in will only.[6] If we have this in mind, then perhaps the 'weakness' becomes strength. The temptation is real and perilous in the extreme on the *moral plane* (for Gawain's own view of the circumstances is all that matters on that plane[7]); yet hanging in the background, for those able to receive the air of 'faerie' in a romance, is a terrible threat of disaster and destruction. The struggle becomes intense to a degree which a merely realistic story of how a pious knight resisted a temptation to adultery (when a guest) could hardly attain.[8] It is one of the properties of Fairy Story thus to enlarge the scene and the actors; or rather it is one of the properties that are distilled by literary alchemy when old deep-rooted stories are rehandled by a real poet with an imagination of his own.

In my view, then, the temptations of Sir Gawain, his behaviour under them, and criticism of his code, were for our author his story, to which all else was subservient. I will not argue this. The weight, length, and detailed elaboration of the Third Fit (and of the end of the Second Fit which defines the situation) are, as I have said, sufficient evidence to show where at least the prime attention of the poet was concentrated.

I will turn then now to the temptation scenes, especially to those points in them that are most significant, as I believe, of the author's views and purpose: the keys to the question 'what is this poem really about?' as it is by him presented. For this purpose it is necessary to have fresh in mind the conversations of Gawain and the Lady of the Castle.

(Here the temptation-scenes were read aloud in translation).[9]

From these scenes I will select some points for comment. On December the 29th the lady comes to Gawain's room before he is fully awake, sits upon his bed-side, and when he arouses puts her arms about him (49.1224-5). She tells him that all is quite safe, and makes her all-out assault. It is, I think, here important to say that though some critics have held this to be a mistake on her part (which can in reality mean only a mistake on the part of the poet), they themselves are certainly mistaken. The lady is very beautiful indeed, Gawain was from the first, as we have seen, greatly attracted by her, and not only is he severely tempted on this occasion, but by the lady's declaration (49.1235-40) *that temptation remains in force throughout his dealings with her.* All their converse and talk slips perpetually towards adultery thereafter.

After the first temptation no private conversation between Gawain and the lady (except in his room) is reported – he is either with at least both the ladies together, or after the lord's home-comings in company – save only in the evening after the second temptation. And we may well consider the change that has occurred, contrasting the scene after supper on December the 30th with the untroubled air at dinner on Christmas Day (which I have already recited, page 80):

> Much gladness and gaiety began then to spring
> round the fire on the hearth, and freely and oft
> at supper and later: many songs of delight,
> such as canticles of Christmas, and new carol-dances,
> amid all the mannerly mirth that men can tell of;
> and ever our noble knight was next to the lady.
> Such glances she gave him of her gracious favour,
> secretly stealing sweet looks that strong man to charm,
> that he was passing perplexed, and ill-pleased at heart.
> Yet he would fain not of his courtesy coldly refuse her,
> but graciously engaged her, however against the grain
> the play.   (66.1652-63)

This I believe to be a fair translation of a passage that contains some verbal, and possibly textual, difficulties; but neither this version nor the original must be misunderstood. Gawain's mood is not that of one who has been 'put off' or disgusted, but of a man who does not know what to do. He is in the throes of temptation. All his breeding constrains him to go on playing the game, but the lady has already exposed the weakness of such 'nurture', that it is a perilous weapon in such a situation, as dangerous as a handful of pretty rockets near a real gunpowder-plot. Immediately afterwards fear or prudence suggests flight, and Gawain tries to get out of his promise to do the lord's bidding and stay three nights longer. But he is caught again by his own courtesy. He has no better excuse to offer than to say that it is very near the time for his appointment, and he had better start in the morning. This the lord easily counters by pretending to think that his own good faith is doubted, and he repeats that he gives his word that Sir Gawain shall reach the Green Chapel in good time. That this attempt at flight on Gawain's part is due to moral wisdom (to fear of himself, that is) and not to disgust is made clear by the sequel.

Apart from this hint, however, in the first two scenes the author has been content to report events and sayings without revealing Gawain's feelings (or his own views). But as soon as we come to the third scene the tone changes. So far Gawain has been engaged mainly in a problem of 'courtesy', and we see him using the wits and good manners for which he was renowned with great skill, and still (until the evening of December the 30th) with a certain confidence. But with stanzas 70 and 71 (lines 1750 ff.) we come to the 'nub' of the affair. Gawain is now in great peril. Wise flight has proved impossible without breaking his word and the rules of courtesy to his host.[10] His sleep has been dark and troubled with the fear of death. And when the lady appears again he welcomes her with sheer pleasure and delight in her beauty. On the last morning of the old year she came again to his room:

in a gay mantle that to the ground was measured
and was fur-lined most fairly with fells well trimmed,
with no comely coif on her head, only the clear jewels
that were twined in her tressure by twenties in clusters;
her noble face and her neck all naked were laid,
her breast bare in front and at the back also.
She came through the chamber-door and closed it behind her,
wide set a window, and to wake him she called,

thus greeting him gaily with her gracious words
>of cheer:
>>'Ah! man, how canst thou sleep,
>>the morning is so clear!'
>>He lay in darkness deep,
>>but her call he then could hear.

In heavy darkness drowsing he dream-words muttered,
as a man whose mind was bemused with many mournful thoughts,
how destiny should his doom on that day bring him
when he at the Green Chapel the great man would meet,
and be obliged his blow to abide without debate at all.
But when so comely she came, he recalled then his wits,
swept aside his slumbers, and swiftly made answer.
The lady in lovely guise came laughing sweetly,
bent down o'er his dear face, and deftly kissed him.
He greeted her graciously with a glad welcome,
seeing her so glorious and gaily attired,
so faultless in her features and so fine in her hues
that at once joy up-welling went warm to his heart.
With smiles sweet and soft they turned swiftly to mirth,
and only brightness and bliss was broached there between them
>so gay.
>>They spoke then speeches good,
>>much pleasure was in that play;
>>great peril between them stood,
>>unless Mary for her knight should pray.   (69–70.1736–69)

And with that we have the re-entry, for the first time since the
pentangle and the shield of Gawain (that is here indeed alluded
to), of *religion*, of something higher than and beyond a code of
polite or polished manners which have proved, and are going again
and finally to prove, not only an ineffectual weapon in the last
resort, but an actual danger, playing into the hands of the
enemy.

Immediately afterwards the word *synne* is introduced, for the
first and only time in this highly moral poem, and so all the more
emphatically; and what is more, a distinction is drawn, Gawain
himself is forced to draw, a distinction between 'sin' (the moral
law) and 'courtesy':

For she, queenly and peerless, pressed him so closely,
led him so near the line, that at last he must needs
either refuse her with offence or her favours there take.
He cared for his courtesy, lest a caitiff[11] he proved,
yet more for his sad case, if he should sin commit
and to the owner of the house, to his host, be a traitor.
'God help me!' said he. 'Happen that shall not!'

(71.1770–6)

The end of the last temptation-scene, with the lady's complete shift of ground after her final defeat on the major (or higher, or only real) issue, is, of course, an added complexity in this complex poem, which must be considered in its place. But we must from this point move at once to the scene that follows the temptation: Gawain's confession (75.1874–84).

Gollancz at least deserves credit for noting the confession,[12] which had previously received little or no attention. But he totally missed the point, or points, involved. These I wish now specially to consider. It is not too much to say that the whole interpretation and valuation of *Sir Gawain and the Green Knight* depends on what one thinks of the thirtieth stanza of the Third Fit [stanza 75]. Either the poet knew what he was about, meant what he said, and placed this stanza where he wished it to be – in which case we must think about it seriously and consider his intentions; or else he did not, and was just a muddler, stringing conventional scenes together, and his work is not worth long consideration at all, except, perhaps, as a lumber-room of old half-forgotten and less than half-understood stories and motives, just a fairy-story for adults, and not a very good one.

Gollancz evidently thought the latter; for in his notes he makes the astonishing remark that *though the poet does not notice it* (!), *Gawain makes a sacrilegious confession. For he conceals the fact that he has accepted the girdle with the intention of retaining it.* This is arrant nonsense. It will not even endure reference to the text, as we shall see. But, first of all, it is quite incredible that a poet of high serious-ness[13] who has already with explicit moral purpose inserted a long digression on the Pentangle and the shield of Sir Gawain, should put in a passage about *confession and absolution* (matters which he regarded with the greatest solemnity, whatever critics may now feel) quite casually, and without 'noticing' such a minor point as 'sacrilege'. If he was such a fool, one wonders why editors trouble to edit his works.

Let us look then at the text. First: since the author does not specify what Gawain confessed, we cannot say what he omitted, and it is therefore gratuitously silly to assert that he concealed anything. We are told, however, that he *schewed his mysdedez, of þe more and þe mynne*, that is, that he confessed all his sins (sc. all that it was necessary to confess) both great and small. If that is not definite enough, it is made still plainer that Gawain's confession was a good one, and not 'sacrilegious', and the absolution effective,[14] by the statement that this was so:

> There he cleanly confessed him and declared his misdeeds,
> both the more and the less, and for mercy he begged,
> to absolve him of them all he besought the good man;
> and he assoiled him and made him as safe and as clean
> as for Doom's Day indeed, were it due on the morrow.
>   (75.1880–4)

And if even this is not enough the poet goes on to describe the consequent lightness of Gawain's heart.

> Thereafter more merry he made among the fair ladies,
> with carol-dances gentle and all kinds of rejoicing,
> than ever he did ere that day, till the darkness of night,
>   in bliss.
>   Each man there said: 'I vow
>   a delight to all he is!
>   Since hither he came till now,
>   he was ne'er so gay as this.'   (75.1885–92)

Need I say that a light heart is certainly not the mood induced by a bad confession and the wilful concealment of sin?

Gawain's confession is represented as a good one, then. Yet the girdle is retained. This cannot be accidental or inadvertent. We are obliged therefore to come to terms with the situation deliberately contrived by the author; we are driven to consider the relation of all these rules of behaviour, these games and courtesies,

to *sin*, morals, the saving of souls, to what the author would have
held to be eternal and universal values. And that, surely, is precisely why the confession is introduced, and at this point. Gawain
in his last perilous extremity was obliged to tear his 'code' in two,
and distinguish its components of good manners and good morals.
We are now compelled to consider these matters further.

The first implication of the confession is seen thus to be that
retention of the girdle was not a *misdeed* or a *sin* on the moral plane
in the author's view. For there are only two alternatives: either
(*a*) Gawain did not mention the girdle at all, being sufficiently
instructed to distinguish between such pastimes and serious
matters; or (*b*) if he did mention it, his confessor *lerned hym better*.
The former is perhaps the less likely, since Gawain's education in
this direction had, we might say, only just begun; whereas we are
told that before he went to confession Gawain asked the advice of
the priest.[15]

We have in fact reached the point of intersection of two different
planes: of a real and permanent, and an unreal and passing world
of values: *morals* on the one hand, and on the other a *code of honour*,
or a game with rules. The personal code of most people was, and
of many still is, like that of Sir Gawain made up of a close blend of
the two; and breaches at any point in that personal code have a
very similar emotional flavour. Only a crisis, or serious thought
without a crisis (which is rare) will serve to disentangle the elements; and the process may be painful, as Gawain discovered.

A 'game with rules' may deal, of course, with trivial matters or
with ones more serious in an ascending scale, as, say, from
games with pieces of cardboard upwards. The more they deal
with or become involved with real affairs and duties, the more
moral bearings they will have; the things 'done' or 'not done' will
have two sides, the ritual or rules of the game, and the eternal
rules; and therefore the more occasions there will be for a *dilemma*,
a conflict of rules. And the more seriously you take your games, the
severer and more painful the dilemma. Sir Gawain belonged (as he
is depicted) by class, tradition, and training to the kind that take
their games with great seriousness. His suffering was acute. He was,
one might say, selected for that reason – by an author who
belonged to the same class and tradition and knew what
it felt like from the inside; but who was interested also in

problems of conduct, and have given some thought to them.

It might be felt a fair question to interject at this moment: 'Is it not a *fault of art*, a poetic blunder, to allow so serious a matter as a real confession and absolution to intrude at this point? To force into the open, and compel the attention of a reader to this divergence of values (in which he may not be much interested)? Indeed to intrude such matters at all at any point into a fairy-story, to subject such absurdities as exchanging venison for a kiss to a serious examination?'

I am not at this time greatly concerned to answer such a question; for I am at the moment chiefly anxious to assert, to show (I hope), that this is what the author of *Sir Gawain and the Green Knight* has in fact done, and that his operations upon his material will be unintelligible or largely misunderstood if that is not recognized. But if the question were raised I would reply: There is a strength and life about this poem which is almost universally admitted. This is more likely to be *due* to the greater seriousness of the author than to have survived in spite of it. But much depends on what you want, or think that you want. Do you demand that the author should have the objects that you would expect him to have, or the views that you would prefer him to hold? That he should, for instance, be an anthropological antiquarian? Or that he should simply devote himself to telling an exciting fairy-story well, in such a way as to produce literary credibility sufficient for entertainment? And how will he do that, in terms of his own time and thought? Surely, if that simple object was his only object (unlikely enough in the complex and didactic fourteenth century), he would in the process of giving life to old legends inevitably slide into the consideration of contemporary, or permanent, problems of conduct? It is by that consideration that he has vivified his charac-ters, and by that has given new life to old tales – totally different to their former significance (about which he probably knew, and certainly cared, much less than some men of this day). It is a case of pouring new wine into old bottles, no doubt, and there are some inevitable cracks and leaks. But I at any rate find this question of ethics both more vivid for its curious and bizarre setting, and in itself more interesting than all the guesses about more primitive times. But then I think the fourteenth century superior to bar-barism, and theology and ethics above folklore.

I do not, of course, insist that the author must have had, as a conscious purpose, any such object as probing into the relation of real and artificial rules of conduct when he began to deal with this story. I imagine this poem took some time to write, was often altered, expanded here and cut down there. But the moral questions are there, inherent in the tale, and they will naturally arise and present themselves for attention in proportion as the tale is realistically handled, and in proportion as the author is a man of thought and intelligence, something more than a tale-pedlar. In any case it is clear that before he achieved his final version the author was fully aware of what he was doing: writing a 'moral' poem, and a study of knightly virtue and manners under strain; for he put in two stanzas ('though it may tarry my story', and though we may not now like it) about the Pentangle, as he sent off his knight to his trial. And before he puts in the passage about confession at the end of the major trial, he has already drawn our attention to the divergence of values, by the clear distinction expressed in lines 1773–4; lines which place the moral law higher than the laws of 'courtesy', and explicitly reject, and make Gawain reject, *adultery* as part of courtesy possible to a perfect knight. A very contemporary and very English point of view![16]

But by the open invitation to adultery of lines 49.1237–40, and that is no doubt one of the reasons why it is placed at the beginning, we are able to see the hollowness of all the courteous fencing that follows. For Gawain from that moment can have no doubt whatever of the lady's object: *to haf wonnen hym to woȝe* ('to allure him to love-making', 61.1550). He is attacked on two fronts, and has in reality abandoned from the outset 'service', the absolute submission of the 'true servant' to the will and wishes of the lady; though he strives throughout to maintain the verbal shadow of it, the gentleness of polite speech and manners.

> By God, I would be glad, if good to you seemed
> whatever I could say, or in service could offer
> to the pleasure of your excellence – it would be pure delight
>
> (50.1245–7)

> But I am proud of the praise you are pleased to give me,
> and as your servant in earnest my sovereign I hold you
>
> (51.1277–8)

All your will I would wish to work, as I am able,
being so beholden in honour, and, so help me the Lord,
desiring ever the servant of yourself to remain   (61.1546–8)

All such expressions have become mere pretences, reduced to a
level hardly above that of the Christmas games, when the *wylnyng*
(1546) of the lady has been and is persistently rejected.

Sheer courtly practice in the game of manners and adroitness of
speech enabled Gawain to avoid being openly *crapayn*, to eschew
'vileinye' in words, that is expressions that were boorish or brutally
outspoken (whether just and true, or not).[17] But even though he
may do it with disarming gracefulness, the law of 'service' to the
lady's wishes is in fact broken. And the motive of the breach, of
all his adroit defence, can from the first only be a moral one,
though this is not stated until 71.1773–4. Had there been no other
way out Gawain would have had to abandon even his technical
courtesy of manners and *lodly refuse* (1772). But he was never
'driven nearer to the line' than to say: 'Nay! lover have I none,
and none will have meanwhile' (71.1790–1), which in spite of his
'smooth smile' is plain enough and *a worde þat worst is of alle*
(72.1792). But the lady drives him no further, for undoubtedly
the author did not wish the gentleness of Gawain to be broken
down. He approved gentle manners and absence of 'vileinye' when
allied to, founded on, virtue, the distillation of the courtesy in
'courtly love' without adultery.[18]

We must then recognize that the intrusion of Sir Gawain's
confession and its precise placing in the poem was deliberate;
and that it is an indication of the author's opinion that *games* and
manners were not important, ultimately (for 'salvation', 75.1879),
and were in any case on an inferior plane to real *virtue*, to which
they must in the case of conflict give way. Even the Green Knight
recognizes the distinction, and declares that Gawain is 'the most
faultless man on earth' (95.2363) with regard to the major moral
issue.

But we have not done with the interesting minor issues. The
Green Knight proceeds: *Bot here yow lakked a lyttel, sir, and lewté yow
wonted* (95.2366). What was this *lewté*? The word is not well translated by 'loyalty', in spite of the kinship of the words; for 'loyalty'
is now chiefly applied to honesty and steadfastness in some

important personal or public relationship or duty (as to king or country, kin or dear friends). 'Legality' would be equally akin and better; for *lewté* might mean no more than 'sticking to the rules' of whatever grade or sanction. Thus our author can call the alliterations that occur in the proper places in a line, according to merely metrical rules, *lel lettres* 'loyal letters' (2.35).

What rules then is Gawain accused of breaking in accepting, keeping, and concealing the girdle? It might be *three*: accepting a gift without returning one; not surrendering it as part of the 'gain' on the third day (according to a jocular pact, definitely called a *layke* or game); using it as a protection at the tryst. It is plain, I think, that the Green Knight is considering only the *second* of these. He says:

> The true shall truly repay,
> for no peril then need he quake.
> Thou didst fail on the third day . . .   (94.2354–6)

> For it is my weed that thou wearest . . .
>
>   (95.2358)

It is as man to man, as opponents in a game, that he is challenging Gawain. And I think that it is plain that in this he expresses the opinion of the author.

For the author was not a simple-minded man. Those who take an ultimately stern and uncompromising moral view are not necessarily simple-minded. He might think the major issue clear in theory, but nothing in his handling of his tale suggests that he thought moral conduct a simple and painless thing in practice. And anyway he was, as we might say, a gentleman and a sportsman, and was intrigued by the minor issue. Indeed the *moralitas* of his poem, if complicated, is yet also enriched by this exhibition of a clash of rules on a lower plane. He has contrived or brought out a very pretty problem.

Gawain is induced to accept a parting gift from the lady. From the technical fault of 'covetousness' (taking without return) he has been explicitly acquitted: he had nothing he could give in return which would not by its disparity in value be insulting (72. 1798 ff.); he had no thought of the beauty or monetary value of the girdle (81.2037–40). But he was led into a position from which he could not withdraw by the thought that it might possibly save his life when he came to the tryst. Now the author nowhere examines the ethics of the Beheading Game; but if we do so, we shall not find that Gawain had broken any article of his covenant in wearing the girdle for that purpose. All he had promised to do was to come in person, not send a substitute (the probable meaning of line 17.384: *wyth no wyȝ ellez on lyue*, 'in the world with none else but me'); to come at an appointed time, and then stand one stroke without resistance. He does not, therefore, on this count need an advocate; though one might quickly point out that Gawain was actually tricked into the covenant, before the Green Knight revealed that he was magically protected; and his promise might well be held ethically void, and even on the level of a mere 'game' a little private magic of his own could only be regarded as perfectly fair. But the author was not considering this case; though he was not unaware of the point, as we see in Gawain's protest:

> But if on floor now falls my head,
> I cannot it restore.   (91.2282–3)

We are thus merely considering the events in the castle, and the sporting pact with the lord. Gawain had accepted the girdle as a gift because of his dread of the beheading. But again he had been caught. The lady's timing was cunning. She pressed the belt on him, and the moment he weakened she gave it to him, and then closed the trap. She begged him not to tell her husband. He agreed. He could hardly do anything else; but with his characteristic generosity, indeed impetuous excess, which we have already noted, he vowed never to tell anyone else in the world.[19] Of course he desired the belt on the chance (he seems never to have rated it higher than that) that it might save him from death; but even if he had not, he would have been in a dilemma of 'courtesy'. To have rejected the belt, once accepted; or to have refused the request: neither would have been 'courteous'. It was not for him to enquire why he must keep the belt secret; presumably it was to save the lady from embarrassment, since there was no reason to suppose that it was not hers to give. At any rate it was quite as much hers to give as her kisses, and in that matter he had protected her already from embarrassment by refusing to say from whom he had obtained them.[20] It is not said at this moment of acceptance and promise that Gawain recalled his game-compact with the lord at all. But he cannot be finally excused on that ground. For he could not long remain forgetful of the point. When the lord came home at night, he was bound to remember. And he did. It is not said so; but we see it clearly in stanza 77: in Gawain's haste to get the business over. 'This time I will pay first' he cries (as usual going further than he need, whether in making or breaking a promise), as he goes to meet the lord half way (lines 1932–4).

It is at this point then, and at this point only, that we may detect Gawain in a fault, such as it is. 'I shall first fulfil the compact that we made,' he says, and for what that compact was worth he does not do so. He says nothing about the girdle. And he is uneasy. 'Enough!' he cries, when the lord (with a significance that he cannot yet perceive, nor we until we have read the whole tale) says that a fox-fell is poor pay for three such precious things as these kisses.

Well, there it is. *Þrid tyme þrowe best*, but *at þe þrid þou fayled þore*. It is not my part to argue that Gawain did not 'fail' at all; for neither was that the thesis of the author. But to consider in what degree and on what plane he failed, in the author's view, so far as it can be discerned; for with such points he was deeply concerned. There were for him, it seems clear to me from his handling of this tale, *three* planes: mere jesting pastimes, such as that played between Gawain and the lord of the castle; 'courtesy',[21] as a code of 'gentle' or polite manners, which included a special mode of deference to women, and could be held to include, as it was by the lady, the more serious, and therefore more dangerous, 'game' of courtly love-making, which might compete with moral laws; and finally real morals, virtues and sins. These might compete one with another. If so, the higher law must be obeyed. From the first arrival of Sir Gawain at the castle situations are being prepared in which such competitions, with dilemmas in conduct, will occur. The author is chiefly interested in the competition between 'courtesy' and virtue (purity and loyalty); he shows us their increasing divergence, and shows us Gawain at the crisis of the temptation recognizing this, and choosing virtue rather than courtesy, yet preserving a graciousness of manner and a gentleness of speech belonging to the true spirit of courtesy. I think it was his intention by the confession also to show that the lowest grade, 'jesting pastime', was not an ultimately important matter at all; but only after he had amused himself, as it were, by exhibiting a dilemma which artificial courtesy could produce even on a lower level. In this case, since questions of sin and virtue did not arise, Gawain placed the rules of courtesy higher, and obeyed the lady, even though it landed him in breaking his word (though that only in a game of no seriousness). But alas! as I think our author would have said, the rules of artificial courtesy could not really excuse him, not being of universal overriding validity, as are those of morality, not even if courtesy alone had been his motive for taking the girdle. But it was not. He would never have been in the position where he was bound to secrecy, contrary to the games-pact, if he had not wanted to possess the girdle for its possible power: he wished to save his life, a simple and honest motive, and by means that were in no way contrary to his original pact with the Green Knight, and conflicted only with the seemingly absurd and purely jocular pact with the lord of the castle. That was his only fault.

We may observe that each of these 'planes' has its own court of judgement. The moral law is referred to the Church. Lewté, 'playing the game' when it is a mere game, as man to man, is referred to the Green Knight, who indeed speaks of the procedure in mock-religious terms, though (it may be noted) he applies these only to the game: the higher matters have been already judged; 'confession' and a 'penance' at the point of his edge. Courtesy is referred to the supreme court of such affairs, the Court of King Arthur of kydde cortaysye; and the case against the defendant is laughed out.

But there is yet another court: Sir Gawain himself, and his own judgement. Let us say at once that he is not competent to judge this case impartially, and his judgement cannot be held valid. He is not unnaturally at first in an emotional state of mind, greatly disturbed, after having not only his whole 'code' pulled to pieces, but receiving sore wounds to his pride. His first outcry against himself is hardly more likely to be just than his bitter generalization against women.[22] But it is none the less very interesting to consider what he has to say; because he is a very roundly drawn character, and not a mere vehicle of opinions and analyses. This poet had skill in character drawing. Though the lady, when she has a reported speaking part, has only a simple role, and only one line to follow (directed by an unexplained 'enmity'), all that she says has an unmistakable tone of her own. Better still is Sir Bertilak, and greater the skill with which he is made to behave and speak credibly both as Green Knight and as Host, so that, if these two had not in fact been one, either would have been adequately drawn as an individual, yet at the end we are well able to believe that we have listened to the same character throughout: it is this as much as anything that makes a reader accept as unquestion-ingly as Gawain their identity without (in this poem) any dis-enchantment or change of shape after the revelation. But both these actors are secondary, and their main function is to provide the situation for Gawain's trial. Gawain has full literary reality.

His 'perfection' is made more human and credible, and there-fore more appreciable as genuine nobility, by the small flaw.[23] But, to my mind, nothing makes him 'come alive' as a real man so much as the depiction of his 'reactions' to the revelation: here that grossly abused word 'reaction' can with some justice be used, for his words and behaviour are largely a matter of instinct and emotion. We may well consider the contrast between the stanzas in which these are exhibited and the lines in which his perilous journeys are described, lines at once picturesque and perfunctory. But this poet was not really interested in fairy-tale or in romance for their own sakes. It is also, I think, a final stroke of art in a poem that is so concentrated on virtue and problems of conduct that it should end with a glimpse of the 'reactions' of a man truly 'gentle', but not deeply reflective, to a fault in a part of his personal code that is not to a cool outside judge essential. That it should indeed end with a glimpse of that twofold scale with which all reasonably charitable people measure: the stricter for oneself, the more lenient for others.[24] *Þe kyng comfortez þe knyȝt, and alle þe court als laȝen loude þerat.*

What does Gawain feel and say? He accuses himself of *couardise* and *couetyse*. He 'stood in a study' a long while

in such grief and disgust he had a grue in his heart;
all the blood from his breast in his blush mingled,
and he shrank into himself with shame at that speech.
The first words on that field that he found then to say

were: 'Cursed be ye, Coveting, and Cowardice also!
In you is vileness, and vice that virtue destroyeth.'
He took then the treacherous thing, and untying the knot
fiercely flung he the belt at the feet of the knight:
'See there the falsifier, and foul be its fate!
Through care for thy blow Cowardice brought me
to consent to Coveting, my true kind[25] to forsake,
which is free-hand and faithful word that are fitting to knights.
Now I am faulty and false, who afraid have been ever
of treachery and troth-breach: the two now my curse
           may bear!   (95.2370–84)

Later, on return to the Court, he recounts his adventures in this
order:[26] his hardships; the way things went at the tryst, and the
bearing of the Green Knight; the love-making of the lady; and
(last of all) the matter of the Girdle. He then showed the scar in
his neck which he got as a rebuke for his *vnleuté*:

> It was torment to tell the truth:
> in his face the blood did flame;
> he groaned for grief and ruth
> when he showed it, to his shame.

'Lo! Lord,' he said at last, and the lace handled,
'This is the band! For this a rebuke I bear in my neck!
This is the grief and disgrace I have got for myself
from the covetousness and cowardice that o'ercame me there!
This is the token of the troth-breach that I am detected in,
and needs must I wear it while in the world I remain.'
                                   (100–1.2501–10)

Two lines follow, of which the first is unclear, but which together
(however interpreted or emended) undoubtedly express Gawain's
feeling that nothing can ever delete this blot. That is in keeping
with his 'excess' when moved; but it is true to the emotions of
many others. For one may believe in the forgiveness of sins (as he
did), even forgive oneself one's own and certainly forget them, but
the sting of shame on morally less important or insignificant levels
will bite still after long years as sharp as new!
    Sir Gawain's emotion is thus one of burning shame; and the

burden of his self-accusation is cowardice and covetousness. Cowardice is the chief, for through it he fell into covetousness. This must mean that as a knight of the Round Table Gawain makes no claim against the Green Knight for the unfairness of the beheading-pact (though he has glanced at it in lines 2282–3), abides by his own words *quat-so bifallez after* (382), and elects to stand trial on the simple ground that this was a test of the absolute courage of a knight of his Order: having given his word he was obliged to keep it even with death as the consequence, and to meet that with straight unflinching human courage. He was by circumstance the representative of the Round Table and should have stood his ground just so, without aids.

On that simple, but very high level, he is ashamed, and as a result emotionally disturbed. He thus calls 'cowardice' his reluctance to throw away his life without striking a blow, or to surrender a talisman that might possibly have saved him. He calls 'covetice' his acceptance of a gift from a lady which he could not immediately repay, though it was pressed on him after two refusals, and in spite of the fact that he did not value it for its costliness. It was indeed only 'covetice' within the terms of the game with the lord of the castle: keeping back any part of the *waith* because he wanted it for himself (for any reason). He calls 'treachery'[27] a breach of the rules of a mere pastime, which he could only have regarded as jocular or whimsical (whatever lay hidden in the proposer of the game), since there could obviously be no real exchange between the gains of a hunter and those of a man idling at home!

And so we end. Beyond that our author does not take us. We have seen a gentle courtly knight learn by bitter experience the perils of Courtesy, and the unreality in the last resort of protestations of complete 'service' to a lady as a 'sovereign' whose will is law;[28] and in that last resort we have seen him prefer a higher law. But though by that higher law he proved 'faultless', the exposure of 'courtesy' of this kind went further, and he has had to suffer the final mortification of discovering that the will of the lady was in fact his own disgrace, and that all her flattering protestations of love were false. In a moment of bitterness he has rejected all his 'cortaysye' and cried against women as deceivers:

a gain 'twould be vast

to love them well and believe them not, if it lay in man's power!
(97.2420–1)

But that has not been all his suffering as a knight: he has been
tricked into 'not playing the game' and breaking his word in a
sport; and we have seen him pass through an agony of emotional
shame at this failure on a lower plane only really fitting to failure
on the higher. This all seems to me vividly true and credible, and
I am not making fun of it, if I say that as a final spectacle we see
Gawain tearing off the School Tie (as unworthy to wear it), and
riding home with a white feather stuck in his cap, only to have that
adopted as the colours of the First Eleven, while the matter ends
with the laughter of the Court of Honour.

But finally, how true it is to the depicted character of Gawain,
this excess of shame, this going beyond all that is required in adopt-
ing a badge of disgrace for all to see always, *in tokenyng he watz tane in
tech of a faute* (100.2488)! And how true also to the whole tone and
air of this poem, so concerned with 'confession' and penance.

> Grace innogh þe mon may haue
> Þat synnez þenne new, ȝif him repente,
> Bot wyth sorȝ and syt he mot it craue,
> And byde þe payne þerto is bent

says the poet in his *Pearl* (661–4).[29] After the shame the repentance,
and then the unreserved confession with sorrow and penance, and
at last not only forgiveness, but the redemption, so that the 'harm'
that is not concealed, and the reproach that is voluntarily borne,
becomes a glory, *euermore after*. And with that the whole scene, for a
time so vivid, so present, even topical, begins to fade back into the
Past. *Gawayn with his olde curteisye* goes back into *Fairye*[30]

> as it is written in the best of the books of romance.
> Thus in Arthur his days happened this marvel,
> as the Book of the Brut beareth us witness;
> since Brutus the bold knight to Britain came first,
> after the siege and the assault had ceased at Troy,
>   I trow,
>   many a marvel such before
>   has happened here ere now.

To his bliss us bring Who bore
the Crown of Thorns on brow!
Amen.   (101.2521–30)

*Postscript: lines 1885–92.**
In the above discussion it was said (p. 88) that Gawain's light
heart was sufficient evidence that he had made a 'good confession'.
By that I meant that gaiety proceeding from a 'lightness of heart'
may be and often is a result of the fitting reception of a sacrament
by one of the faithful, and that quite independently of other pains
or cares: such as, in Gawain's case, fear of the blow, fear of death.
But this may be, and has been, queried. It has been asked: Is not
his gaiety due rather to having the belt, and so being no longer
afraid of the tryst? Or it has been suggested that Gawain's mood is
due rather to despair: let me eat and be merry, for tomorrow I die!
    We are not dealing with a simple-minded author, nor with a
simple-minded period, and it is not necessary to assume that
only one explanation of Gawain's mood is possible (i.e. was in the
poet's mind). Gawain is being drawn with understanding, and
he is made to feel, speak, and behave as such a man would in his
situation as a whole: consolation of religion, magic belt (or at
least a belief that such a thing was possible), and approaching
mortal peril, and all. But I think, nonetheless, that the placing
of the lines describing his mood immediately after the absolution
(*And syþen* 1885), and the use of the words *ioye* and *blys*, are
sufficient to show that the author intended the confession to be
the chief reason of Gawain's increased mirth; and was not
thinking at all of a wild gaiety of despair.
    But the belt requires more attention. I think it is significant
that Gawain nowhere ever shows confidence in the girdle's
efficacy, certainly not even *hope* in it sufficient to cause care-free
joy! In fact his hope in it seems to have continually decreased
from the time of his confession. It is true that, at the time of
acceptance and before his visit to the priest, he thanked the lady
abundantly and heartily for it (one so courteous could hardly do
less!), but even at the moment when the idea of help in escaping
from death first wakes in his mind (lines 1855 ff.) and is strongest,

* Cited above in translation, p. 88.

before he has had time to reflect, all that the poet strictly reports
him as thinking is: 'It would be a marvellous thing to have in the
desperate business allotted to me. If I could somehow escape
being slain, it would be a splendid trick.' It does not sound
confident enough, as an explanation of his being merrier that
day than ever before. In any case that night he sleeps very badly,
and hears every cock crow, dreading the hour of the tryst. In
lines 83.2075–6 we read of *þat tene place þer þe ruful race he schulde
resayue* ('that grievous place where he is due to endure the
dolorous blow'), which is plainly meant to be Gawain's reflexion
as he and his guide set out. In lines 85.2138–9 he openly declares
to his guide that his trust is in God, whose servant he is.[31]
Similarly in lines 86.2158–9, with reference certainly to his
confession and preparedness for death, he says: *to Goddez wylle I
am ful bayn, and to hym I haf me tone.* Again in lines 88.2208–11 he
overcomes fear not by any thought or mention of the 'jewel for
the jeopardy' but by submission to God's will. In lines 90.2255 ff.
he is in great fear of imminent death, and is at pains to conceal
it, but does not quite succeed. In lines 91.2265–7 he expected
the stroke to kill him. And finally in lines 92.2307–8 we read:
no meruayle þaȝ hym myslyke þat hoped of no rescowe.

Now all this fear, and this summoning up of courage to meet
death, is perfectly consonant with the consolation of religion and
with a mood of joy after being assoiled, but it does not accord at
all with possession of a talisman that is *believed in* as a protection
against bodily harm, according to the words of the temptress:

> For whoever goes girdled with this green riband,
> while he keeps it well clasped closely about him,
> there is none so hardy under heaven that to hew him were
>   able;
> for he could not be killed by any cunning of hand.   (74.1851–4)

We may fairly say, then, that from the moment of its acceptance,
certainly from the moment of his absolution, the Girdle seems
to have been of no comfort to Gawain.[32] If it were not for lines
81.2030–40, where Gawain puts on the Girdle *for gode of hymseluen*,
we might well have supposed that he had, after confession,
resolved not to use it, though he could not now in courtesy hand

it back or break his promise of secrecy. From Gawain's setting out to his shame at the revelation the poet has at any rate ignored the Girdle, or has represented Gawain as doing so. Such comfort and strength as he has beyond his own natural courage is derived only from *religion*. It is no doubt possible to dislike this moral and religious outlook, but the poet has it; and if one does not (with or without dislike) recognize this, the purport and point of the poem will be missed, the point at any rate that the author intended.

Nonetheless it may be objected that I am here pressing the author too hard. If Gawain had shown *no* fear, but had been cheerfully confident in his magic belt (*no more mate ne dismayd for hys mayn dintez* than the Green Knight confident in the magic of Morgan le Fay), then the last scene, the tryst, would have lost all savour. Also granted magic, and even a general belief in the possibility of enchanted belts and the like, it would have needed a very lively faith in this particular belt to take a man to such a tryst without even a shudder of the shoulders! Well, let us concede that. In fact it only goes to strengthen the point that I put forward. Gawain is *not* depicted as having a very lively faith in the Girdle, even if that is only, or partly, for mere reasons of narrative. Therefore his 'joy' on New Year's Eve is not derived from it. Therefore that must be derived from the absolution, to which it is appended, and Gawain is shown as a man with a 'good conscience' and the confession was not 'sacrilegious'.

But quite apart from narrative technique, the poet evidently intended to emphasize the moral and (if you will) higher sides of Gawain's character. For that is simply what he has consistently done throughout, whether with complete appropriateness to his inherited story-material or not. And so, while Gawain does not accept the Girdle solely out of courtesy, and is tempted by the hope of magic aid, and when arming does not forget it, but puts it on *for gode of hymseluen* and *to sauen hymself*, this motive is minimized, and Gawain is not represented as relying on it at all when coming to the desperate point – for it, no less than the horrible Green Knight, and his *faierie*, and all *faierie*, is ultimately under God. A reflexion which makes the magic Girdle seem rather feeble, as no doubt the poet intended that it should.

We are meant then to look on Sir Gawain, after his last confession, as clear in conscience, and so able as much as any other brave and pious man (if not as much as a saint) to support himself in the expectation of death with the thought of God's ultimate protection of the righteous. This implies not only that he has survived the lady's temptations, but that his whole adventure and tryst are *for him* righteous, or at least justified and lawful. We now see the great importance of the description in the First Fit of the way in which Sir Gawain became involved in the affair, and the purpose of the remarkable criticisms of King Arthur voiced in the court (in the Second Fit, stanza 29). In these ways Gawain is shown to have become imperilled not out of *nobelay*, nor because of any fantastic custom or vainglorious vow, nor because of pride in prowess or rating himself as the best knight of his Order – all the possible motives that from a strictly moral point of view might make the whole affair for him foolish or reprehensible, a mere wilful risk or waste of life for no sufficient cause. The wilfulness and the pride are cast on the King; Gawain is involved out of humility, and as a matter of duty to his king and kinsman.

We can imagine indeed the author inserting this curious passage after reflexion. After making Gawain's conduct in his adventure the subject of moral analysis on a serious plane, he would see that in that case the adventure must be for Gawain praiseworthy, as judged on the same level. In fact the author has taken this story, or blend of stories, with all its improbabilities, its lack of secure rational motives, and its incoherence, and endeavoured to make it the *machinery* by which a virtuous man is involved in a mortal peril which it is noble, or at least proper (not wrong or silly), for him to face; and is thus drawn into consequent temptations which he does not wilfully or wittingly incur. And in the end he survives all with plain moral weapons. The Pentangle is thus seen to replace the Gryphon on Gawain's shield as part of a deliberate plan throughout – throughout the final version which we have, at any rate. That plan, and that choice and emphasis, must be recognized.

It is another question whether this treatment is either justified, or artistically successful. For myself, I would say that the criticism of Arthur, and the making of Gawain a proxy of the king with wholly humble and unselfish motives, is for this poem[33] necessary, and successful, and realistic. The Pentangle is justified, and only unsuccessful (at least to my taste, and to that I suppose of many of my period) because it is 'pedantic', very fourteenth-century, almost Chaucerian, in its pedantry indeed, and over long and elaborate, and (most of all) because it proved too difficult for the author's skill with the alliterative verse that he uses. The treatment of the Girdle, hesitating between belief and disregard, is reasonably successful, if one does not scrutinize this matter too closely. A degree of belief in it is necessary for the last temptation-scene; and it proves the only effective bait that the lady has for her traps, thus leading to the one 'flaw' (on the lowest plane of 'playing the game') which makes the actual conduct of Gawain and his near-perfection so much more credible than the mathematical perfection of the Pentangle.

But this belief, or hope, must be played down at the beginning of the last Fit, even if it were in a mere romance unconcerned with moral issues, for confidence in the Girdle would even in such a tale spoil the last scenes. The weakness of the Girdle, as a talisman able (or believed able) to defend a man from wounds, is inherent. Actually this weakness is *less* glaring than it might be, precisely because of the seriousness of the author and the piety which he has ascribed to his pattern of knights; for the disregard of the talisman at the crisis is more credible in such a character as the Gawain of this poem than in a mere adventurer. And yet I regret, not the flaw in Gawain, not that the lady found one little bait for her victim, but that the poet could not think of anything else which Gawain might have accepted and been induced to conceal, and yet one which would not have affected his view of his perilous tryst. But I cannot think of one; so that such criticism, *kesting such cavillacioun*, is idle.

Sir Gawain and the Green Knight remains the best conceived and shaped narrative poem of the Fourteenth Century, indeed of the Middle Age, in English, with one exception only. It has a rival, a claimant to equality not superiority, in Chaucer's masterpiece *Troilus and Criseyde*. That is larger, longer, more intricate, and perhaps more subtle, though no wiser or more perceptive, and certainly less noble. And both these poems deal, from different angles, with the problems that so much occupied the English mind: the relations of Courtesy and Love with morality and Christian morals and the Eternal Law.

NOTES

1   Of this name *pentangle* he is the first recorded user in the vernacular, the only user indeed in Middle English. Yet he claims that the English call it everywhere the Endless Knot. This much at least may be said: the lack of record must be accidental, for the form that he uses, *penta(u)ngel*, is one that shows already clear traces of popular use, being altered from the correct learned *pentaculum* by association with 'angle'. Moreover, though much concerned with the symbolism, he speaks as if his audience could visualize the shape of the figure.

2   The attempt to describe the complex figure and its symbolism was actually too much even for our poet's considerable skill with the long alliterative line. In any case, since part of its significance was the *interrelation* of religious faith, piety, and courtesy in human relations, the attempt to enumerate 'virtues' brings out the arbitrariness of their division and their individual names at any one time, and the constant flux of the meaning of these names (such as *pité* or *fraunchyse*) from age to age.

3   And why the pentangle is proper to that prince so noble
        I intend now to tell you, though it may tarry my story.   (27.623–4)

4   Though actually it has, I think, tended to be over-elaborated in criticism. One point only has been neglected, as far as my knowledge goes: the author has taken care to show that the lord himself in person, not the hunt generally, slew and obtained the *waith* that he surrendered to Gawain. This is of course clear in the cases of the boar and the fox. But even in the first hunt it is indicated: 'When the sun began to slope he had slain such a number / of does and other deer one might doubt it were true' (53.1321–2). But (since there appear to have been no other persons of rank at the hunt) the lord of the castle is probably the *best* of 1325, who supervises the cutting up of his own selected 'quarry'. In this case *didden* of 1327 is one of the many errors of the MS, with plural substituted for singular according to the immediate suggestion of a context not wholly clear to the copyist. It was the lord who chose the fattest of his own 'kill' and gave orders for their proper dressing ready for the presentation of *his venysoun* (1375). This may seem a minute point, and remote from the things that are here being considered, but it is, I believe, related to the topic of *lewté* and keeping one's word which is to be examined.

5   Unless perhaps in the minds of those with too much literary experience. Yet even they must realise that we are supposed to see things with Gawain's eyes, and sense the air with his senses, and he has plainly no suspicions.

6   I mean, if we had posed the author with this question, he would have had an answer, for he had thought the whole thing out, especially all that had a moral aspect; and I think that his answer would have been, in the idiom of his time, the one that I am trying to give.

7   His resistance thus actually redounds all the more to his credit, for he is unaware of any peril save that of 'sin', and he resists on plain moral grounds, unaided by the fear of magic powers or even of discovery.

8   The text as typed had: 'could not attain. Or would not. For this [is] a mode of making felt the real tension that one should feel in a narrative of moral struggle.' When 'could not attain' was changed to 'could hardly attain' the following sentence was bracketed as if for exclusion. [Ed.]

9   This statement is the author's. On this matter see the Foreword. [Ed.]

10   Written in pencil on the typescript: 'a sacrifice he is not yet prepared to make' – to be placed either at the end of the sentence or after 'without breaking his word'. [Ed.]

11   A cad and a boor.

12   The reference is to *Sir Gawain and the Green Knight* edited by Sir Israel Gollancz, Early English Text Society 1940, p. 123, note to line 1880. [Ed.]

13 And one, it may be added, who beyond any real doubt also wrote *Pearl*, not to mention *Purity* and *Patience*.

14 Since the effectiveness of confession is wholly dependent on the dispositions of the penitent, and no words of the priest can remedy bad intentions, or the wilful concealment of recollected sin.

15 I do not assert, of course, that a *genuine compact*, even in sport, has never any moral implications, and never involves any obligations. But I do mean that in the author's view 'Christmas games' such as those played by the lord and Gawain are not of that order. To that point I will return.

16 That Gawain appends to *synne* a consideration that makes the sin more heinous or odious, the treachery of a guest to his host, is both ethically sound, and true to character. It is also very proper to this poem which is concerned with *loyalty* on every plane. Here we find Gawain rejecting a *disloyalty* that would really have been sinful, so that we may view the *lack of loyalty* of which he is after accused in its proper scale.

17 So Chaucer reports of his *perfit gentil knight* that *he neuer yet no vileinye ne sayde . . . vnto no maner wight;* and later defends himself speciously against a charge of *vileinye* (precisely low and coarse speech) that might be levelled against his ignoble tales and characters.

18 Whether he would have called the lady's invitation *vileinye* is another matter. The actions of the lord and lady are not in fact judged at all. It is only Gawain's conduct, as the representative of Courtesy and Piety, that is scrutinized. The deeds and words of others are in the main used solely to provide the situations in which his character and behaviour will be exhibited.

19 Which he later expiates, in the same spirit, by telling everyone.

20 Though we might feel, if we were disposed to subject this fairy-tale detail to a scrutiny it is hardly substantial enough to bear, that a kiss cannot be paid away, and at any rate if its source is not named, then a wife's kiss cannot rightly be said to have been surrendered to the husband. But even this point has not been unnoted by the author. The two feinted blows may have been *boute scape* (94.2353), as far as Gawain's flesh went, but they were painful to endure. The Green Knight (or Sir Bertilak) does not seem to have felt that taking kisses from his wife was a matter entirely negligible, even if 'courtesy' was the reason for their acceptance.

21 In the ordinary mundane senses. If our author also wrote the *Pearl* (as seems to me certain), he has complicated matters, for those who wish to consider his mind and views as a whole, by there using 'courtesy' in a more elevated sense: the manners not of earthly courts, but of the Court of Heaven; the Divine Generosity and Grace, and the unalloyed humility and charity of the Blessed; the spirit, that is, from which even mundane 'courtesy' must proceed, if it is to be alive and sincere, and also pure. There is probably a trace of this to be seen in the conjunction of *clannes* and *cortaysye* (28.653) in the 'fifth five' of the Pentangle which is concerned with virtue in human relationships.

22 This may appear at first to be a blemish, even if the only serious blemish in this poem. It is indeed, I think, put into a form hardly suitable to Gawain, so that it reads rather more like a sentence of *auctor*, a piece of clerkly pedantry. But fundamentally it is in character, true to the general character of Gawain as depicted, and credible to his 'reaction' at the particular moment. Gawain always tends to go a little further than the case requires. He only needs to say: many greater men than I have been deceived by women, so there is some excuse for me. He need not proceed to say that it would be vastly to men's profit if they could love women and yet never trust them at all. But he does. And that is not only very like this Gawain, but not unnatural in any 'courtier' whose very courtesy and pride in it has been made the means of exposing him to shame. Let it be a mere game and pretence, then! he cries – at that moment.

23 Though one may reflect that his near-perfection would not have been attained

unless he had set before himself as an ideal the absolute or mathematical perfection symbolized by the Pentangle.

24   The more charitable, the wider often the divergence, as may be seen in the self-stern saints.

25   By the word *kynde* in the original the author may intend Gawain's natural character; but the less introspective sense 'my sort', the proper behaviour of members of his order (knights), is perhaps better.

26   The order is probably not significant (nor strictly possible), except the reservation of the Girdle to the last.

27   Not always so strong a word as now, however, when the association with 'treason' and 'traitor' (originally unconnected) has made it applicable only to acts of great baseness and serious injury.

28   Unless she herself obeys some higher law than herself or than 'love'.

29   In my father's translation of *Pearl* these lines are rendered:

> Grace enow may the man receive
> Who sins anew, if he repent;
> But craving it he must sigh and grieve
> And abide what pains are consequent. [Ed.]

30   Chaucer, *The Squire's Tale*, lines 95–6. The passage in which these lines occur was (in part) the basis for my father's view, mentioned at the beginning of this lecture (p. 73), that Chaucer knew *Sir Gawain and the Green Knight*. [Ed.]

31   Though God's instrument could indeed be the Girdle, in a world where such things were possible, and lawful.

32   It is an interesting point, which cannot have been unintended on the part of the poet, that the belt for which Gawain broke the rules of his game, and so made the only flaw in the perfection of his conduct on all levels, was never in fact of any use to him at all, not even as a hope.

33   It might be regarded as regrettable in Arthurian Romance as a whole. Personally I do not think that belittling of the King (as *sumquat childgered*, and the like) does that any good at all.

ON FAIRY-STORIES

I propose to speak about fairy-stories, though I am aware that this is a rash adventure. Faërie is a perilous land, and in it are pitfalls for the unwary and dungeons for the overbold. And overbold I may be accounted, for though I have been a lover of fairy-stories since I learned to read, and have at times thought about them, I have not studied them professionally. I have been hardly more than a wandering explorer (or trespasser) in the land, full of wonder but not of information.

The realm of fairy-story is wide and deep and high and filled with many things: all manner of beasts and birds are found there; shoreless seas and stars uncounted; beauty that is an enchantment, and an ever-present peril; both joy and sorrow as sharp as swords. In that realm a man may, perhaps, count himself fortunate to have wandered, but its very richness and strangeness tie the tongue of a traveller who would report them. And while he is there it is dangerous for him to ask too many questions, lest the gates should be shut and the keys be lost.

There are, however, some questions that one who is to speak about fairy-stories must expect to answer, or attempt to answer, whatever the folk of Faërie may think of his impertinence. For instance: What are fairy-stories? What is their origin? What is the use of them? I will try to give answers to these questions, or such hints of answers to them as I have gleaned – primarily from the stories themselves, the few of all their multitude that I know.

FAIRY-STORY

What is a fairy-story? In this case you will turn to the *Oxford English Dictionary* in vain. It contains no reference to the combination *fairy-story*, and is unhelpful on the subject of *fairies* generally. In the Supplement, *fairy-tale* is recorded since the year

1750, and its leading sense is said to be (*a*) a tale about fairies, or generally a fairy legend; with developed senses, (*b*) an unreal or incredible story, and (*c*) a falsehood.

The last two senses would obviously make my topic hopelessly vast. But the first sense is too narrow. Not too narrow for an essay; it is wide enough for many books, but too narrow to cover actual usage. Especially so, if we accept the lexicographer's definition of *fairies*: 'supernatural beings of diminutive size, in popular belief supposed to possess magical powers and to have great influence for good or evil over the affairs of man'.

Supernatural is a dangerous and difficult word in any of its senses, looser or stricter. But to fairies it can hardly be applied, unless *super* is taken merely as a superlative prefix. For it is man who is, in contrast to fairies, supernatural (and often of diminutive stature); whereas they are natural, far more natural than he. Such is their doom. The road to fairyland is not the road to Heaven; nor even to Hell, I believe, though some have held that it may lead thither indirectly by the Devil's tithe.

> O see ye not yon narrow road
>   So thick beset wi' thorns and briers?
> That is the path of Righteousness,
>   Though after it but few inquires.
>
> And see ye not yon braid, braid road
>   That lies across the lily leven?
> That is the path of Wickedness,
>   Though some call it the Road to Heaven.
>
> And see ye not yon bonny road
>   That winds about yon fernie brae?
> That is the road to fair Elfland,
>   Where thou and I this night maun gae.

As for *diminutive size*: I do not deny that the notion is a leading one in modern use. I have often thought that it would be interesting to try to find out how that has come to be so; but my knowledge is not sufficient for a certain answer. Of old there were indeed some inhabitants of Faërie that were small (though hardly diminutive), but smallness was not characteristic of that people as a whole. The diminutive being, elf or fairy, is (I guess) in England largely a sophisticated product of literary fancy.[1] It is perhaps not unnatural that in England, the land where the love of the delicate and fine has often reappeared in art, fancy should in this matter turn towards the dainty and diminutive, as in France it went to court and put on powder and diamonds. Yet I suspect that this flower-and-butterfly minuteness was also a product of 'rationalisation', which transformed the glamour of Elf-land into mere finesse, and invisibility into a fragility that could hide in a cowslip or shrink behind a blade of grass. It seems to become fashionable soon after the great voyages had begun to make the world seem too narrow to hold both men and elves; when the magic land of Hy Breasail in the West had become the mere Brazils, the land of red-dye-wood.[2] In any case it was largely a literary business in which William Shakespeare and Michael Drayton played a part.[3] Drayton's *Nymphidia* is one ancestor of that long line of flower-fairies and fluttering sprites with antennae that I so disliked as a child, and which my children in their turn detested. Andrew Lang had similar feelings. In the preface to the *Lilac Fairy Book* he refers to the tales of tiresome contemporary authors: 'they always begin with a little boy or girl who goes out and meets the fairies of polyanthuses and gardenias and appleblossom . . . These fairies try to be funny and fail; or they try to preach and succeed.'

But the business began, as I have said, long before the nineteenth century, and long ago achieved tiresomeness, certainly the tiresomeness of trying to be funny and failing. Drayton's *Nymphidia* is, considered as a fairy-story (a story about fairies), one of the worst ever written. The palace of Oberon has walls of spider's legs,

---

[1] I am speaking of developments before the growth of interest in the folk-lore of other countries. The English words, such as *elf*, have long been influenced by French (from which *fay* and *faërie*, *fairy* are derived); but in later times, through their use in translation, both *fairy* and *elf* have acquired much of the atmosphere of German, Scandinavian, and Celtic tales, and many characteristics of the *huldu-fólk*, the *daoine-sithe*, and the *tylwyth teg*.

[2] For the probability that the Irish *Hy Breasail* played a part in the naming of Brazil see Nansen, *In Northern Mists*, ii, 223–30.

[3] Their influence was not confined to England. German *Elf*, *Elfe* appears to be derived from *A Midsummer-night's Dream*, in Wieland's translation (1764).

And windows of the eyes of cats,
And for the roof, instead of slats,
Is covered with the wings of bats.

The knight Pigwiggen rides on a frisky earwig, and sends his
love, Queen Mab, a bracelet of emmets' eyes, making an assigna-
tion in a cowslip-flower. But the tale that is told amid all this
prettiness is a dull story of intrigue and sly go-betweens; the
gallant knight and angry husband fall into the mire, and their
wrath is stilled by a draught of the waters of Lethe. It would have
been better if Lethe had swallowed the whole affair. Oberon,
Mab, and Pigwiggen may be diminutive elves or fairies, as
Arthur, Guinevere, and Lancelot are not; but the good and evil
story of Arthur's court is a 'fairy-story' rather than this tale of
Oberon.

Fairy, as a noun more or less equivalent to *elf*, is a relatively
modern word, hardly used until the Tudor period. The first
quotation in the *Oxford Dictionary* (the only one before A.D. 1450)
is significant. It is taken from the poet Gower: *as he were a faierie*.
But this Gower did not say. He wrote *as he were of faierie*, 'as if he
were come from Faërie'. Gower was describing a young gallant
who seeks to bewitch the hearts of the maidens in church.

> His croket kembd and thereon set
> A Nouche with a chapelet,
> Or elles one of grene leves
> Which late com out of the greves,
> Al for he sholde seme freissh;
>
> And thus he loketh on the fleissh,
> Riht as an hauk which hath a sihte
> Upon the foul ther he schal lihte,
> And as he were of faierie
> He scheweth him tofore here yhe.[1]

This is a young man of mortal blood and bone; but he gives a
much better picture of the inhabitants of Elfland than the
definition of a 'fairy' under which he is, by a double error, placed.

---

[1] *Confessio Amantis*, v. 7065 ff.

For the trouble with the real folk of Faërie is that they do not always look like what they are; and they put on the pride and beauty that we would fain wear ourselves. At least part of the magic that they wield for the good or evil of man is power to play on the desires of his body and his heart. The Queen of Elfland, who carried off Thomas the Rhymer upon her milk-white steed swifter than the wind, came riding by the Eildon Tree as a lady, if one of enchanting beauty. So that Spenser was in the true tradition when he called the knights of his Faërie by the name of Elfe. It belonged to such knights as Sir Guyon rather than to Pigwiggen armed with a hornet's sting.

Now, though I have only touched (wholly inadequately) on *elves* and *fairies*, I must turn back; for I have digressed from my proper theme: fairy-stories. I said the sense 'stories about fairies' was too narrow.[1] It is too narrow, even if we reject the diminutive size, for fairy-stories are not in normal English usage stories *about* fairies or elves, but stories about Fairy, that is *Faërie*, the realm or state in which fairies have their being. *Faërie* contains many things besides elves and fays, and besides dwarfs, witches, trolls, giants, or dragons: it holds the seas, the sun, the moon, the sky; and the earth, and all things that are in it: tree and bird, water and stone, wine and bread, and ourselves, mortal men, when we are enchanted.

Stories that are actually concerned primarily with 'fairies', that is with creatures that might also in modern English be called 'elves', are relatively rare, and as a rule not very interesting. Most good 'fairy-stories' are about the *aventures* of men in the Perilous Realm or upon its shadowy marches. Naturally so; for if elves are true, and really exist independently of our tales about them, then this also is certainly true: elves are not primarily concerned with us, nor we with them. Our fates are sundered, and our paths seldom meet. Even upon the borders of Faërie we encounter them only at some chance crossing of the ways.[2]

---

[1] Except in special cases such as collections of Welsh or Gaelic tales. In these the stories about the 'Fair Family' or the Shee-folk are sometimes distinguished as 'fairy-tales' from 'folk-tales' concerning other marvels. In this use 'fairy-tales' or 'fairy-lore' are usually short accounts of the appearances of 'fairies' or their intrusions upon the affairs of men. But this distinction is a product of translation.

[2] This is true also, even if they are only creations of Man's mind, 'true' only as reflecting in a particular way one of Man's visions of Truth.

The definition of a fairy-story – what it is, or what it should be – does not, then, depend on any definition or historical account of elf or fairy, but upon the nature of *Faërie*: the Perilous Realm itself, and the air that blows in that country. I will not attempt to define that, nor to describe it directly. It cannot be done. Faërie cannot be caught in a net of words; for it is one of its qualities to be indescribable, though not imperceptible. It has many ingredients, but analysis will not necessarily discover the secret of the whole. Yet I hope that what I have later to say about the other questions will give some glimpses of my own imperfect vision of it. For the moment I will say only this: a 'fairy-story' is one which touches on or uses Faërie, whatever its own main purpose may be: satire, adventure, morality, fantasy. Faërie itself may perhaps most nearly be translated by Magic[1] – but it is magic of a peculiar mood and power, at the furthest pole from the vulgar devices of the laborious, scientific, magician. There is one proviso: if there is any satire present in the tale, one thing must not be made fun of, the magic itself. That must in that story be taken seriously, neither laughed at nor explained away. Of this seriousness the medieval *Sir Gawain and the Green Knight* is an admirable example.

But even if we apply only these vague and ill-defined limits, it becomes plain that many, even the learned in such matters, have used the term 'fairy-tale' very carelessly. A glance at those books of recent times that claim to be collections of 'fairy-stories' is enough to show that tales about fairies, about the fair family in any of its houses, or even about dwarfs and goblins, are only a small part of their content. That, as we have seen, was to be expected. But these books also contain many tales that do not use, do not even touch upon, Faërie at all; that have in fact no business to be included.

I will give one or two examples of the expurgations I would perform. This will assist the negative side of definition. It will also be found to lead on to the second question: what are the origins of fairy-stories?

The number of collections of fairy-stories is now very great. In English none probably rival either the popularity, or the inclusiveness, or the general merits of the twelve books of twelve

[1] See further below, pp 142–3.

colours which we owe to Andrew Lang and to his wife. The first
of these appeared more than fifty years ago (1889), and is still in
print. Most of its contents pass the test more or less clearly. I will
not analyse them, though an analysis might be interesting, but I
note in passing that of the stories in this *Blue Fairy Book* none are
primarily about 'fairies', few refer to them. Most of the tales are
taken from French sources: a just choice in some ways at that
time, as perhaps it would be still (though not to my taste, now or
in childhood). At any rate, so powerful has been the influence
of Charles Perrault, since his *Contes de ma Mère l'Oye* were first
Englished in the eighteenth century, and of such other excerpts
from the vast storehouse of the *Cabinet des Fées* as have become
well known, that still, I suppose, if you asked a man to name at
random a typical 'fairy-story', he would be most likely to name
one of these French things: such as *Puss-in-Boots, Cinderella,* or
Little Red Riding Hood. With some people *Grimm's Fairy Tales*
might come first to mind.

But what is to be said of the appearance in the *Blue Fairy Book*
of *A Voyage to Lilliput*? I will say this: it is *not* a fairy-story, neither
as its author made it, nor as it here appears 'condensed' by Miss
May Kendall. It has no business in this place. I fear that it was
included merely because Lilliputians are small, even diminutive –
the only way in which they are at all remarkable. But smallness
is in Faërie, as in our world, only an accident. Pygmies are no
nearer to fairies than are Patagonians. I do not rule this story
out because of its satirical intent: there is satire, sustained or
intermittent, in undoubted fairy-stories, and satire may often
have been intended in traditional tales where we do not now
perceive it. I rule it out, because the vehicle of the satire, brilliant
invention though it may be, belongs to the class of travellers' tales.
Such tales report many marvels, but they are marvels to be seen
in this mortal world in some region of our own time and space;
distance alone conceals them. The tales of Gulliver have no more
right of entry than the yarns of Baron Munchausen; or than, say,
The First Men in the Moon or *The Time-Machine.* Indeed, for the
Eloi and the Morlocks there would be a better claim than for the
Lilliputians. Lilliputians are merely men peered down at,
sardonically, from just above the house-tops. Eloi and Morlocks
live far away in an abyss of time so deep as to work an enchantment

upon them; and if they are descended from ourselves, it may be remembered that an ancient English thinker once derived the *ylfe*, the very elves, through Cain from Adam.[1] This enchantment of distance, especially of distant time, is weakened only by the preposterous and incredible Time Machine itself. But we see in this example one of the main reasons why the borders of fairy-story are inevitably dubious. The magic of Faërie is not an end in itself, its virtue is in its operations: among these are the satisfaction of certain primordial human desires. One of these desires is to survey the depths of space and time. Another is (as will be seen) to hold communion with other living things. A story may thus deal with the satisfaction of these desires, with or without the operation of either machine or magic, and in proportion as it succeeds it will approach the quality and have the flavour of fairy-story.

Next, after travellers' tales, I would also exclude, or rule out of order, any story that uses the machinery of Dream, the dreaming of actual human sleep, to explain the apparent occurrence of its marvels. At the least, even if the reported dream was in other respects in itself a fairy-story, I would condemn the whole as gravely defective: like a good picture in a disfiguring frame. It is true that Dream is not unconnected with Faërie. In dreams strange powers of the mind may be unlocked. In some of them a man may for a space wield the power of Faërie, that power which, even as it conceives the story, causes it to take living form and colour before the eyes. A real dream may indeed sometimes be a fairy-story of almost elvish ease and skill – while it is being dreamed. But if a waking writer tells you that his tale is only a thing imagined in his sleep, he cheats deliberately the primal desire at the heart of Faërie: the realisation, independent of the conceiving mind, of imagined wonder. It is often reported of fairies (truly or lyingly, I do not know) that they are workers of illusion, that they are cheaters of men by 'fantasy'; but that is quite another matter. That is their affair. Such trickeries happen, at any rate, inside tales in which the fairies are not themselves illusions; behind the fantasy real wills and powers exist, independent of the minds and purposes of men.

It is at any rate essential to a genuine fairy-story, as distinct

[1] *Beowulf*, 111–12.

from the employment of this form for lesser or debased purposes, that it should be presented as 'true'. The meaning of 'true' in this connection I will consider in a moment. But since the fairy-story deals with 'marvels', it cannot tolerate any frame or machinery suggesting that the whole story in which they occur is a figment or illusion. The tale itself may, of course, be so good that one can ignore the frame. Or it may be successful and amusing as a dream-story. So are Lewis Carroll's *Alice* stories, with their dream-frame and dream-transitions. For this (and other reasons) they are not fairy-stories.[1]

There is another type of marvellous tale that I would exclude from the title 'fairy-story', again certainly not because I do not like it: namely pure 'Beast-fable'. I will choose an example from Lang's Fairy Books: *The Monkey's Heart*, a Swahili tale which is given in the *Lilac Fairy Book*. In this story a wicked shark tricked a monkey into riding on his back, and carried him half-way to his own land, before he revealed the fact that the sultan of that country was sick and needed a monkey's heart to cure his disease. But the monkey outwitted the shark, and induced him to return by convincing him that the heart had been left behind at home, hanging in a bag on a tree.

The beast-fable has, of course, a connection with fairy-stories. Beasts and birds and other creatures often talk like men in real fairy-stories. In some part (often small) this marvel derives from one of the primal 'desires' that lie near the heart of Faërie: the desire of men to hold communion with other living things. But the speech of beasts in the beast-fable, as developed into a separate branch, has little reference to that desire, and often wholly forgets it. The magical understanding by men of the proper languages of birds and beasts and trees, that is much nearer to the true purposes of Faërie. But in stories in which no human being is concerned; or in which the animals are the heroes and heroines, and men and women, if they appear, are mere adjuncts; and above all those in which the animal form is only a mask upon a human face, a device of the satirist or the preacher, in these we have beast-fable and not fairy-story: whether it be *Reynard the Fox*, or *The Nun's Priest's Tale*, or *Brer Rabbit*, or merely *The Three Little Pigs*. The stories of Beatrix Potter lie near the borders of Faërie, but outside

[1] See Note A at the end (p. 157).

it, I think, for the most part.[1] Their nearness is due largely to their strong moral element: by which I mean their inherent morality, not any allegorical *significatio*. But *Peter Rabbit*, though it contains a prohibition, and though there are prohibitions in fairyland (as, probably, there are throughout the universe on every plane and in every dimension), remains a beast-fable.

Now *The Monkey's Heart* is also plainly only a beast-fable. I suspect that its inclusion in a 'Fairy Book' is due not primarily to its entertaining quality, but precisely to the monkey's heart supposed to have been left behind in a bag. That was significant to Lang, the student of folk-lore, even though this curious idea is here used only as a joke; for, in this tale, the monkey's heart was in fact quite normal and in his breast. None the less this detail is plainly only a secondary use of an ancient and very widespread folk-lore notion, which does occur in fairy-stories;[2] the notion that the life or strength of a man or creature may reside in some other place or thing; or in some part of the body (especially the heart) that can be detached and hidden in a bag, or under a stone, or in an egg. At one end of recorded folk-lore history this idea was used by George MacDonald in his fairy story *The Giant's Heart*, which derives this central motive (as well as many other details) from well-known traditional tales. At the other end, indeed in what is probably one of the oldest stories in writing, it occurs in *The Tale of the Two Brothers* in the Egyptian D'Orsigny papyrus. There the younger brother says to the elder:

'I shall enchant my heart, and I shall place it upon the top of the flower of the cedar. Now the cedar will be cut down and my heart will fall to the ground, and thou shalt come to seek for it, even though thou pass seven years in seeking it; but when thou hast found it, put it into a vase of cold water, and in very truth I shall live.'[3]

---

[1] *The Tailor of Gloucester* perhaps comes nearest. *Mrs Tiggywinkle* would be as near, but for the hinted dream-explanation. I would also include *The Wind in the Willows* in beast-fable.

[2] Such as, for instance: *The Giant that had no Heart* in Dasent's *Popular Tales from the Norse*; or *The Sea-Maiden* in Campbell's *Popular Tales of the West Highlands* (no. iv, cf. also no. i); or more remotely *Die Kristallkugel* in Grimm.

[3] Budge, *Egyptian Reading Book*, p. xxi.

But that point of interest and such comparisons as these bring us to the brink of the second question: What are the origins of 'fairy-stories'? That must, of course, mean: the origin or origins of the fairy elements. To ask what is the origin of stories (however qualified) is to ask what is the origin of language and of the mind.

ORIGINS

Actually the question: What is the origin of the fairy element? lands us ultimately in the same fundamental inquiry; but there are many elements in fairy-stories (such as this detachable heart, or swan-robes, magic rings, arbitrary prohibitions, wicked step-mothers, and even fairies themselves) that can be studied without tackling this main question. Such studies are, however, scientific (at least in intent); they are the pursuit of folklorists or anthropologists: that is of people using the stories not as they were meant to be used, but as a quarry from which to dig evidence, or information, about matters in which they are interested. A perfectly legitimate procedure in itself -- but ignorance or forgetfulness of the nature of a story (as a thing told in its entirety) has often led such inquirers into strange judgements. To investigators of this sort recurring similarities (such as this matter of the heart) seem specially important. So much so that students of folk-lore are apt to get off their own proper track, or to express themselves in a misleading 'shorthand': misleading in particular, if it gets out of their monographs into books about literature. They are inclined to say that any two stories that are built round the same folklore motive, or are made up of a generally similar combination of such motives, are 'the same stories'. We read that *Beowulf* 'is only a version of *Dat Erdmänneken*'; that '*The Black Bull of Norroway* is *Beauty and the Beast*', or 'is the same story as *Eros and Psyche*'; that the Norse *Mastermaid* (or the Gaelic *Battle of the Birds*[1] and its many congeners and variants) is 'the same story as the Greek tale of Jason and Medea'.

Statements of that kind may express (in undue abbreviation) some element of truth; but they are not true in a fairy-story sense, they are not true in art or literature. It is precisely the colouring,

[1] See Campbell, op. cit., vol. i.

the atmosphere, the unclassifiable individual details of a story, and above all the general purport that informs with life the undissected bones of the plot, that really count. Shakespeare's *King Lear* is not the same as Layamon's story in his *Brut*. Or to take the extreme case of *Red Riding Hood*: it is of merely secondary interest that the re-told versions of this story, in which the little girl is saved by wood-cutters, is directly derived from Perrault's story in which she was eaten by the wolf. The really important thing is that the later version has a happy ending (more or less, and if we do not mourn the grandmother overmuch), and that Perrault's version had not. And that is a very profound difference, to which I shall return.

Of course, I do not deny, for I feel strongly, the fascination of the desire to unravel the intricately knotted and ramified history of the branches on the Tree of Tales. It is closely connected with the philologists' study of the tangled skein of Language, of which I know some small pieces. But even with regard to language it seems to me that the essential quality and aptitudes of a given language in a living moment is both more important to seize and far more difficult to make explicit than its linear history. So with regard to fairy-stories, I feel that it is more interesting, and also in its way more difficult, to consider what they are, what they have become for us, and what values the long alchemic processes of time have produced in them. In Dasent's words I would say: 'We must be satisfied with the soup that is set before us, and not desire to see the bones of the ox out of which it has been boiled.'[1] Though, oddly enough, Dasent by 'the soup' meant a mishmash of bogus pre-history founded on the early surmises of Comparative Philology; and by 'desire to see the bones' he meant a demand to see the workings and the proofs that led to these theories. By 'the soup' I mean the story as it is served up by its author or teller, and by 'the bones' its sources or material – even when (by rare luck) those can be with certainty discovered. But I do not, of course, forbid criticism of the soup as soup.

I shall therefore pass lightly over the question of origins. I am too unlearned to deal with it in any other way; but it is the least important of the three questions for my purpose, and a few

---

[1] *Popular Tales from the Norse*, p. xviii.

remarks will suffice. It is plain enough that fairy-stories (in wider
or in narrower sense) are very ancient indeed. Related things
appear in very early records; and they are found universally,
wherever there is language. We are therefore obviously confronted
with a variant of the problem that the archaeologist encounters,
or the comparative philologist: with the debate between *independent
evolution* (or rather *invention*) of the similar; *inheritance* from a
common ancestry; and *diffusion* at various times from one or more
centres. Most debates depend on an attempt (by one or both
sides) at over-simplification; and I do not suppose that this
debate is an exception. The history of fairy-stories is probably
more complex than the physical history of the human race, and as
complex as the history of human language. All three things:
independent invention, inheritance, and diffusion, have evidently
played their part in producing the intricate web of Story. It is
now beyond all skill but that of the elves to unravel it.[1] Of these
three *invention* is the most important and fundamental, and so
(not surprisingly) also the most mysterious. To an inventor, that
is to a storymaker, the other two must in the end lead back.
Diffusion (borrowing in space), whether of an artefact or a story,
only refers the problem of origin elsewhere. At the centre of the
supposed diffusion there is a place where once an inventor lived.
Similarly with *inheritance* (borrowing in time): in this way we
arrive at last only at an ancestral inventor. While if we believe
that sometimes there occurred the independent striking out of
similar ideas and themes or devices, we simply multiply the
ancestral inventor but do not in that way the more clearly
understand his gift.

Philology has been dethroned from the high place it once had
in this court of inquiry. Max Müller's view of mythology as a
'disease of language' can be abandoned without regret. Mythology
is not a disease at all, though it may like all human things become
diseased. You might as well say that thinking is a disease of the

---

[1] Except in particularly fortunate cases; or in a few occasional details. It is indeed
easier to unravel a single *thread* – an incident, a name, a motive – than to trace the
history of any *picture* defined by many threads. For with the picture in the tapestry a new
element has come in: the picture is greater than, and not explained by, the sum of the
component threads. Therein lies the inherent weakness of the analytic (or 'scientific')
method: it finds out much about things that occur in stories, but little or nothing about
their effect in any given story.

mind. It would be more near the truth to say that languages, especially modern European languages, are a disease of mythology. But Language cannot, all the same, be dismissed. The incarnate mind, the tongue, and the tale are in our world coeval. The human mind, endowed with the powers of generalisation and abstraction, sees not only *green-grass*, discriminating it from other things (and finding it fair to look upon), but sees that it is *green* as well as being *grass*. But how powerful, how stimulating to the very faculty that produced it, was the invention of the adjective: no spell or incantation in Faërie is more potent. And that is not surprising: such incantations might indeed be said to be only another view of adjectives, a part of speech in a mythical grammar. The mind that thought of *light, heavy, grey, yellow, still, swift*, also conceived of magic that would make heavy things light and able to fly, turn grey lead into yellow gold, and the still rock into swift water. If it could do the one, it could do the other; it inevitably did both. When we can take green from grass, blue from heaven, and red from blood, we have already an enchanter's power – upon one plane; and the desire to wield that power in the world external to our minds awakes. It does not follow that we shall use that power well upon any plane. We may put a deadly green upon a man's face and produce a horror; we may make the rare and terrible blue moon to shine; or we may cause woods to spring with silver leaves and rams to wear fleeces of gold, and put hot fire into the belly of the cold worm. But in such 'fantasy', as it is called, new form is made; Faërie begins; Man becomes a sub-creator.

An essential power of Faërie is thus the power of making immediately effective by the will the visions of 'fantasy'. Not all are beautiful or even wholesome, not at any rate the fantasies of fallen Man. And he has stained the elves who have this power (in verity or fable) with his own stain. This aspect of 'mythology' – sub-creation, rather than either representation or symbolic interpretation of the beauties and terrors of the world – is, I think, too little considered. Is that because it is seen rather in Faërie than upon Olympus? Because it is thought to belong to the 'lower mythology' rather than to the 'higher'? There has been much debate concerning the relations of these things, of *folk-tale* and *myth*; but, even if there had been no debate, the question would require some notice in any consideration of origins, however brief.

At one time it was a dominant view that all such matter was derived from 'nature-myths'. The Olympians were *personifications* of the sun, of dawn, of night, and so on, and all the stories told about them were originally *myths* (*allegories* would have been a better word) of the greater elemental changes and processes of nature. Epic, heroic legend, saga, then localised these stories in real places and humanised them by attributing them to ancestral heroes, mightier than men and yet already men. And finally these legends, dwindling down, became folk-tales, *Märchen*, fairy-stories – nursery-tales.

That would seem to be the truth almost upside down. The nearer the so-called 'nature-myth', or allegory of the large processes of nature, is to its supposed archetype, the less interesting it is, and indeed the less is it of a myth capable of throwing any illumination whatever on the world. Let us assume for the moment, as this theory assumes, that nothing actually exists corresponding to the 'gods' of mythology: no personalities, only astronomical or meteorological objects. Then these natural objects can only be arrayed with a personal significance and glory by a gift, the gift of a person, of a man. Personality can only be derived from a person. The gods may derive their colour and beauty from the high splendours of nature, but it was Man who obtained these for them, abstracted them from sun and moon and cloud; their personality they get direct from him; the shadow or flicker of divinity that is upon them they receive through him from the invisible world, the Supernatural. There is no fundamental distinction between the higher and lower mythologies. Their peoples live, if they live at all, by the same life, just as in the mortal world do kings and peasants.

Let us take what looks like a clear case of Olympian nature-myth: the Norse god Thórr. His name is Thunder, of which Thórr is the Norse form; and it is not difficult to interpret his hammer, Miöllnir, as lightning. Yet Thórr has (as far as our late records go) a very marked character, or personality, which cannot be found in thunder or in lightning, even though some details can, as it were, be related to these natural phenomena: for instance, his red beard, his loud voice and violent temper, his blundering and smashing strength. None the less it is asking a question without much meaning, if we inquire: Which came first, nature-allegories about personalized thunder in the mountains, splitting rocks and trees; or stories about an irascible, not very clever, red-beard farmer, of a strength beyond common measure, a person (in all but mere stature) very like the Northern farmers, the *bœndr* by whom Thórr was chiefly beloved? To a picture of such a man Thórr may be held to have 'dwindled', or from it the god may be held to have been enlarged. But I doubt whether either view is right – not by itself, not if you insist that one of these things must precede the other. It is more reasonable to suppose that the farmer popped up in the very moment when Thunder got a voice and face; that there was a distant growl of thunder in the hills every time a story-teller heard a farmer in a rage.

Thórr must, of course, be reckoned a member of the higher aristocracy of mythology: one of the rulers of the world. Yet the tale that is told of him in *Thrymskvitha* (in the Elder Edda) is certainly just a fairy-story. It is old, as far as Norse poems go, but that is not far back (say A.D. 900 or a little earlier, in this case). But there is no real reason for supposing that this tale is 'un-primitive', at any rate in quality: that is, because it is of folk-tale kind and not very dignified. If we could go backwards in time, the fairy-story might be found to change in details, or to give way to other tales. But there would always be a 'fairy-tale' as long as there was any Thórr. When the fairy-tale ceased, there would be just thunder, which no human ear had yet heard.

Something really 'higher' is occasionally glimpsed in mythology: Divinity, the right to power (as distinct from its possession), the due of worship; in fact 'religion'. Andrew Lang said, and is by some still commended for saying,[1] that mythology and religion (in the strict sense of that word) are two distinct things that have become inextricably entangled, though mythology is in itself almost devoid of religious significance.[2]

[1] For example, by Christopher Dawson in *Progress and Religion*.
[2] This is borne out by the more careful and sympathetic study of 'primitive' peoples: that is, peoples still living in an inherited paganism, who are not, as we say, civilised. The hasty survey finds only their wilder tales; a closer examination finds their cosmo-logical myths; only patience and inner knowledge discovers their philosophy and religion: the truly worshipful, of which the 'gods' are not necessarily an embodiment at all, or only in a variable measure (often decided by the individual).

Yet these things have in fact become entangled – or maybe they were sundered long ago and have since groped slowly, through a labyrinth of error, through confusion, back towards re-fusion. Even fairy-stories as a whole have three faces: the Mystical towards the Supernatural; the Magical towards Nature; and the Mirror of scorn and pity towards Man. The essential face of Faërie is the middle one, the Magical. But the degree in which the others appear (if at all) is variable, and may be decided by the individual story-teller. The Magical, the fairy-story, may be used as a *Mirour de l'Omme*; and it may (but not so easily) be made a vehicle of Mystery. This at least is what George Mac-Donald attempted, achieving stories of power and beauty when he succeeded, as in *The Golden Key* (which he called a fairy-tale); and even when he partly failed, as in *Lilith* (which he called a romance).

For a moment let us return to the 'Soup' that I mentioned above. Speaking of the history of stories and especially of fairy-stories we may say that the Pot of Soup, the Cauldron of Story, has always been boiling, and to it have continually been added new bits, dainty and undainty. For this reason, to take a casual example, the fact that a story resembling the one known as *The Goosegirl* (*Die Gänsemagd* in Grimm) is told in the thirteenth century of Bertha Broadfoot, mother of Charlemagne, really proves nothing either way: neither that the story was (in the thirteenth century) descending from Olympus or Asgard by way of an already legendary king of old, on its way to become a *Hausmärchen*; nor that it was on its way up. The story is found to be widespread, unattached to the mother of Charlemagne or to any historical character. From this fact by itself we certainly cannot deduce that it is not true of Charlemagne's mother, though that is the kind of deduction that is most frequently made from that kind of evidence. The opinion that the story is not true of Bertha Broadfoot must be founded on something else: on features in the story which the critic's philosophy does not allow to be possible in 'real life', so that he would actually disbelieve the tale, even if it were found nowhere else; or on the existence of good historical evidence that Bertha's actual life was quite different, so that he would disbelieve the tale, even if his philosophy allowed that it was perfectly possible in 'real life'. No one, I fancy, would discredit a story that the Archbishop of Canterbury slipped on a banana skin merely because he found that a similar comic mishap had been reported of many people, and especially of elderly gentlemen of dignity. He might disbelieve the story, if he discovered that in it an angel (or even a fairy) had warned the Archbishop that he would slip if he wore gaiters on a Friday. He might also disbelieve the story, if it was stated to have occurred in the period between, say, 1940 and 1945. So much for that. It is an obvious point, and it has been made before; but I venture to make it again (although it is a little beside my present purpose), for it is constantly neglected by those who concern themselves with the origins of tales.

But what of the banana skin? Our business with it really only begins when it has been rejected by historians. It is more useful when it has been thrown away. The historian would be likely to say that the banana-skin story 'became attached to the Archbishop', as he does say on fair evidence that 'the Goosegirl *Märchen* became attached to Bertha'. That way of putting it is harmless enough, in what is commonly known as 'history'. But is it really a good description of what is going on and has gone on in the history of story-making? I do not think so. I think it would be nearer the truth to say that the Archbishop bcame attached to the banana skin, or that Bertha was turned into the Goosegirl. Better still: I would say that Charlemagne's mother and the Archbishop were put into the Pot, in fact got into the Soup. They were just new bits added to the stock. A considerable honour, for in that soup were many things older, more potent, more beautiful, comic, or terrible than they were in themselves (considered simply as figures of history).

It seems fairly plain that Arthur, once historical (but perhaps as such not of great importance), was also put into the Pot. There he was boiled for a long time, together with many other older figures and devices, of mythology and Faërie, and even some other stray bones of history (such as Alfred's defence against the Danes), until he emerged as a King of Faërie. The situation is similar in the great Northern 'Arthurian' court of the Shield-Kings of Denmark, the *Scyldingas* of ancient English tradition. King Hrothgar and his family have many manifest marks of true history, far more than Arthur; yet even in the older (English) accounts of them they are associated with many figures and events of fairy-story: they have been in the Pot. But I refer now to the remnants of the oldest recorded English tales of Faërie (or its borders), in spite of the fact that they are little known in England, not to discuss the turning of the bear-boy into the knight Beowulf, or to explain the intrusion of the ogre Grendel into the royal hall of Hrothgar. I wish to point to something else that these traditions contain: a singularly suggestive example of the relation of the 'fairy-tale element' to gods and kings and nameless men, illustrating (I believe) the view that this element does not rise or fall, but is there, in the Cauldron of Story, waiting for the great figures of Myth and History, and for the yet nameless He or She, waiting for the moment when they are cast into the simmering stew, one by one or all together, without consideration of rank or precedence.

The great enemy of King Hrothgar was Froda, King of the Heathobards. Yet of Hrothgar's daughter Freawaru we hear echoes of a strange tale – not a usual one in Northern heroic legend: the son of the enemy of her house, Ingeld son of Froda, fell in love with her and wedded her, disastrously. But that is extremely interesting and significant. In the background of the ancient feud looms the figure of that god whom the Norsemen called Frey (the Lord) or Yngvi-frey, and the Angles called Ing: a god of the ancient Northern mythology (and religion) of Fertility and Corn. The enmity of the royal houses was connected with the sacred site of a cult of that religion. Ingeld and his father bear names belonging to it. Freawaru herself is named 'Protection of the Lord (of Frey)'. Yet one of the chief things told later (in Old Icelandic) about Frey is the story in which he falls in love from afar with the daughter of the enemies of the gods, Gerdr, daughter of the giant Gymir, and weds her. Does this prove that Ingeld and Freawaru, or their love, are 'merely mythical'? I think not. History often resembles 'Myth', because they are both ultimately of the same stuff. If indeed Ingeld and Freawaru never lived, or at least never loved, then it is ultimately from nameless man and woman that they get their tale, or rather into whose tale they have entered. They have been put into the Cauldron, where so many potent things lie simmering agelong on the fire, among them Love-at-first-sight. So too of the god. If no young man had ever fallen in love by chance meeting with a maiden, and found old enmities to stand between him and his love, then the god Frey would never have seen Gerdr the giant's daughter from the high-seat of Odin. But if we speak of a Cauldron, we must not wholly forget the Cooks. There are many things in the Cauldron, but the Cooks do not dip in the ladle quite blindly. Their selection is important. The gods are after all gods, and it is a matter of some moment what stories are told of them. So we must freely admit that a tale of love is more likely to be told of a prince in history, indeed is more likely actually to happen in an historical family whose traditions are those of golden Frey and the Vanir, rather than those of Odin the Goth, the Necromancer, glutter of the crows, Lord of the Slain. Small wonder that *spell* means both a story told, and a formula of power over living men.

But when we have done all that research – collection and comparison of the tales of many lands – can do; when we have explained many of the elements commonly found embedded in fairy-stories (such as stepmothers, enchanted bears and bulls, cannibal witches, taboos on names, and the like) as relics of ancient customs once practised in daily life, or of beliefs once held as beliefs and not as 'fancies' – there remains still a point too often forgotten: that is the effect produced *now* by these old things in the stories as they are.

For one thing they are now *old*, and antiquity has an appeal in itself. The beauty and horror of *The Juniper Tree* (*Von dem Machandelboom*), with its exquisite and tragic beginning, the abominable cannibal stew, the gruesome bones, the gay and vengeful bird-spirit coming out of a mist that rose from the tree, has remained with me since childhood; and yet always the chief flavour of that tale lingering in the memory was not beauty or horror, but distance and a great abyss of time, not measurable even by *twe tusend Johr*. Without the stew and the bones – which children are now too often spared in mollified versions of Grimm[1] – that vision would largely have been lost. I do not think I was harmed by the horror *in the fairy-tale setting*, out of whatever dark beliefs and practices of the past it may have come. Such stories have now a mythical or total (unanalysable) effect, an effect

---

[1] They should not be spared it – unless they are spared the whole story until their digestions are stronger.

quite independent of the findings of Comparative Folk-lore, and one which it cannot spoil or explain; they open a door on Other Time, and if we pass through, though only for a moment, we stand outside our own time, outside Time itself, maybe.

If we pause, not merely to note that such old elements have been preserved, but to think *how* they have been preserved, we must conclude, I think, that it has happened, often if not always, precisely because of this literary effect. It cannot have been we, or even the brothers Grimm, that first felt it. Fairy-stories are by no means rocky matrices out of which the fossils cannot be prised except by an expert geologist. The ancient elements can be knocked out, or forgotten and dropped out, or replaced by other ingredients with the greatest ease: as any comparison of a story with closely related variants will show. The things that are there must often have been retained (or inserted) because the oral narrators, instinctively or consciously, felt their literary 'significance'[1]. Even where a prohibition in a fairy-story is guessed to be derived from some taboo once practised long ago, it has probably been preserved in the later stages of the tale's history because of the great mythical significance of prohibition. A sense of that significance may indeed have lain behind some of the taboos themselves. Thou shalt not — or else thou shalt depart beggared into endless regret. The gentlest 'nursery-tales' know it. Even Peter Rabbit was forbidden a garden, lost his blue coat, and took sick. The Locked Door stands as an eternal Temptation.

CHILDREN

I will now turn to children, and so come to the last and most important of the three questions: what, if any, are the values and functions of fairy-stories *now*? It is usually assumed that children are the natural or the specially appropriate audience for fairy-stories. In describing a fairy-story which they think adults might possibly read for their own entertainment, reviewers frequently indulge in such waggeries as: 'this book is for children from the ages of six to sixty'. But I have never yet seen the puff of a new motor-model that began thus: 'this toy will amuse infants from seventeen to seventy'; though that to my mind would be much

[1] See Note B at end (p. 157).

more appropriate. Is there any *essential* connection between children and fairy-stories? Is there any call for comment, if an adult reads them for himself? *Reads* them as tales, that is, not *studies* them as curios. Adults are allowed to collect and study anything, even old theatre-programmes or paper bags.

Among those who still have enough wisdom not to think fairy-stories pernicious, the common opinion seems to be that there is a natural connection between the minds of children and fairy-stories, of the same order as the connection between children's bodies and milk. I think this is an error; at best an error of false sentiment, and one that is therefore most often made by those who, for whatever private reason (such as childlessness), tend to think of children as a special kind of creature, almost a different race, rather than as normal, if immature, members of a particular family, and of the human family at large.

Actually, the association of children and fairy-stories is an accident of our domestic history. Fairy-stories have in the modern lettered world been relegated to the 'nursery', as shabby or old-fashioned furniture is relegated to the playroom, primarily because the adults do not want it, and do not mind if it is misused.[1] It is not the choice of the children which decides this. Children as a class – except in a common lack of experience they are not one – neither like fairy-stories more, nor understand them better than adults do; and no more than they like many other things. They are young and growing, and normally have keen appetites, so the fairy-stories as a rule go down well enough. But in fact only some children, and some adults, have any special taste for them; and when they have it, it is not exclusive, nor even necessarily dominant.[2] It is a taste, too, that would not appear, I think, very early in childhood without artificial stimulus; it is certainly one that does not decrease but increases with age, if it is innate.

It is true that in recent times fairy-stories have usually been written or 'adapted' for children. But so may music be, or verse,

---

[1] In the case of stories and other nursery lore, there is also another factor. Wealthier families employed women to look after their children, and the stories were provided by these nurses, who were sometimes in touch with rustic and traditional lore forgotten by their 'betters'. It is long since this source dried up, at any rate in England; but it once had some importance. But again there is no proof of the special fitness of children as the recipients of this vanishing 'folk-lore'. The nurses might just as well (or better) have been left to choose the pictures and furniture.

[2] See Note C at end (p. 158).

or novels, or history, or scientific manuals. It is a dangerous process, even when it is necessary. It is indeed only saved from disaster by the fact that the arts and sciences are not as a whole relegated to the nursery; the nursery and schoolroom are merely given such tastes and glimpses of the adult thing as seem fit for them in adult opinion (often much mistaken). Any one of these things would, if left altogether in the nursery, become gravely impaired. So would a beautiful table, a good picture, or a useful machine (such as a microscope), be defaced or broken, if it were left long unregarded in a schoolroom. Fairy-stories banished in this way, cut off from a full adult art, would in the end be ruined; indeed in so far as they have been so banished, they have been ruined.

The value of fairy-stories is thus not, in my opinion, to be found by considering children in particular. Collections of fairy-stories are, in fact, by nature attics and lumber-rooms, only by temporary and local custom play-rooms. Their contents are disordered, and often battered, a jumble of different dates, purposes, and tastes; but among them may occasionally be found a thing of permanent virtue: an old work of art, not too much damaged, that only stupidity would ever have stuffed away.

Andrew Lang's *Fairy Books* are not, perhaps, lumber-rooms. They are more like stalls in a rummage-sale. Someone with a duster and a fair eye for things that retain some value has been round the attics and box-rooms. His collections are largely a by-product of his adult study of mythology and folk-lore; but they were made into and presented as books for children.[1] Some of the reasons that Lang gave are worth considering.

The introduction to the first of the series speaks of 'children to whom and for whom they are told'. 'They represent', he says, 'the young age of man true to his early loves, and have his un-blunted edge of belief, a fresh appetite for marvels.' ' "Is it true?" ' he says, 'is the great question children ask.'

I suspect that *belief* and *appetite for marvels* are here regarded as identical or as closely related. They are radically different, though the appetite for marvels is not at once or at first differentiated by a growing human mind from its general appetite. It seems fairly

---

[1] By Lang and his helpers. It is not true of the majority of the contents in their original (or oldest surviving) forms.

clear that Lang was using *belief* in its ordinary sense: belief that a thing exists or can happen in the real (primary) world. If so, then I fear that Lang's words, stripped of sentiment, can only imply that the teller of marvellous tales to children, must, or may, or at any rate does trade on their *credulity*, on the lack of experience which makes it less easy for children to distinguish fact from fiction in particular cases, though the distinction in itself is fundamental to the sane human mind, and to fairy-stories.

Children are capable, of course, of *literary belief*, when the story-maker's art is good enough to produce it. That state of mind has been called 'willing suspension of disbelief'. But this does not seem to me a good description of what happens. What really happens is that the story-maker proves a successful 'sub-creator'. He makes a Secondary World which your mind can enter. Inside it, what he relates is 'true': it accords with the laws of that world. You therefore believe it, while you are, as it were, inside. The moment disbelief arises, the spell is broken; the magic, or rather art, has failed. You are then out in the Primary World again, looking at the little abortive Secondary World from outside. If you are obliged, by kindliness or circumstance, to stay, then disbelief must be suspended (or stifled), otherwise listening and looking would become intolerable. But this suspension of disbelief is a substitute for the genuine thing, a subterfuge we use when condescending to games or make-believe, or when trying (more or less willingly) to find what virtue we can in the work of an art that has for us failed.

A real enthusiast for cricket is in the enchanted state: Secondary Belief. I, when I watch a match, am on the lower level. I can achieve (more or less) willing suspension of disbelief, when I am held there and supported by some other motive that will keep away boredom: for instance, a wild, heraldic, preference for dark blue rather than light. This suspension of disbelief may thus be a somewhat tired, shabby, or sentimental state of mind, and so lean to the 'adult'. I fancy it is often the state of adults in the presence of a fairy-story. They are held there and supported by sentiment (memories of childhood, or notions of what childhood ought to be like); they think they ought to like the tale. But if they really liked it, for itself, they would not have to suspend disbelief: they would believe – in this sense.

Now if Lang had meant anything like this there might have been some truth in his words. It may be argued that it is easier to work the spell with children. Perhaps it is, though I am not sure of this. The appearance that it is so is often, I think, an adult illusion produced by children's humility, their lack of critical experience and vocabulary and their voracity (proper to their rapid growth). They like or try to like what is given to them: if they do not like it, they cannot well express their dislike or give reasons for it (and so may conceal it); and they like a great mass of different things indiscriminately, without troubling to analyse the planes of their belief. In any case I doubt if this potion – the enchantment of the effective fairy-story – is really one of the kind that becomes 'blunted' by use, less potent after repeated draughts.

' "Is it true?" is the great question children ask', Lang said. They do ask that question, I know; and it is not one to be rashly or idly answered.[1] But that question is hardly evidence of 'un-blunted belief', or even of the desire for it. Most often it proceeds from the child's desire to know which kind of literature he is faced with. Children's knowledge of the world is often so small that they cannot judge, off-hand and without help, between the fantastic, the strange (that is rare or remote facts), the nonsensical, and the merely 'grown-up' (that is ordinary things of their parents' world, much of which still remains unexplored). But they recognize the different classes, and may like all of them at times. Of course the borders between them are often fluctuating or confused; but that is not only true for children. We all know the differences in kind, but we are not always sure how to place anything that we hear. A child may well believe a report that there are ogres in the next county; many grown-up persons find it easy to believe of another country; and as for another planet, very few adults seem able to imagine it as peopled, if at all, by anything but monsters of iniquity.

Now I was one of the children whom Andrew Lang was addressing – I was born at about the same time as the *Green Fairy Book* – the children for whom he seemed to think that fairy-stories were the equivalent of the adult novel, and of whom he said:

---

[1] Far more often they have asked me: 'Was he good? Was he wicked?' That is, they were more concerned to get the Right side and the Wrong side clear. For that is a question equally important in History and in Faërie.

'Their taste remains like the taste of their naked ancestors thousands of years ago; and they seem to like fairy-tales better than history, poetry, geography, or arithmetic.'[1] But do we really know much about these 'naked ancestors', except that they were certainly not naked? Our fairy-stories, however old certain elements in them may be, are certainly not the same as theirs. Yet if it is assumed that we have fairy-stories because they did, then probably we have history, geography, poetry, and arithmetic because they liked these things too, as far as they could get them, and in so far as they had yet separated the many branches of their general interest in everything.

And as for children of the present day, Lang's description does not fit my own memories, or my experience of children. Lang may have been mistaken about the children he knew, but if he was not, then at any rate children differ considerably, even within the narrow borders of Britain, and such generalisations which treat them as a class (disregarding their individual talents, and the influences of the countryside they live in, and their upbringing) are delusory. I had no special childish 'wish to believe'. I wanted to know. Belief depended on the way in which stories were presented to me, by older people, or by the authors, or on the inherent tone and quality of the tale. But at no time can I remember that the enjoyment of a story was dependent on belief that such things could happen, or had happened, in 'real life'. Fairy-stories were plainly not primarily concerned with possibility, but with desirability. If they awakened *desire*, satisfying it while often whetting it unbearably, they succeeded. It is not necessary to be more explicit here, for I hope to say something later about this desire, a complex of many ingredients, some universal, some particular to modern men (including modern children), or even to certain kinds of men. I had no desire to have either dreams or adventures like *Alice*, and the account of them merely amused me. I had very little desire to look for buried treasure or fight pirates, and *Treasure Island* left me cool. Red Indians were better: there were bows and arrows (I had and have a wholly unsatisfied desire to shoot well with a bow), and strange languages, and glimpses of an archaic mode of life, and, above all, forests in such stories. But the land of Merlin and

[1] Preface to the *Violet Fairy Book*.

Arthur was better than these, and best of all the nameless North of Sigurd of the Völsungs, and the prince of all dragons. Such lands were pre-eminently desirable. I never imagined that the dragon was of the same order as the horse. And that was not solely because I saw horses daily, but never even the footprint of a worm.[1] The dragon had the trade-mark *Of Faërie* written plain upon him. In whatever world he had his being it was an Other-world. Fantasy, the making or glimpsing of Other-worlds, was the heart of the desire of Faërie. I desired dragons with a profound desire. Of course, I in my timid body did not wish to have them in the neighbourhood, intruding into my relatively safe world, in which it was, for instance, possible to read stories in peace of mind, free from fear.[2] But the world that contained even the imagination of Fáfnir was richer and more beautiful, at whatever cost of peril. The dweller in the quiet and fertile plains may hear of the tormented hills and the unharvested sea and long for them in his heart. For the heart is hard though the body be soft.

All the same, important as I now perceive the fairy-story element in early reading to have been, speaking for myself as a child, I can only say that a liking for fairy-stories was not a dominant characteristic of early taste. A real taste for them awoke after 'nursery' days, and after the years, few but long-seeming, between learning to read and going to school. In that (I nearly wrote 'happy' or 'golden', it was really a sad and troublous) time I liked many other things as well, or better: such as history, astronomy, botany, grammar, and etymology. I agreed with Lang's generalised 'children' not at all in principle, and only in some points by accident: I was, for instance, in-sensitive to poetry, and skipped it if it came in tales. Poetry I discovered much later in Latin and Greek, and especially through being made to try and translate English verse into classical verse. A real taste for fairy-stories was wakened by philology on the threshold of manhood, and quickened to full life by war.

I have said, perhaps, more than enough on this point. At least it will be plain that in my opinion fairy-stories should not be *specially* associated with children. They are associated with them:

[1] See Note D at end (p. 158).
[2] This is, naturally, often enough what children mean when they ask: 'Is it true?' They mean: 'I like this, but is it contemporary? Am I safe in my bed?' The answer: 'There is certainly no dragon in England today', is all that they want to hear.

naturally, because children are human and fairy-stories are a natural human taste (though not necessarily a universal one); accidentally, because fairy-stories are a large part of the literary lumber that in latter-day Europe has been stuffed away in attics; unnaturally, because of erroneous sentiment about children, a sentiment that seems to increase with the decline in children.

It is true that the age of childhood-sentiment has produced some delightful books (especially charming, however, to adults) of the fairy kind or near to it; but it has also produced a dreadful undergrowth of stories written or adapted to what was or is conceived to be the measure of children's minds and needs. The old stories are mollified or bowdlerised, instead of being reserved; the imitations are often merely silly, Pigwiggenry without even the intrigue; or patronising; or (deadliest of all) covertly sniggering, with an eye on the other grown-ups present. I will not accuse Andrew Lang of sniggering, but certainly he smiled to himself, and certainly too often he had an eye on the faces of other clever people over the heads of his child-audience – to the very grave detriment of the *Chronicles of Pantouflia*.

Dasent replied with vigour and justice to the prudish critics of his translations from Norse popular tales. Yet he committed the astonishing folly of particularly *forbidding* children to read the last two in his collection. That a man could study fairy-stories and not learn better than that seems almost incredible. But neither criticism, rejoinder, nor prohibition would have been necessary if children had not unnecessarily been regarded as the inevitable readers of the book.

I do not deny that there is a truth in Andrew Lang's words (sentimental though they may sound): 'He who would enter into the Kingdom of Faërie should have the heart of a little child.' For that possession is necessary to all high adventure, into kingdoms both less and far greater than Faërie. But humility and innocence – these things 'the heart of a child' must mean in such a context – do not necessarily imply an uncritical wonder, nor indeed an uncritical tenderness. Chesterton once remarked that the children in whose company he saw Maeterlinck's *Blue Bird* were dissatisfied 'because it did not end with a Day of Judgement, and it was not revealed to the hero and the heroine that the Dog had been faithful and the Cat faithless'. 'For children', he says, 'are innocent and love justice; while most of us are wicked and naturally prefer mercy.'

Andrew Lang was confused on this point. He was at pains to defend the slaying of the Yellow Dwarf by Prince Ricardo in one of his own fairy-stories. 'I hate cruelty,' he said, '. . . but that was in fair fight, sword in hand, and the dwarf, peace to his ashes! died in harness.' Yet it is not clear that 'fair fight' is less cruel than 'fair judgement'; or that piercing a dwarf with a sword is more just than the execution of wicked kings and evil stepmothers – which Lang abjures: he sends the criminals (as he boasts) to retirement on ample pensions. That is mercy untempered by justice. It is true that this plea was not addressed to children but to parents and guardians, to whom Lang was recommending his own *Prince Prigio* and *Prince Ricardo* as suitable for their charges.[1] It is parents and guardians who have classified fairy-stories as *Juvenilia*. And this is a small sample of the falsification of values that results.

If we use *child* in a good sense (it has also legitimately a bad one) we must not allow that to push us into the sentimentality of only using *adult* or *grown-up* in a bad sense (it has also legitimately a good one). The process of growing older is not necessarily allied to growing wickeder, though the two do often happen together. Children are meant to grow up, and not to become Peter Pans. Not to lose innocence and wonder; but to proceed on the appointed journey: that journey upon which it is certainly not better to travel hopefully than to arrive, though we must travel hopefully if we are to arrive. But it is one of the lessons of fairy-stories (if we can speak of the lessons of things that do not lecture) that on callow, lumpish, and selfish youth peril, sorrow, and the shadow of death can bestow dignity, and even sometimes wisdom.

Let us not divide the human race into Eloi and Morlocks: pretty children – 'elves' as the eighteenth century often idiotically called them – with their fairy-tales (carefully pruned), and dark Morlocks tending their machines. If fairy-story as a kind is worth reading at all it is worthy to be written for and read by adults. They will, of course, put more in and get more out than children can. Then, as a branch of a genuine art, children may hope to

[1] Preface to the *Lilac Fairy Book*.

get fairy-stories fit for them to read and yet within their measure; as they may hope to get suitable introductions to poetry, history, and the sciences. Though it may be better for them to read some things, especially fairy-stories, that are beyond their measure rather than short of it. Their books like their clothes should allow for growth, and their books at any rate should encourage it.

Very well, then. If adults are to read fairy-stories as a natural branch of literature – neither playing at being children, nor pretending to be choosing for children, nor being boys who would not grow up – what are the values and functions of this kind? That is, I think, the last and most important question. I have already hinted at some of my answers. First of all: if written with art, the prime value of fairy-stories will simply be that value which, as literature, they share with other literary forms. But fairy-stories offer also, in a peculiar degree or mode, these things: Fantasy, Recovery, Escape, Consolation, all things of which children have, as a rule, less need than older people. Most of them are nowadays very commonly considered to be bad for anybody. I will consider them briefly, and will begin with *Fantasy*.

FANTASY

The human mind is capable of forming mental images of things not actually present. The faculty of conceiving the images is (or was) naturally called Imagination. But in recent times, in technical not normal language, Imagination has often been held to be something higher than the mere image-making, ascribed to the operations of Fancy (a reduced and depreciatory form of the older word Fantasy); an attempt is thus made to restrict, I should say misapply, Imagination to 'the power of giving to ideal creations the inner consistency of reality'.

Ridiculous though it may be for one so ill-instructed to have an opinion on this critical matter, I venture to think the verbal distinction philologically inappropriate, and the analysis in-accurate. The mental power of image-making is one thing, or aspect; and it should appropriately be called Imagination. The perception of the image, the grasp of its implications, and the control, which are necessary to a successful expression, may vary in vividness and strength: but this is a difference of degree in

Imagination, not a difference in kind. The achievement of the expression, which gives (or seems to give) 'the inner consistency of reality',[1] is indeed another thing, or aspect, needing another name: Art, the operative link between Imagination and the final result, Sub-creation. For my present purpose I require a word which shall embrace both the Sub-creative Art in itself and a quality of strangeness and wonder in the Expression, derived from the Image: a quality essential to fairy-story. I propose, therefore, to arrogate to myself the powers of Humpty-Dumpty, and to use Fantasy for this purpose: in a sense, that is, which combines with its older and higher use as an equivalent of Imagination the derived notions of 'unreality' (that is, of un-likeness to the Primary World), of freedom from the domination of observed 'fact', in short of the fantastic. I am thus not only aware but glad of the etymological and semantic connections of *fantasy* with *fantastic*: with images of things that are not only 'not actually present', but which are indeed not to be found in our primary world at all, or are generally believed not to be found there. But while admitting that, I do not assent to the depreciative tone. That the images are of things not in the primary world (if that indeed is possible) is a virtue not a vice. Fantasy (in this sense) is, I think, not a lower but a higher form of Art, indeed the most nearly pure form, and so (when achieved) the most potent.

Fantasy, of course, starts out with an advantage: arresting strangeness. But that advantage has been turned against it, and has contributed to its disrepute. Many people dislike being 'arrested'. They dislike any meddling with the Primary World, or such small glimpses of it as are familiar to them. They, therefore, stupidly and even maliciously confound Fantasy with Dreaming, in which there is no Art;[2] and with mental disorders, in which there is not even control: with delusion and hallucination.

But the error or malice, engendered by disquiet and consequent dislike, is not the only cause of this confusion. Fantasy has also an essential drawback: it is difficult to achieve. Fantasy may be, as I think, not less but more sub-creative; but at any rate it is

---

[1] That is: which commands or induces Secondary Belief.
[2] This is not true of all dreams. In some Fantasy seems to take a part. But this is exceptional. Fantasy is a rational not an irrational activity.

found in practice that 'the inner consistency of reality' is more difficult to produce, the more unlike are the images and the rearrangements of primary material to the actual arrangements of the Primary World. It is easier to produce this kind of 'reality' with more 'sober' material. Fantasy thus, too often, remains undeveloped; it is and has been used frivolously, or only half-seriously, or merely for decoration: it remains merely 'fanciful'. Anyone inheriting the fantastic device of human language can say *the green sun*. Many can then imagine or picture it. But that is not enough – though it may already be a more potent thing than many a 'thumbnail sketch' or 'transcript of life' that receives literary praise.

To make a Secondary World inside which the green sun will be credible, commanding Secondary Belief, will probably require labour and thought, and will certainly demand a special skill, a kind of elvish craft. Few attempt such difficult tasks. But when they are attempted and in any degree accomplished then we have a rare achievement of Art: indeed narrative art, story-making in its primary and most potent mode.

In human art Fantasy is a thing best left to words, to true literature. In painting, for instance, the visible presentation of the fantastic image is technically too easy; the hand tends to outrun the mind, even to overthrow it.[1] Silliness or morbidity are frequent results. It is a misfortune that Drama, an art fundamentally distinct from Literature, should so commonly be considered together with it, or as a branch of it. Among these misfortunes we may reckon the depreciation of Fantasy. For in part at least this depreciation is due to the natural desire of critics to cry up the forms of literature or 'imagination' that they themselves, innately or by training, prefer. And criticism in a country that has produced so great a Drama, and possesses the works of William Shakespeare, tends to be far too dramatic. But Drama is naturally hostile to Fantasy. Fantasy, even of the simplest kind, hardly ever succeeds in Drama, when that is presented as it should be, visibly and audibly acted. Fantastic forms are not to be counterfeited. Men dressed up as talking animals may achieve buffoonery or mimicry, but they do not achieve Fantasy. This is, I think, well illustrated by the failure of

[1] See Note E at end (p. 159).

the bastard form, pantomime. The nearer it is to 'dramatised fairy-story' the worse it is. It is only tolerable when the plot and its fantasy are reduced to a mere vestigiary framework for farce, and no 'belief' of any kind in any part of the performance is required or expected of anybody. This is, of course, partly due to the fact that the producers of drama have to, or try to, work with mechanism to represent either Fantasy or Magic. I once saw a so-called 'children's pantomime', the straight story of *Puss-in-Boots*, with even the metamorphosis of the ogre into a mouse. Had this been mechanically successful it would either have terrified the spectators or else have been just a turn of high-class conjuring. As it was, though done with some ingenuity of lighting, disbelief had not so much to be suspended as hung, drawn, and quartered.

In *Macbeth*, when it is read, I find the witches tolerable: they have a narrative function and some hint of dark significance; though they are vulgarised, poor things of their kind. They are almost intolerable in the play. They would be quite intolerable, if I were not fortified by some memory of them as they are in the story as read. I am told that I should feel differently if I had the mind of the period, with its witch-hunts and witch-trials. But that is to say: if I regarded the witches as possible, indeed likely, in the Primary World; in other words, if they ceased to be 'Fantasy'. That argument concedes the point. To be dissolved, or to be degraded, is the likely fate of Fantasy when a dramatist tries to use it, even such a dramatist as Shakespeare. *Macbeth* is indeed a work by a playwright who ought, at least on this occasion, to have written a story, if he had the skill or patience for that art.

A reason, more important, I think, than the inadequacy of stage-effects, is this: Drama has, of its very nature, already attempted a kind of bogus, or shall I say at least substitute, magic: *the visible and audible presentation of imaginary men in a story*. That is in itself an attempt to counterfeit the magician's wand. To introduce, even with mechanical success, into this quasi-magical secondary world a further fantasy or magic is to demand, as it were, an inner or tertiary world. It is a world too much. To make such a thing may not be impossible. I have never seen it done with success. But at least it cannot be claimed as the proper mode of drama, in which walking and talking people have been found to be the natural instruments of Art and illusion.[1]

For this precise reason – that the characters, and even the scenes, are in Drama not imagined but actually beheld – Drama is, even though it uses a similar material (words, verse, plot), an art fundamentally different from narrative art. Thus, if you prefer Drama to Literature (as many literary critics plainly do), or form your critical theories primarily from dramatic critics, or even from Drama, you are apt to misunderstand pure story-making, and to constrain it to the limitations of stage-plays. You are, for instance, likely to prefer characters, even the basest and dullest, to things. Very little about trees as trees can be got into a play.

Now 'Faërian Drama' – those plays which according to abundant records the elves have often presented to men – can produce Fantasy with a realism and immediacy beyond the compass of any human mechanism. As a result their usual effect (upon a man) is to go beyond Secondary Belief. If you are present at a Faërian drama you yourself are, or think that you are, bodily inside its Secondary World. The experience may be very similar to Dreaming and has (it would seem) sometimes (by men) been confounded with it. But in Faërian drama you are in a dream that some other mind is weaving, and the knowledge of that alarming fact may slip from your grasp. To experience *directly* a Secondary World: the potion is too strong, and you give to it Primary Belief, however marvellous the events. You are deluded – whether that is the intention of the elves (always or at any time) is another question. They at any rate are not themselves deluded. This is for them a form of Art, and distinct from Wizardry or Magic, properly so called. They do not live in it, though they can, perhaps, afford to spend more time at it than human artists can. The Primary World, Reality, of elves and men is the same, if differently valued and perceived.

We need a word for this elvish craft, but all the words that have been applied to it have been blurred and confused with other things. Magic is ready to hand, and I have used it above (p. 114), but I should not have done so: Magic should be reserved for the operations of the Magician. Art is the human process that

[1] See Note F at end (p. 159).

produces by the way (it is not its only or ultimate object) Secondary Belief. Art of the same sort, if more skilled and effortless, the elves can also use, or so the reports seem to show; but the more potent and specially elvish craft I will, for lack of a less debatable word, call Enchantment. Enchantment produces a Secondary World into which both designer and spectator can enter, to the satisfaction of their senses while they are inside; but in its purity it is artistic in desire and purpose. Magic produces, or pretends to produce, an alteration in the Primary World. It does not matter by whom it is said to be practised, fay or mortal, it remains distinct from the other two; it is not an art but a technique; its desire is *power* in this world, domination of things and wills.

To the elvish craft, Enchantment, Fantasy aspires, and when it is successful of all forms of human art most nearly approaches. At the heart of many man-made stories of the elves lies, open or concealed, pure or alloyed, the desire for a living, realised sub-creative art, which (however much it may outwardly resemble it) is inwardly wholly different from the greed for self-centred power which is the mark of the mere Magician. Of this desire the elves, in their better (but still perilous) part, are largely made; and it is from them that we may learn what is the central desire and aspiration of human Fantasy – even if the elves are, all the more in so far as they are, only a product of Fantasy itself. That creative desire is only cheated by counterfeits, whether the innocent but clumsy devices of the human dramatist, or the malevolent frauds of the magicians. In this world it is for men unsatisfiable, and so imperishable. Uncorrupted it does not seek delusion, nor bewitchment and domination; it seeks shared enrichment, partners in making and delight, not slaves.

To many, Fantasy, this sub-creative art which plays strange tricks with the world and all that is in it, combining nouns and redistributing adjectives, has seemed suspect, if not illegitimate. To some it has seemed at least a childish folly, a thing only for peoples or for persons in their youth. As for its legitimacy I will say no more than to quote a brief passage from a letter I once wrote to a man who described myth and fairy-story as 'lies'; though to do him justice he was kind enough and confused enough to call fairy-story making 'Breathing a lie through Silver'.

'Dear Sir,' I said – 'Although now long estranged,
Man is not wholly lost nor wholly changed.
Dis-graced he may be, yet is not de-throned,
and keeps the rags of lordship once he owned:
Man, Sub-creator, the refracted Light
through whom is splintered from a single White
to many hues, and endlessly combined
in living shapes that move from mind to mind.
Though all the crannies of the world we filled
with Elves and Goblins, though we dared to build
Gods and their houses out of dark and light,
and sowed the seed of dragons – 'twas our right
(used or misused). That right has not decayed:
we make still by the law in which we're made.'

Fantasy is a natural human activity. It certainly does not destroy or even insult Reason; and it does not either blunt the appetite for, nor obscure the perception of, scientific verity. On the contrary. The keener and the clearer is the reason, the better fantasy will it make. If men were ever in a state in which they did not want to know or could not perceive truth (facts or evidence), then Fantasy would languish until they were cured. If they ever get into that state (it would not seem at all impossible), Fantasy will perish, and become Morbid Delusion.

For creative Fantasy is founded upon the hard recognition that things are so in the world as it appears under the sun; on a recognition of fact, but not a slavery to it. So upon logic was founded the nonsense that displays itself in the tales and rhymes of Lewis Carroll. If men really could not distinguish between frogs and men, fairy-stories about frog-kings would not have arisen.

Fantasy can, of course, be carried to excess. It can be ill done. It can be put to evil uses. It may even delude the minds out of which it came. But of what human thing in this fallen world is that not true? Men have conceived not only of elves, but they have imagined gods, and worshipped them, even worshipped those most deformed by their authors' own evil. But they have made false gods out of other materials: their notions, their banners, their monies; even their sciences and their social and economic theories have demanded human sacrifice. *Abusus non tollit usum.*

Fantasy remains a human right: we make in our measure and in our derivative mode, because we are made: and not only made, but made in the image and likeness of a Maker.

RECOVERY, ESCAPE, CONSOLATION

As for old age, whether personal or belonging to the times in which we live, it may be true, as is often supposed, that this imposes disabilities (cf. p. 131). But it is in the main an idea produced by the mere *study* of fairy-stories. The analytic study of fairy-stories is as bad a preparation for the enjoying or the writing of them as would be the historical study of the drama of all lands and times for the enjoyment or writing of stage-plays. The study may indeed become depressing. It is easy for the student to feel that with all his labour he is collecting only a few leaves, many of them now torn or decayed, from the countless foliage of the Tree of Tales, with which the Forest of Days is carpeted. It seems vain to add to the litter. Who can design a new leaf? The patterns from bud to unfolding, and the colours from spring to autumn were all discovered by men long ago. But that is not true. The seed of the tree can be replanted in almost any soil, even in one so smoke-ridden (as Lang said) as that of England. Spring is, of course, not really less beautiful because we have seen or heard of other like events: like events, never from world's beginning to world's end the same event. Each leaf, of oak and ash and thorn, is a unique embodiment of the pattern, and for some this very year may be *the* embodiment, the first ever seen and recognized, though oaks have put forth leaves for countless generations of men.

We do not, or need not, despair of drawing because all lines must be either curved or straight, nor of painting because there are only three 'primary' colours. We may indeed be older now, in so far as we are heirs in enjoyment or in practice of many generations of ancestors in the arts. In this inheritance of wealth there may be a danger of boredom or of anxiety to be original, and that may lead to a distaste for fine drawing, delicate pattern, and 'pretty' colours, or else to mere manipulation and over-elaboration of old material, clever and heartless. But the true road of escape from such weariness is not to be found in the wilfully awkward, clumsy, or misshapen, not in making all things dark or unremittingly violent; nor in the mixing of colours on through subtlety to drabness, and the fantastical complication of shapes to the point of silliness and on towards delirium. Before we reach such states we need recovery. We should look at green again, and be startled anew (but not blinded) by blue and yellow and red. We should meet the centaur and the dragon, and then perhaps suddenly behold, like the ancient shepherds, sheep, and dogs, and horses -- and wolves. This recovery fairy-stories help us to make. In that sense only a taste for them may make us, or keep us, childish.

Recovery (which includes return and renewal of health) is a re-gaining – regaining of a clear view. I do not say 'seeing things as they are' and involve myself with the philosophers, though I might venture to say 'seeing things as we are (or were) meant to see them' – as things apart from ourselves. We need, in any case, to clean our windows; so that the things seen clearly may be freed from the drab blur of triteness or familiarity – from possessiveness. Of all faces those of our *familiares* are the ones both most difficult to play fantastic tricks with, and most difficult really to see with fresh attention, perceiving their likeness and unlikeness: that they are faces, and yet unique faces. This triteness is really the penalty of 'appropriation': the things that are trite, or (in a bad sense) familiar, are the things that we have appropriated, legally or mentally. We say we know them. They have become like the things which once attracted us by their glitter, or their colour, or their shape, and we laid hands on them, and then locked them in our hoard, acquired them, and acquiring ceased to look at them.

Of course, fairy-stories are not the only means of recovery, or prophylactic against loss. Humility is enough. And there is (especially for the humble) *Mooreeffoc*, or Chestertonian Fantasy. *Mooreeffoc* is a fantastic word, but it could be seen written up in every town in this land. It is Coffee-room, viewed from the inside through a glass door, as it was seen by Dickens on a dark London day; and it was used by Chesterton to denote the queerness of things that have become trite, when they are seen suddenly from a new angle. That kind of 'fantasy' most people would allow to be wholesome enough; and it can never lack for material. But it has, I think, only a limited power; for the reason that recovery of freshness of vision is its only virtue. The word *Mooreeffoc* may cause you suddenly to realise that England is an utterly alien land, lost either in some remote past age glimpsed by history, or in some strange dim future to be reached only by a time-machine; to see the amazing oddity and interest of its inhabitants and their customs and feeding-habits; but it cannot do more than that: act as a time-telescope focused on one spot. Creative fantasy, because it is mainly trying to do something else (make something new), may open your hoard and let all the locked things fly away like cage-birds. The gems all turn into flowers or flames, and you will be warned that all you had (or knew) was dangerous and potent, not really effectively chained, free and wild; no more yours than they were you.

The 'fantastic' elements in verse and prose of other kinds, even when only decorative or occasional, help in this release. But not so thoroughly as a fairy-story, a thing built on or about Fantasy, of which Fantasy is the core. Fantasy is made out of the Primary World, but a good craftsman loves his material, and has a knowledge and feeling for clay, stone and wood which only the art of making can give. By the forging of Gram cold iron was revealed; by the making of Pegasus horses were ennobled; in the Trees of the Sun and Moon root and stock, flower and fruit are manifested in glory.

And actually fairy-stories deal largely, or (the better ones) mainly, with simple or fundamental things, untouched by Fantasy, but these simplicities are made all the more luminous by their setting. For the story-maker who allows himself to be 'free with' Nature can be her lover not her slave. It was in fairy-stories that I first divined the potency of the words, and the wonder of the things, such as stone, and wood, and iron; tree and grass; house and fire; bread and wine.

I will now conclude by considering Escape and Consolation, which are naturally closely connected. Though fairy-stories are of course by no means the only medium of Escape, they are today one of the most obvious and (to some) outrageous forms of 'escapist' literature; and it is thus reasonable to attach to a consideration of them some considerations of this term 'escape' in criticism generally.

I have claimed that Escape is one of the main functions of

fairy-stories, and since I do not disapprove of them, it is plain that I do not accept the tone of scorn or pity with which 'Escape' is now so often used: a tone for which the uses of the word outside literary criticism give no warrant at all. In what the misusers of Escape are fond of calling Real Life, Escape is evidently as a rule very practical, and may even be heroic. In real life it is difficult to blame it, unless it fails; in criticism it would seem to be the worse the better it succeeds. Evidently we are faced by a misuse of words, and also by a confusion of thought. Why should a man be scorned, if, finding himself in prison, he tries to get out and go home? Or if, when he cannot do so, he thinks and talks about other topics than jailers and prison-walls? The world outside has not become less real because the prisoner cannot see it. In using Escape in this way the critics have chosen the wrong word, and, what is more, they are confusing, not always by sincere error, the Escape of the Prisoner with the Flight of the Deserter. Just so a Party-spokesman might have labelled departure from the misery of the Führer's or any other Reich and even criticism of it as treachery. In the same way these critics, to make confusion worse, and so to bring into contempt their opponents, stick their label of scorn not only on to Desertion, but on to real Escape, and what are often its companions, Disgust, Anger, Condemnation, and Revolt. Not only do they confound the escape of the prisoner with the flight of the deserter; but they would seem to prefer the acquiescence of the 'quisling' to the resistance of the patriot. To such thinking you have only to say 'the land you loved is doomed' to excuse any treachery, indeed to glorify it.

For a trifling instance: not to mention (indeed not to parade) electric street-lamps of mass-produced pattern in your tale is Escape (in that sense). But it may, almost certainly does, proceed from a considered disgust for so typical a product of the Robot Age, that combines elaboration and ingenuity of means with ugliness, and (often) with inferiority of result. These lamps may be excluded from the tale simply because they are bad lamps; and it is possible that one of the lessons to be learnt from the story is the realization of this fact. But out comes the big stick: 'Electric lamps have come to stay', they say. Long ago Chesterton truly remarked that, as soon as he heard that anything 'had come to stay', he knew that it would be very soon replaced – indeed regarded as pitiably obsolete and shabby. 'The march of Science, its tempo quickened by the needs of war, goes inexorably on . . . making some things obsolete, and foreshadowing new developments in the utilization of electricity': an advertisement. This says the same thing only more menacingly. The electric street-lamp may indeed be ignored, simply because it is so insignificant and transient. Fairy-stories, at any rate, have many more permanent and fundamental things to talk about. Lightning, for example. The escapist is not so subservient to the whims of evanescent fashion as these opponents. He does not make things (which it may be quite rational to regard as bad) his masters or his gods by worshipping them as inevitable, even 'inexorable'. And his opponents, so easily contemptuous, have no guarantee that he will stop there: he might rouse men to pull down the street-lamps. Escapism has another and even wickeder face: Reaction.

Not long ago – incredible though it may seem – I heard a clerk of Oxenford declare that he 'welcomed' the proximity of mass-production robot factories, and the roar of self-obstructive mechanical traffic, because it brought his university into 'contact with real life'. He may have meant that the way men were living and working in the twentieth century was increasing in barbarity at an alarming rate, and that the loud demonstration of this in the streets of Oxford might serve as a warning that it is not possible to preserve for long an oasis of sanity in a desert of unreason by mere fences, without actual offensive action (practical and intellectual). I fear he did not. In any case the expression 'real life' in this context seems to fall short of academic standards. The notion that motor-cars are more 'alive' than, say, centaurs or dragons is curious; that they are more 'real' than, say, horses is pathetically absurd. How real, how startlingly alive is a factory chimney compared with an elm tree: poor obsolete thing, insubstantial dream of an escapist!

For my part, I cannot convince myself that the roof of Bletchley station is more 'real' than the clouds. And as an artefact I find it less inspiring than the legendary dome of heaven. The bridge to platform 4 is to me less interesting than Bifröst guarded by Heimdall with the Gjallarhorn. From the wildness of my heart I cannot exclude the question whether railway-engineers, if they had been brought up on more fantasy, might not have done better with all their abundant means than they commonly do. Fairy-stories might be, I guess, better Masters of Arts than the academic person I have referred to.

Much that he (I must suppose) and others (certainly) would call 'serious' literature is no more than play under a glass roof by the side of a municipal swimming-bath. Fairy-stories may invent monsters that fly the air or dwell in the deep, but at least they do not try to escape from heaven or the sea.

And if we leave aside for a moment 'fantasy', I do not think that the reader or the maker of fairy-stories need even be ashamed of the 'escape' of archaism: of preferring not dragons but horses, castles, sailing-ships, bows and arrows; not only elves, but knights and kings and priests. For it is after all possible for a rational man, after reflection (quite unconnected with fairy-story or romance), to arrive at the condemnation, implicit at least in the mere silence of 'escapist' literature, of progressive things like factories, or the machine-guns and bombs that appear to be their most natural and inevitable, dare we say 'inexorable', products.

'The rawness and ugliness of modern European life' – that real life whose contact we should welcome – 'is the sign of a biological inferiority, of an insufficient or false reaction to environment.'[1] The maddest castle that ever came out of a giant's bag in a wild Gaelic story is not only much less ugly than a robot-factory, it is also (to use a very modern phrase) 'in a very real sense' a great deal more real. Why should we not escape from or condemn the 'grim Assyrian' absurdity of top-hats, or the Morlockian horror of factories? They are condemned even by the writers of that most escapist form of all literature, stories of Science fiction. These prophets often foretell (and many seem to yearn for) a world like one big glass-roofed railway-station. But from them it is as a rule very hard to gather what men in such a world-town will *do*. They may abandon the 'full Victorian panoply' for loose garments (with zip-fasteners), but

[1] Christopher Dawson, *Progress and Religion*, pp. 58, 59. Later he adds: 'The full Victorian panoply of top-hat and frock-coat undoubtedly expressed something essential in the nineteenth-century culture, and hence it has with that culture spread all over the world, as no fashion of clothing has ever done before. It is possible that our descendants will recognise in it a kind of grim Assyrian beauty, fit emblem of the ruthless and great age that created it; but however that may be, it misses the direct and inevitable beauty that all clothing should have, because like its parent culture it was out of touch with the life of nature and of human nature as well.'

will use this freedom mainly, it would appear, in order to play with mechanical toys in the soon-cloying game of moving at high speed. To judge by some of these tales they will still be as lustful, vengeful, and greedy as ever; and the ideals of their idealists hardly reach farther than the splendid notion of building more towns of the same sort on other planets. It is indeed an age of 'improved means to deteriorated ends'. It is part of the essential malady of such days – producing the desire to escape, not indeed from life, but from our present time and self-made misery – that we are acutely conscious both of the ugliness of our works, and of their evil. So that to us evil and ugliness seem indissolubly allied. We find it difficult to conceive of evil and beauty together. The fear of the beautiful fay that ran through the elder ages almost eludes our grasp. Even more alarming: goodness is itself bereft of its proper beauty. In Faërie one can indeed conceive of an ogre who possesses a castle hideous as a nightmare (for the evil of the ogre wills it so), but one cannot conceive of a house built with a good purpose – an inn, a hostel for travellers, the hall of a virtuous and noble king – that is yet sickeningly ugly. At the present day it would be rash to hope to see one that was not – unless it was built before our time.

This, however, is the modern and special (or accidental) 'escapist' aspect of fairy-stories, which they share with romances and other stories out of or about the past. Many stories out of the past have only become 'escapist' in their appeal through surviving from a time when men were as a rule delighted with the work of their hands into our time when many men feel disgust with man-made things.

But there are also other and more profound 'escapisms' that have always appeared in fairy-tale and legend. There are other things more grim and terrible to fly from than the noise, stench, ruthlessness, and extravagance of the internal-combustion engine. There are hunger, thirst, poverty, pain, sorrow, injustice, death. And even when men are not facing hard things such as these, there are ancient limitations from which fairy-stories offer a sort of escape, and old ambitions and desires (touching the very roots of fantasy) to which they offer a kind of satisfaction and consolation. Some are pardonable weaknesses or curiosities: such as the desire to visit, free as a fish, the deep sea; or the longing for the noiseless, gracious, economical flight of a bird, that longing which the aeroplane cheats, except in rare moments, seen high and by wind and distance noiseless, turning in the sun: that is, precisely when imagined and not used. There are profounder wishes: such as the desire to converse with other living things. On this desire, as ancient as the Fall, is largely founded the talking of beasts and creatures in fairy-tales, and especially the magical understanding of their proper speech. This is the root, and not the 'confusion' attributed to the minds of men of the unrecorded past, an alleged 'absence of the sense of separation of ourselves from beasts'.[1] A vivid sense of that separation is very ancient; but also a sense that it was a severance: a strange fate and a guilt lies on us. Other creatures are like other realms with which Man has broken off relations, and sees now only from the outside at a distance, being at war with them, or on the terms of an uneasy armistice. There are a few men who are privileged to travel abroad a little; others must be content with travellers' tales. Even about frogs. In speaking of that rather odd but widespread fairy-story *The Frog King* Max Müller asked in his prim way: 'How came such a story ever to be invented? Human beings were, we may hope, at all times sufficiently enlightened to know that a marriage between a frog and the daughter of a queen was absurd.' Indeed we may hope so! For if not, there would be no point in this story at all, depending as it does essentially on the sense of the absurdity. Folk-lore origins (or guesses about them) are here quite beside the point. It is of little avail to consider totemism. For certainly, whatever customs or beliefs about frogs and wells lie behind this story, the frog-shape was and is preserved in the fairy-story[2] precisely because it was so queer and the marriage absurd, indeed abominable. Though, of course, in the versions which concern us, Gaelic, German, English,[3] there is in fact no wedding between a princess and a frog: the frog was an enchanted prince. And the point of the story lies not in thinking frogs possible mates, but in the necessity of keeping promises (even those with intolerable consequences) that, together with observing prohibitions, runs through all

[1] See Note G at end (p. 160).
[2] Or group of similar stories.
[3] *The Queen who sought drink from a certain Well and the Lorgann* (Campbell, xxiii); *Der Froschkönig*; *The Maid and the Frog*.

Fairyland. This is one of the notes of the horns of Elfland, and not a dim note.

And lastly there is the oldest and deepest desire, the Great Escape: the Escape from Death. Fairy-stories provide many examples and modes of this – which might be called the genuine *escapist*, or (I would say) *fugitive* spirit. But so do other stories (notably those of scientific inspiration), and so do other studies. Fairy-stories are made by men not by fairies. The human stories of the elves are doubtless full of the Escape from Deathlessness. But our stories cannot be expected always to rise above our common level. They often do. Few lessons are taught more clearly in them than the burden of that kind of immortality, or rather endless serial living, to which the 'fugitive' would fly. For the fairy-story is specially apt to teach such things, of old and still today. Death is the theme that most inspired George MacDonald.

But the 'consolation' of fairy-tales has another aspect than the imaginative satisfaction of ancient desires. Far more important is the Consolation of the Happy Ending. Almost I would venture to assert that all complete fairy-stories must have it. At least I would say that Tragedy is the true form of Drama, its highest function; but the opposite is true of Fairy-story. Since we do not appear to possess a word that expresses this opposite – I will call it *Eucatastrophe*. The *eucatastrophic* tale is the true form of fairy-tale, and its highest function.

The consolation of fairy-stories, the joy of the happy ending: or more correctly of the good catastrophe, the sudden joyous 'turn' (for there is no true end to any fairy-tale):[1] this joy, which is one of the things which fairy-stories can produce supremely well, is not essentially 'escapist', nor 'fugitive'. In its fairy-tale – or otherworld – setting, it is a sudden and miraculous grace: never to be counted on to recur. It does not deny the existence of *dyscatastrophe*, of sorrow and failure: the possibility of these is necessary to the joy of deliverance; it denies (in the face of much evidence, if you will) universal final defeat and in so far is *evangelium*, giving a fleeting glimpse of Joy, Joy beyond the walls of the world, poignant as grief.

It is the mark of a good fairy-story, of the higher or more complete kind, that however wild its events, however fantastic

[1] See Note H at end (p. 160).

or terrible the adventures, it can give to child or man that hears it, when the 'turn' comes, a catch of the breath, a beat and lifting of the heart, near to (or indeed accompanied by) tears, as keen as that given by any form of literary art, and having a peculiar quality.

Even modern fairy-stories can produce this effect sometimes. It is not an easy thing to do; it depends on the whole story which is the setting of the turn, and yet it reflects a glory backwards. A tale that in any measure succeeds in this point has not wholly failed, whatever flaws it may possess, and whatever mixture or confusion of purpose. It happens even in Andrew Lang's own fairy-story, *Prince Prigio*, unsatisfactory in many ways as that is. When 'each knight came alive and lifted his sword and shouted "long live Prince Prigio" ', the joy has a little of that strange mythical fairy-story quality, greater than the event described. It would have none in Lang's tale, if the event described were not a piece of more serious fairy-story 'fantasy' than the main bulk of the story, which is in general more frivolous, having the half-mocking smile of the courtly, sophisticated *Conte*.[1] Far more powerful and poignant is the effect in a serious tale of Faërie.[2] In such stories when the sudden 'turn' comes we get a piercing glimpse of joy, and heart's desire, that for a moment passes outside the frame, rends indeed the very web of story, and lets a gleam come through.

> Seven long years I served for thee,
> The glassy hill I clamb for thee,
> The bluidy shirt I wrang for thee,
> And wilt thou not wauken and turn to me?

He heard and turned to her.[3]

---

[1] This is characteristic of Lang's wavering balance. On the surface the story is a follower of the 'courtly' French *conte* with a satirical twist, and of Thackeray's *Rose and the Ring* in particular – a kind which being superficial, even frivolous, by nature, does not produce or aim at producing anything so profound; but underneath lies the deeper spirit of the romantic Lang.

[2] Of the kind which Lang called 'traditional', and really preferred.

[3] *The Black Bull of Norroway.*

EPILOGUE

This 'joy' which I have selected as the mark of the true fairy-story (or romance), or as the seal upon it, merits more consideration.

Probably every writer making a secondary world, a fantasy, every sub-creator, wishes in some measure to be a real maker, or hopes that he is drawing on reality: hopes that the peculiar quality of this secondary world (if not all the details)[1] are derived from Reality, or are flowing into it. If he indeed achieves a quality that can fairly be described by the dictionary definition: 'inner consistency of reality', it is difficult to conceive how this can be, if the work does not in some way partake of reality. The peculiar quality of the 'joy' in successful Fantasy can thus be explained as a sudden glimpse of the underlying reality or truth. It is not only a 'consolation' for the sorrow of this world, but a satisfaction, and an answer to that question, 'Is it true?' The answer to this question that I gave at first was (quite rightly): 'If you have built your little world well, yes: it is true in that world.' That is enough for the artist (or the artist part of the artist). But in the 'eucatastrophe' we see in a brief vision that the answer may be greater – it may be a far-off gleam or echo of *evangelium* in the real world. The use of this word gives a hint of my epilogue. It is a serious and dangerous matter. It is presumptuous of me to touch upon such a theme; but if by grace what I say has in any respect any validity, it is, of course, only one facet of a truth incalculably rich: finite only because the capacity of Man for whom this was done is finite.

I would venture to say that approaching the Christian Story from this direction, it has long been my feeling (a joyous feeling) that God redeemed the corrupt making-creatures, men, in a way fitting to this aspect, as to others, of their strange nature. The Gospels contain a fairy-story, or a story of a larger kind which embraces all the essence of fairy-stories. They contain many marvels – peculiarly artistic,[2] beautiful, and moving: 'mythical' in their perfect, self-contained significance; and among the

---

[1] For all details may not be 'true': it is seldom that the 'inspiration' is so strong and lasting that it leavens all the lump, and does not leave much that is mere uninspired 'invention'.

[2] The Art is here in the story itself rather than in the telling; for the Author of the story was not the evangelists.

marvels is the greatest and most complete conceivable eucatastrophe. But this story has entered History and the primary world; the desire and aspiration of sub-creation has been raised to the fulfilment of Creation. The Birth of Christ is the eucatastrophe of Man's history. The Resurrection is the eucatastrophe of the story of the Incarnation. This story begins and ends in joy. It has pre-eminently the 'inner consistency of reality'. There is no tale ever told that men would rather find was true, and none which so many sceptical men have accepted as true on its own merits. For the Art of it has the supremely convincing tone of Primary Art, that is, of Creation. To reject it leads either to sadness or to wrath.

It is not difficult to imagine the peculiar excitement and joy that one would feel, if any specially beautiful fairy-story were found to be 'primarily' true, its narrative to be history, without thereby necessarily losing the mythical or allegorical significance that it had possessed. It is not difficult, for one is not called upon to try and conceive anything of a quality unknown. The joy would have exactly the same quality, if not the same degree, as the joy which the 'turn' in a fairy-story gives: such joy has the very taste of primary truth. (Otherwise its name would not be joy.) It looks forward (or backward: the direction in this regard is unimportant) to the Great Eucatastrophe. The Christian joy, the *Gloria*, is of the same kind; but it is pre-eminently (infinitely, if our capacity were not finite) high and joyous. Because this story is supreme; and it is true. Art has been verified. God is the Lord, of angels, and of men – and of elves. Legend and History have met and fused.

But in God's kingdom the presence of the greatest does not depress the small. Redeemed Man is still man. Story, fantasy, still go on, and should go on. The Evangelium has not abrogated legends; it has hallowed them, especially the 'happy ending'. The Christian has still to work, with mind as well as body, to suffer, hope, and die; but he may now perceive that all his bents and faculties have a purpose, which can be redeemed. So great is the bounty with which he has been treated that he may now, perhaps, fairly dare to guess that in Fantasy he may actually assist in the effoliation and multiple enrichment of creation. All tales may come true; and yet, at the last, redeemed, they may be as like and as unlike the forms that we give them as Man, finally redeemed, will be like and unlike the fallen that we know.

NOTES

A (p. 117)

The very root (not only the use) of their 'marvels' is satiric, a mockery of unreason; and the 'dream' element is not a mere machinery of introduction and ending, but inherent in the action and transitions. These things children can perceive and appreciate, if left to themselves. But to many, as it was to me, *Alice* is presented as a fairy-story and while this misunderstanding lasts, the distaste for the dream-machinery is felt. There is no suggestion of dream in *The Wind in the Willows*. 'The Mole had been working very hard all the morning, spring-cleaning his little house.' So it begins, and that correct tone is maintained. It is all the more remarkable that A. A. Milne, so great an admirer of this excellent book, should have prefaced to his dramatised version a 'whimsical' opening in which a child is seen telephoning with a daffodil. Or perhaps it is not very remarkable, for a perceptive admirer (as distinct from a great admirer) of the book would never have attempted to dramatise it. Naturally only the simpler ingredients, the pantomime, and the satiric beast-fable elements, are capable of presentation in this form. The play is, on the lower level of drama, tolerably good fun, especially for those who have not read the book; but some children that I took to see *Toad of Toad Hall* brought away as their chief memory nausea at the opening. For the rest they preferred their recollections of the book.

B (p. 129)

Of course, these details, as a rule, got into the tales, *even in the days when they were real practices*, because they had a story-making value. If I were to write a story in which it happened that a man was hanged, that *might* show in later ages, if the story survived – in itself a sign that the story possessed some permanent, and more than local or temporary, value – that it was written at a period when men were really hanged, as a legal practice. *Might*: the inference would not, of course, in that future time be certain. For certainty on that point the future inquirer would have to know definitely when hanging was practised and when I lived. I could have borrowed the incident from other times and places, from other stories; I could simply have invented it. But even if this inference happened to be correct, the hanging-scene would only occur in the story, (*a*) because I was aware of the dramatic, tragic, or macabre force of this incident in my tale, and (*b*) because those who handed it down felt this force enough to make them keep the incident in. Distance of time, sheer antiquity and alienness, might later sharpen the edge of the tragedy or the horror; but the edge must be there even for the elvish hone of antiquity to whet it. The least useful question, therefore, for literary critics at any rate, to ask or to answer about Iphigeneia, daughter of Agamemnon, is: Does the legend of her sacrifice at Aulis come down from a time when human-sacrifice was commonly practised?

I say only 'as a rule', because it is conceivable that what is now regarded as a 'story' was once something different in intent: e.g. a record of fact or ritual. I mean 'record' strictly. A story invented to explain a ritual (a process that is sometimes supposed to have frequently occurred) remains primarily a story. It takes form as such, and will survive (long after the ritual evidently) only because of its story-values. In some cases details that now are notable merely because they are strange may have once been so everyday and unregarded that they were slipped in casually: like mentioning that a man 'raised his hat', or 'caught a train'. But such casual details will not long survive change in everyday habits. Not in a period of oral transmission. In a period of writing (and of rapid changes in habits) a story may remain unchanged long enough for even its casual details to acquire the value of quaintness or queerness. Much of Dickens now has this air. One can open today an edition of a novel of his that was bought and first read when things were so in everyday life as they are in the story, though these everyday details are now already as remote from our daily habits as the Eliza-bethan period. But that is a special modern situation. The anthropologists and folk-lorists do not imagine any conditions of that kind. But if they are dealing with unlettered oral transmission, then they should all the more reflect that in that case they are dealing with items whose primary object was story-building, and whose primary reason for survival was the same. The Frog King (see p. 152) is not a *Credo*, nor a manual of totem-law: it is a queer tale with a plain moral.

C (p. 130)

As far as my knowledge goes, children who have an early bent for writing have no special inclination to attempt the writing of fairy-stories, unless that has been almost the sole form of literature presented to them; and they fail most markedly when they try. It is not an easy form. If children have any special leaning it is to Beast-fable, which adults often confuse with Fairy-story. The best stories by children that I have seen have been either 'realistic' (in intent), or have had as their characters animals and birds, who were in the main the zoomorphic human beings usual in Beast-fable. I imagine that this form is so often adopted principally because it allows a large measure of realism: the representation of domestic events and talk that children really know. The form itself is, however, as a rule, suggested or imposed by adults. It has a curious preponderance in the literature, good and bad, that is nowadays commonly presented to young children: I suppose it is felt to go with 'Natural History', semi-scientific books about beasts and birds that are also considered to be proper pabulum for the young. And it is reinforced by the bears and rabbits that seem in recent times almost to have ousted human dolls from the play-rooms even of little girls. Children make up sagas, often long and elaborate, about their dolls. If these are shaped like bears, bears will be the characters of the sagas; but they will talk like people.

D (p. 135)

I was introduced to zoology and palaeontology ('for children') quite as early as to Faërie. I saw pictures of living beasts and of true (so I was told) prehistoric animals. I liked the 'prehistoric' animals best: they had at least lived long ago, and hypothesis (based on somewhat slender evidence) cannot avoid a gleam of fantasy. But I did not like being told that these creatures were 'dragons'. I can still re-feel the irritation that I felt in childhood at assertions of instructive relatives (or their gift-books) such as these: 'snowflakes are fairy jewels', or 'are more beautiful than fairy jewels'; 'the marvels of the ocean depths are more wonderful than fairyland'. Children expect the differences they feel but cannot analyse to be explained by their elders, or at least recognized, not to be ignored or denied. I was keenly alive to the beauty of 'Real things', but it seemed to me quibbling to confuse this with the wonder of 'Other things'. I was eager to study Nature, actually more eager than I was to read most fairy-stories; but I did not want to be quibbled into Science and cheated out of Faërie by people who seemed to assume that by some kind of original sin I should prefer fairy-tales, but according to some kind of new religion I ought to be induced to like science. Nature is no doubt a life-study, or a study for eternity (for those so gifted); but there is a part of man which is not 'Nature', and which therefore is not obliged to study it, and is, in fact, wholly unsatisfied by it.

E (p. 140)

There is, for example, in surrealism commonly present a morbidity or un-ease very rarely found in literary fantasy. The mind that produced the depicted images may often be suspected to have been in fact already morbid; yet this is not a necessary explanation in all cases. A curious disturbance of the mind is often set up by the very act of drawing things of this kind, a state similar in quality and consciousness of morbidity to the sensations in a high fever, when the mind develops a distressing fecundity and facility in figure-making, seeing forms sinister or grotesque in all visible objects about it.

I am speaking here, of course, of the primary expression of Fantasy in 'pictorial' arts, not of 'illustrations'; nor of the cinematograph. However good in themselves, illustrations do little good to fairy-stories. The radical distinction between all art (including drama) that offers a *visible* presentation and true literature is that it imposes one visible form. Literature works from mind to mind and is thus more progenitive. It is at once more universal and more poignantly particular. If it speaks of *bread* or *wine* or *stone* or *tree*, it appeals to the whole of these things, to their ideas; yet each hearer will give to them a peculiar personal embodiment in his imagination. Should the story say 'he ate bread', the dramatic producer or painter can only show 'a piece of bread' according to his taste or fancy, but the hearer of the story will think of bread in general and picture it in some form of his own. If a story says 'he climbed a hill and saw a river in the valley below', the illustrator may catch, or nearly catch, his own vision of such a scene; but every hearer of the words will have his own picture, and it will be made out of all the hills and rivers and dales he has ever seen, but specially out of The Hill, The River, The Valley which were for him the first embodiment of the word.

F (p. 142)

I am referring, of course, primarily to fantasy of forms and visible shapes. Drama can be made out of the impact upon human characters of some event of Fantasy, or Faërie, that requires no machinery, or that can be assumed or reported to have happened. But that is not fantasy in dramatic result; the human characters hold the stage and upon them attention is concentrated. Drama of this sort (exemplified by some of Barrie's plays) can be used frivolously, or it can be used for satire, or for conveying such 'messages' as the playwright may have in his mind – for men. Drama is anthropocentric. Fairy-story and Fantasy need not be. There are, for instance, many stories telling how men and women have disappeared and spent years among the fairies, without noticing the passage of time, or appearing to grow older. In *Mary Rose* Barrie wrote a play on this theme. No fairy is seen. The cruelly tormented human beings are there all the time. In spite of the sentimental star and the angelic voices at the end (in the printed version) it is a painful play, and can easily be made diabolic: by substituting (as I have seen it done) the elvish call for 'angel voices' at the end. The non-dramatic fairy-stories, in so far as they are concerned with the human victims, can also be pathetic or horrible. But they need not be. In most of them the fairies are also there, on equal terms. In some stories they are the real interest. Many of the short folk-lore accounts of such incidents purport to be just pieces of 'evidence' about fairies, items in an agelong accumulation of 'lore' concerning them and the modes of their existence. The sufferings of human beings who come into contact with them (often enough, wilfully) are thus seen in quite a different perspective. A drama could be made about the sufferings of a victim of research in radiology, but hardly about radium itself. But it is possible to be primarily interested in radium (not radiologists) – or primarily interested in Faërie, not tortured mortals. One interest will produce a scientific book, the other a fairy-story. Drama cannot well cope with either.

G (p. 152)

The absence of this sense is a mere hypothesis concerning men of the lost past, whatever wild confusions men of today, degraded or deluded, may suffer. It is just as legitimate an hypothesis, and one more in agreement with what little is recorded concerning the thoughts of men of old on this subject, that this sense was once stronger. That fantasies which blended the human form with animal and vegetable forms, or gave human faculties to beasts, are ancient is, of course, no evidence for confusion at all. It is, if anything, evidence to the contrary. Fantasy does not blur the sharp outlines of the real world; for it depends on them. As far as our western, European, world is concerned, this 'sense of separation' has in fact been attacked and weakened in modern times not by fantasy but by scientific theory. Not by stories of centaurs or werewolves or enchanted bears, but by the hypotheses (or dogmatic guesses) of scientific writers who classed Man not only as 'an animal' – that correct classification is ancient – but as 'only an animal'. There has been a consequent distortion of sentiment. The natural love of men not wholly corrupt for beasts, and the human desire to 'get inside the skin' of living things, has run riot. We now get men who love animals more than men; who pity sheep so much that they curse shepherds as wolves; who weep over a slain warhorse and vilify dead soldiers. It is now, not in the days when fairy-stories were begotten, that we get 'an absence of the sense of separation'.

H (p. 153)

The verbal ending – usually held to be as typical of the end of fairy-stories as 'once upon a time' is of the beginning – 'and they lived happily ever after' is an artificial device. It does not deceive anybody. End-phrases of this kind are to be compared to the margins and frames of pictures, and are no more to be thought of as the real end of any particular fragment of the seamless Web of Story than the frame is of the visionary scene, or the casement of the Outer World. These phrases may be plain or elaborate, simple or extravagant, as artificial and as necessary as frames plain, or carved, or gilded. 'And if they have not gone away they are there still.' 'My story is done – see there is a little mouse; anyone who catches it may make himself a fine fur cap of it.' 'And they lived happily ever after.' 'And when the wedding was over, they sent me home with little paper shoes on a causeway of pieces of glass.'

Endings of this sort suit fairy-stories, because such tales have a greater sense and grasp of the endlessness of the World of Story than most modern 'realistic' stories, already hemmed within the narrow confines of their own small time. A sharp cut in the endless tapestry is not unfittingly marked by a formula, even a grotesque or comic one. It was an irresistible development of modern illustration (so largely photographic) that borders should be abandoned and the 'picture' end only with the paper. This method may be suitable for photographs; but it is altogether inappropriate for the pictures that illustrate or are inspired by fairy-stories. An enchanted forest requires a margin, even an elaborate border. To print it conterminous with the page, like a 'shot' of the Rockies in *Picture Post*, as if it were indeed a 'snap' of fairyland or a 'sketch by our artist on the spot', is a folly and an abuse.

As for the beginnings of fairy-stories: one can scarcely improve on the formula *Once upon a time*. It has an immediate effect. This effect can be appreciated by reading, for instance, the fairy-story *The Terrible Head* in the *Blue Fairy Book*. It is Andrew Lang's own adaptation of the story of Perseus and the Gorgon. It begins 'once upon a time', and it does not name any year or land or person. Now this treatment does something which could be called 'turning mythology into fairy-story'. I should prefer to say that it turns high fairy-story (for such is the Greek tale) into a particular form that is at present familiar in our land: a nursery or 'old wives' form. Namelessness is not a virtue but an accident, and should not have been imitated; for vagueness in this regard is a debasement, a corruption due to forgetfulness and lack of skill. But not so, I think, the timelessness. That beginning is not poverty-stricken but significant. It produces at a stroke the sense of a great uncharted world of time.

ENGLISH AND WELSH

To be invited to give a lecture under the O'Donnell Trust, and
especially to give the first lecture in Oxford of this series, is an
honour; but it is one which I hardly deserve. In any case a less
dilatory performance of the duty might have been expected.
But the years 1953 to 1955 have for me been filled with a great
many tasks, and their burden has not been decreased by the
long-delayed appearance of a large 'work', if it can be called that,
which contains, in the way of presentation that I find most
natural, much of what I personally have received from the study
of things Celtic.

However, this lecture is only, was only by the Electors intended,
I think, to be an Introduction, a curtain-raiser to what will, I
hope, be a long series of lectures by eminent scholars. Each of
these will, no doubt, enlighten or challenge even the experts.
But one purpose the series will have, so far as the intentions of
the munificent founder, the late Charles James O'Donnell, can
be discerned: that is, to arouse or strengthen the interest of the
English in various departments of Celtic studies, especially those
that are concerned with the origins and connexions of the peoples
and languages of Britain and Ireland. It is in fact to a certain
extent a missionary enterprise.

In a missionary enterprise a converted heathen may be a good
exhibit; and as such, I suppose, I was asked to appear. As such
anyway I am here now: a philologist in the Anglo-Saxon and
Germanic field. Indeed a Saxon in Welsh terms, or in our own
one of the English of Mercia. And yet one who has always felt
the attraction of the ancient history and pre-history of these
islands, and most particularly the attraction of the Welsh
language in itself.

I have tried to some extent to follow that attraction. I was
advised to do so indeed by a Germanic philologist, a great
encourager and adviser of the young, born 100 years ago this

month: Joseph Wright. It was characteristic of him that this advice was given in the form: 'Go in for Celtic, lad; there's money in it.' That the last part of the admonition was hardly true matters little; for those who knew Wright well, as an elder friend rather than as an official, knew also that this motive was not really the dominant one in his heart.

Alas! in spite of his advice I have remained a Saxon, knowing only enough to feel the strength of John Fraser's maxim – which he used to propound to me, with a gleam in his eye of special malice towards myself (as it seemed): 'A little Welsh is a dangerous thing.'

Dangerous certainly, especially if you do not know it for what it is worth, mistaking it for the much that would be much better. Dangerous, and yet desirable. I would say, for most students of English, essential. Mr C. S. Lewis, addressing students of literature, has asserted that the man who does not know Old English literature 'remains all his life a child among real students of English'. I would say to the English philologists that those who have no first-hand acquaintance with Welsh and its philology lack an experience necessary to their business. As necessary, if not so obviously and immediately useful, as a knowledge of Norse or French.

Preachers usually address the converted, and this value of Celtic (particularly Welsh) philology is perhaps more widely recognized now than when Joseph Wright gave me his advice. I know many scholars, here and elsewhere, whose official field is in English or Germanic, who have drunk much more than I from this particular well of knowledge. But they often remain, as it were, secret drinkers.

If by that furtive or at least apologetic attitude they disclaim possession of more than the dangerous little, not presuming to enter the litigious lists of the accredited Celtic scholars, they are perhaps wise. Welsh at least is still a spoken language, and it may well be true that its intimate heart cannot be reached by those who come to it as aliens, however sympathetic. But a man should look over the fences of a neighbouring farm or garden – a piece of the country which he himself inhabits and tills – even if he does not presume to offer advice. There is much to learn short of the inner secrets.

Anyway, I grant that I am myself a 'Saxon', and that therefore my tongue is not long enough to compass the language of Heaven. There lies, it seems, a long silence before me, unless I reach a destination more in accordance with merit than with Mercy. Or unless that story is to be credited, which I first met in the pages of Andrew Boord, physician of Henry VIII, that tells how the language of Heaven was changed. St Peter, instructed to find a cure for the din and chatter which disturbed the celestial mansions, went outside the Gates and cried *caws bobi*, and slammed the Gates to again before the Welshmen that had surged out discovered that this was a trap without cheese.

But Welsh still survives on earth, and so possibly elsewhere also; and a prudent Englishman will use such opportunities for speech as remain to him. For this tale has little authority. It is related rather to the contemporary effort of the English Government to destroy Welsh on earth as well as in Heaven.

As William Salesbury said in 1547, in a prefatory address to *Henry the eyght: your excellent wysdome . . . hath causede to be enactede and stablyshede by your moste cheffe & heghest counsayl of the parlyament that there shal herafter be no difference in lawes and language bytwyxte youre subiectes of youre principalyte of Wales and your other subiectes of your Royalme of Englande.*

This was made the occasion, or the pretext, for the publication of *A Dictionary in Englyshe and Welshe*. The first, and therefore, as Salesbury says, *rude (as all thinges be at their furst byginnynge)*. Its avowed object was to teach the literate Welsh English, enabling them to learn it even without the help of an English-speaking master, and it contained advice that would certainly have aided the Royal Will, that the English language should ultimately drive out the Welsh from Wales. But though Salesbury may have had a sincere admiration for English, *iaith gyflawn o ddawn a buddygoliaeth*, he was (I suppose) in fact concerned that the literate Welsh should escape the disabilities of a monoglot Welshman under the tyranny of the law. For Henry VIII's *Act for certain Ordinances in the King's Majesty's Dominion and Principality of Wales* laid it down that all ancient Welsh laws and customs at variance with English law should be held void in courts of justice, and that all legal proceedings must be conducted in English. This last and most oppressive rule was maintained until recent times (1830).

Salesbury was in any case a Welsh scholar, if a pedantic one, and the author of a translation into Welsh of the New Testament (1567), and joint author of a translation of the Prayer Book (1567, 1586). The Welsh New Testament played a considerable part in preserving to recent times, as a literary norm above the colloquial and the divergent dialects, the language of an earlier age. But fortunately in the Bible of 1588, by Dr William Morgan, most of Salesbury's pedantries were abandoned. Among these was Salesbury's habit of spelling words of Latin origin (real or supposed) as if they had not changed: as, for example, *eccles* for *eglwys*, from *ecclēsia*.

But in one point of spelling Salesbury's influence was important. He gave up the use of the letter *k* (in the New Testament), which had in medieval Welsh been used more frequently than *c*. Thus was established one of the visible characteristics of modern Welsh in contrast with English: the absence of *k*, even before *e*, *i*, and *y*. Students of English, familiar with the similar orthographic usage of Anglo-Saxon scribes derived from Ireland, often assume that there is a connexion between Welsh and ancient English spelling in this point. But there is in fact no direct connexion; and Salesbury, in answer to his critics (for the loss of *k* was not liked), replied: *C for K, because the printers have not so many as the Welsh requireth.* It was thus the English printers who were really responsible for spelling *Kymry* with a *C*.

It is curious that this legal oppression of the Welsh language should have occurred under the Tudors, proud of their Welsh ancestry, and in times when the authority and favour of the politically powerful were given to what we might call 'The Brut and all that', and Arthurian 'history' was official. It was hardly safe to express in public doubt of its veracity.

The eldest son of Henry VII was called Arthur. His survival, whether he had fulfilled any Arthurian prophecies or not, might (it may be surmised) have much changed the course of history. His brother Henry might have been remembered chiefly in the realms of music and poetry, and as the patron of such ingenious Welshmen as that numerologist and musician, John Lloyd of Caerleon, whom Mr Thurston Dart has studied and is studying.[1] Music indeed might well be considered by O'Donnell lecturers as one of the points of closest contact between Wales and England; but I am quite incompetent to deal with it.

However, as things turned out, music and verse were only the toys of a powerful monarch. No Arthurian romance would avail to protect Welsh custom and Welsh law, if it came to a choice between them and effective power. They would weigh no more in the balance than the head of Thomas More against a single castle in France.

Governments – or far-seeing civil servants from Thomas Cromwell onwards – understand the matter of language well enough, for their purposes. Uniformity is naturally neater; it is also very much more manageable. A hundred-per-cent Englishman is easier for an English government to handle. It does not matter what he *was*, or what his fathers were. Such an 'Englishman' is any man who speaks English natively, and has lost any effective tradition of a different and more independent past. For though cultural and other traditions may accompany a difference of language, they are chiefly maintained and preserved by language. Language is the prime differentiator of peoples – not of 'races', whatever that much-misused word may mean in the long-blended history of western Europe.

Málin eru höfuðeinkenni þjóðanna – 'Languages are the chief distinguishing marks of peoples. No people in fact comes into being until it speaks a language of its own; let the languages perish and the peoples perish too, or become different peoples. But that never happens except as the result of oppression and distress.'

These are the words of a little-known Icelander of the early nineteenth century, Sjéra Tómas Sæmundsson. He had, of course, primarily in mind the part played by the cultivated Icelandic language, in spite of poverty, lack of power, and insignificant numbers, in keeping the Icelanders in being in desperate times. But the words might as well apply to the Welsh of Wales, who have also loved and cultivated their language for its own sake (not as an aspirant for the ruinous honour of becoming the lingua franca of the world), and who by it and with it maintain their identity.

As a mere introducer or curtain-raiser, not as an expert, I will speak now a little further about these two languages, English and Welsh, in their contact and contrast, as coinhabitants of Britain. My glance will be directed to the past. Today English and Welsh are still in close contact (in Wales), little for the good of Welsh one might say who loves the idiom and the beautiful word-form of uncontaminated *Cymraeg*. But though these pathological developments are of great interest to philologists, as are diseases to doctors, they require for their treatment a native speaker of the modern tongue. I speak only as an amateur, and address the *Saeson* and not the *Cymry*; my view is that of a *Sayce* and not a *Waugh*.

I use these surnames – both well known (the first especially in the annals of philology) – since *Sayce* is probably a name of Welsh origin (*Sais*) but means an Englishman, while *Waugh* is certainly of English origin (*Walh*) but means a Welshman; it is in fact the singular of *Wales*. These two surnames may serve both to remind students of the great interest of the surnames current in England, to which Welsh is often the key, and to symbolize the age-long interpenetration of the peoples speaking English and Welsh.

Of peoples, not races. We are dealing with events that are primarily a struggle between languages. Here I will put in an aside, not unconnected with my main theme. If one keeps one's eye on language as such, then one must regard certain kinds of research with caution, or at least not misapply their results.

Among the things envisaged by Mr O'Donnell, one of the lines of inquiry that seems indeed to have specially attracted him, was nomenclature, particularly personal and family names. Now English surnames have received some attention, though not much of it has been well informed or conducted scientifically. But even such an essay as that of Max Förster in 1921 (*Keltisches Wortgut im Englischen*) shows that many 'English' surnames, ranging from the rarest to the most familiar, are linguistically derived from Welsh (or British), from place-names, patronymics, personal names, or nick-names; or are in part so derived, even when that origin is no longer obvious. Names such as Gough, Dewey, Yarnal, Merrick, Onions, or Vowles, to mention only a few.

This kind of inquiry is, of course, significant for the purpose of discovering the etymological origin of elements current in English speech, and characteristic of modern Englishry, of which names and surnames are a very important feature even though they do not appear in ordinary dictionaries. But for other purposes its significance is less certain.

One must naturally first set aside the names derived from places long anglicized in language. For example, even if *Harley* in Shropshire could be shown to be beyond doubt of the same origin as *Harlech* (*Harddlech*) in Wales, nothing instructive concerning the relations of the English and Welsh peoples arises from the occurrence of Harley (derived from the Shropshire place) as a family name in England. The etymology of *Harley* remains an item in place-names research, and such evidence as it affords for the relations of Welsh (or British) and English refers to the distant past, for which the later surname has no significance. Similarly with the surname *Eccles*, even when that place-name or place-name element is not under suspicion of having nothing to do with *ecclesia*.

The case may be different when a name is derived from a place actually in Wales; but even such names could migrate far and early. A probable example is Gower: best known to English students as the name of a fourteenth-century poet whose language was strongly tinctured with the dialect of Kent, the whole breadth of Ynys Prydain from the region of Gŵyr. But with regard to such names, and indeed to others not derived from place-names, the Welsh origin of which is more certain or more obvious – such as *Griffiths, Lloyd, Meredith*, or *Cadwallader* – one should reflect that the patrilinear descent of names makes them misleading.

English or Anglo-Norman names were no doubt adopted in Wales far more freely and extensively than were Welsh names at any period on the other side; but it is, I suppose, hazardous to assume that everyone who bore a Welsh name in the past, from which eventually a surname might be derived – Howell or Maddock or Meredith or the like – was necessarily of Welsh origin or a Welsh-speaker. It is in the early modern period that names of this sort first become frequent in English records, but caution is, no doubt, necessary even in dealing with ancient times and the beginning of the contact between the two languages.

The enormous popularity, to which place-names and other records bear witness, of the *Cad/Chad* group of names or name elements in early England must be held to indicate the adoption of a name as such. The anglicization of its form (from which the *Chad* variety proceeds) further supports this view. The West-Saxon royal genealogy begins with the 'Celtic' name *Cerdic*, and contains both *Cadda/Ceadda* and *Ceadwalla*. Leaving aside the problems which this genealogy presents to historians, a point to note in the present context is not so much the appearance of late British names in a supposedly 'Teutonic' royal house, as their appearance in a markedly anglicized form that must be due to their being borrowed as names, and to their accommodation like ordinary loan-words to English speech-habits. One deduction at least can be safely made: the users of these names had changed their language and spoke English, not any kind of British.[2] In themselves these names prove only that foreign names like foreign words were easily and early adopted by the English. There is, of course, no doubt that the view of the process which established the English language in Britain as a simple case of 'Teutons' driving out and dispossessing 'Celts' is altogether too simple. There was fusion and confusion. But from names alone without other evidence deductions concerning 'race' or indeed language are insecure.

So it was again when new invaders came to Britain. In later times it cannot be assumed that a man who bore a 'Danish' name was (in whole or part) of Scandinavian 'blood' or language, or even of Danish sympathies. *Ulfcytel* is as Norse a name as *Ceadwalla* is British, yet it was borne by a most valiant opponent of the Danes, the alderman of East Anglia, of whom it is recorded that the Danes themselves said that no man *on Angelcynne* had ever done them more damage in fighting.[3] Not every Brián and Niál in Iceland had Irish blood in his veins.

Mixture of peoples is, of course, one of the ways in which the borrowing of names takes place. Mothers have, no doubt, always played an important part in this process. Yet one should reflect that even when the adoption of a name was due in the first instance to, say, intermarriage, this may have been an event of small general importance. And once a name has been adopted it may spread quite independently. When we come to patrilinear surnames it is obvious that these may multiply without any addition to the 'blood' to which their etymology would seem to testify, indeed rather with the extinction of it as an effective ingredient in the make-up, physical or mental, of the bearers of the name.

I am not a German, though my surname is German (anglicized like Cerdic) – my other names are Hebrew, Norse, Greek, and French. I have inherited with my surname nothing that originally belonged to it in language or culture, and after 200 years the 'blood' of Saxony and Poland is probably a negligible physical ingredient.

I do not know what Mr O'Donnell would have said to this. I suspect that to him anyone who spoke a Celtic language was a Celt, even if his name was not Celtic, but anyone who had a Celtic name was a Celt whatever he spoke; and so the Celts won on both the swings and the roundabouts.

But if we leave such terms as Celtic and Teutonic (or Germanic) aside, reserving them for their only useful purpose, linguistic classification, it remains an evident conclusion from history that apart from language the inhabitants of Britain are made of the same 'racial' ingredients, though the mixing of these has not been uniform. It is still patchy. The observable differences are, however, difficult or impossible to relate to language.

The eastern region, especially in the south-east (where the breach with the Continent is narrowest), is the area where the newer layers lie thicker and the older things are thinner and more submerged. So it must have been for many ages, since this island achieved more or less its present peculiar shape. So, if these parts are now considered the most English, or the most Danish, they must once have been the most Celtic, or British, or Belgic. There still endures the ancient pre-English, pre-Roman name of Kent.

For neither Celtic nor Germanic forms of speech belong in origin to these islands. They are both invaders, and by similar routes. The bearers of these languages have clearly never extirpated the peoples of other language that they found before them. This, however, is, I think, an interesting point to note, when we consider the present position (that is, all that has followed since the fifth century A.D.): there is no evidence at all for the survival in the areas which we now call England and Wales of any pre-Celtic speech.[4] In place-names we may find fragments of long-forgotten Neolithic or Bronze Age tongues, celticized, romanized, anglicized, ground down by the wear of time. It is likely enough. For if pre-English names, especially of mountains or rivers, survived the coming of the North Sea pirates, they may as well have survived the coming of the Celtic Iron Age warriors. Yet when the place-names expert hazards a pre-Celtic origin, it in fact only means that from our defective material he cannot devise any etymology fit to print.

This eradication of pre-Indo-European language is interesting, even if its cause or causes remain uncertain. It might be thought to reflect a natural superiority of Indo-European kinds of language; so that the first bringers of that type of speech were eventually completely successful linguistically, while successors bringing languages of the same order, contesting with their linguistic peers, were less so. But even if one admits that languages (like other art-forms or styles) have a virtue of their own, independent of their immediate inheritors – a thing which I believe – one has to admit that other factors than linguistic excellence contribute to their propagation. Weapons, for instance. While the completion of a process may be due simply to the fact that it has gone on for a very long time.

But whatever the success of the imported languages, the inhabitants of Britain, during recorded history, must have been in large part neither Celtic nor Germanic: that is, *not* derived physically from the original speakers of those varieties of language, nor even from the already racially more mixed invaders who planted them in Britain.

In that case they are and were not either 'Celts' or 'Teutons' according to the modern myth that still holds such an attraction for many minds. In this legend Celts and Teutons are primeval and immutable creatures, like a triceratops and a stegosaurus (bigger than a rhinoceros and more pugnacious, as popular palaeontologists depict them), fixed not only in shape but in innate and mutual hostility, and endowed even in the mists of antiquity, as ever since, with the peculiarities of mind and temper which can be still observed in the Irish or the Welsh on the one hand and the English on the other: the wild incalculable poetic Celt, full of vague and misty imaginations, and the Saxon, solid and practical when not under the influence of beer. Unlike most myths this myth seems to have no value at all.

According to such a view *Beowulf*, though in English, must, I should say, be far more Celtic – being full of dark and twilight, and laden with sorrow and regret – than most things that I have met written in a Celtic language.

Should you wish to describe the riding to hunt of the Lord of the Underworld in 'Celtic' fashion (according to this view of the word), you would have to employ an Anglo-Saxon poet. It is easy to imagine how he would have managed it: ominous, colourless, with the wind blowing, and a *wóma* in the distance, as the half-seen hounds came baying in the gloom, huge shadows pursuing shadows to the brink of a bottomless pool.

We have, alas! no Welsh of a like age to compare with it; but we may glance none the less at the White Book of Rhydderch (containing the so-called *Mabinogion*). This manuscript, though its date is of the early fourteenth century, no doubt contains matter composed long before, much of which had come down to the author from times still more remote. In it at the beginning of the *mabinogi* of Pwyll Prince of Dyfed we read how Pwyll set out to hunt in Glyn Cuch:

> And he sounded his horn and began to muster the hunt, and followed after the dogs and lost his companions; and while he was listening to the cry of the pack, he could hear the cry of another pack, but they had not the same cry and were coming to meet his own pack.
>
> And he could see a clearing in the wood as of a level field, and as his pack reached the edge of the clearing he could see a stag in front of the other pack. And towards the middle of the clearing lo! the pack that was pursuing it overtaking it and bringing it to the ground. And then he looked at the colour of the pack, without troubling to look at the stag; and of all the hounds he had seen in the world he had seen no dogs the same colour as these. The colour that was on them was a

brilliant shining white, and their ears red; and as the
exceeding whiteness of the dogs glittered so glittered the
exceeding redness of their ears. And he came to the
dogs and drove away the dogs that had killed the stag,
and baited his own pack upon it.

But these dogs that the prince had driven off were the hounds
of Arawn, King of Annwn, Lord of the Underworld.

A very practical man, with a keen feeling for bright colour,
was this Pwyll, or the writer who described him. Can he have
been a 'Celt'? He had never heard of the word, we may feel sure;
but he spoke and wrote with skill what we now classify as a
Celtic language: Cymraeg, which we call Welsh.

That is all that I have to say at this time about the confusion
between language (and nomenclature) and 'race'; and the
romantic misapplication of the terms Celtic and Teutonic (or
Germanic). Even so I have spent too long on these points for
the narrow limits of my theme and time; and my excuse must
be that, though the dogs that I have been beating may seem to
most of those who are listening to me dead, they are still alive
and barking in this land at large.

I will turn now to the Celtic language in Britain. But even if I
were fully qualified, I should not now be giving a sketch of
Celtic philology. I am trying only to indicate some of the points
in which this study may offer special attraction to the speakers
of English, points which have specially attracted me. So I will
pass over 'P and Q': I mean the difficult and absorbing problems
that are presented by the linguistic and archaeological evidence
concerning the immigrations from the European mainland,
connected or supposed to be connected with the coming of
different varieties of Celtic speech to Britain and Ireland. I am
concerned in any case only with 'P-Celts' and among those with
the speech-ancestors of the Welsh.

The first point that I think should be considered is this: the
antiquity in Britain of Celtic language. Part of Britain we now
call England, the land of the Angles; and yet all the days of the
English in it, from Hengest to Elizabeth II, are short on an
archaeological scale, short even on a Celtic scale. When our

speech-ancestors began their effective linguistic conquests – no doubt much later than their first tentative settlements in such regions as the Sussex coast – in the fifth century A.D. the Celtic occupation had probably some thousand years behind it: a length of time as long as that which separates us from King Alfred.

The English adventure was interrupted and modified, after hardly more than 300 years, by the intrusion of a new element, a different though related variety of Germanic coming from Scandinavia. This is a complication which occurred in historically documented times, and we know a good deal about it. But similar things, historically and linguistically undocumented, though conjectured by archaeology, must have occurred in the course of the celticizing of Britain. The result may be capable of a fairly simple generalization: that the whole of Britain south of the Forth–Clyde line by the first century A.D. shared a British or 'Brittonic' civilization, 'which so far as language goes formed a single linguistic province from Dumbarton and Edinburgh to Cornwall and Kent'.[5] But the processes by which this linguistic state was achieved were no doubt as complicated, differing in pace, mode, and effect, in different areas, as were those of the subsequent process, which has at length achieved a result which 2,000 years hence might be generalized in almost the same terms, though referring to the spread not of 'Brittonic' but of English. (But parts of Wales would have still to be excepted.)

For instance, I do not know what linguistic complications were introduced, or may be thought to have been introduced, by the 'Belgic' invasion, interrupted by Julius Caesar's ill-considered and deservedly ill-fated incursion; but they could, I suppose, have involved dialectal differences within Celtic as considerable as those which divided ninth-century Norse from the older Germanic layer which we now call 'Anglo-Saxon'.[6] But 2,000 years hence those differences which now appear marked and important to English philologists may be insignificant or unrecognizable.

None the less, far off and now obscure as the Celtic adventures may seem, their surviving linguistic traces should be to us, who live here in this coveted and much-contested island, of deep interest, as long as antiquity continues to attract the minds of men. Through them we may catch a glimpse or echo of the past which archaeology alone cannot supply, the past of the land which we call our home.

Of this I may perhaps give an illustration, though it is well known. There stands still in what is now England the ruinous fragment of an ancient monument that we have long called in our English fashion *Stonehenge*, 'the suspended stones', remembering nothing of its history. Archaeologists with the aid of geologists may record the astonishing fact that some of its stones must certainly have been brought from Pembrokeshire, and we may ponder what this great feat of transport must imply: whether in veneration of the site, or in numbers of the population, or in organization of so-called primitive peoples long ago. But when we find 'Celtic' legend, presumably without the aid of precise geological knowledge, recording in its fashion the carrying of stones from Pembroke to Stonehenge, then we must also ponder what that must imply: in the absorption by Celtic-speakers of the traditions of predecessors, and the echoes of ancient things that can still be heard in the seemingly wild and distorted tales that survive enshrined in Celtic tongues.

The variety of Celtic language that we are at present concerned with was one whose development went on at about the same pace as that of spoken Latin – with which it was ultimately related. The distance between the two was greater, of course, than that separating even the most divergent forms of Germanic speech; but the language of southern Britain would appear to have been one whose sounds and words were capable of representation *more Romano* in Latin letters less unsatisfactorily than those of other languages with which the Romans came in contact.

It had entered Britain – and this seems to me an important point – in an *archaic state*. This requires some closer definition. The languages of Indo-European kind in Europe do not, of course, all shift at the same pace, either throughout their organization or in any given department (such as phonetic structure). But there is none the less a general and similar movement of change that achieves successively similar stages or modes.

Of the primitive modes of the major branches – the hypothetical common Indo-European wholly escapes us – we have now no records. But we may use 'archaic' with reference to the states of those languages that are earliest recorded. If we say that classical Latin, substantially the form of that language just before the beginning of our present era, is still an example of the European archaic mode, we may call it an 'old' language. Gothic, though it is recorded later, still qualifies for that title. It is still an example of 'Old Germanic'.

That even so limited a record is preserved, at this stage, of any Germanic language, even of one comparatively well advanced in change,[7] is of great importance to Germanic philology.[8] Anything comparable that represented, say, even one of the dialects of Gaul would have profound effects on Celtic philology.

Unfortunately, for departmental convenience in classifying the periods of the individual languages of later times, we obscure this point by our use of 'old' for the earliest period of their effective records. Old Welsh is used for the scanty records of a time roughly equivalent to that of the documents of Anglo-Saxon; and this we call Old English.

But Old English and Old Welsh were not on a European basis old at all. English certainly, even when we first meet it in the eighth century, is a 'middle' speech, well advanced into the second stage, though its temporary elevation as a learned and cultured language retarded for a time its movement towards a third.[9] The same might be said for Old Welsh, no doubt, if we had enough of it. Though the movement of Welsh was naturally not the same as that of English. It resembled far more closely the movement of the Romance languages – for example, in the loss of a neuter gender; the early disappearance of declensions contrasted with the preservation in verbs of distinct personal inflexions and a fairly elaborate system of tenses and moods.

More than 200 years passed in the dark between the beginning of the linguistic invasion of Britain by English and our first records of its form. Records of the fifth and early sixth centuries would certainly produce some surprises in detail for philologists (as no doubt would those of Welsh for a like period); yet the evidence seems to me clear that already in the days of Hengest and Horsa, at the moment of its first entry, English was in the 'middle' stage.

On the other hand, British forms of language had entered

Britain in an archaic state; indeed, if we place their first arrival some centuries before the beginning of our era, in a mode far more archaic than that of the earliest Latin. The whole of its transformation, therefore, from a language of very ancient mode, an elaborately inflected and recognizable dialect of western Indo-European, to a middle and a modern speech has gone on in this island. It has, and had long ago, become, as it were, acclimatized to and naturalized in Britain; so that it belonged to the land in a way with which English could not compete, and still belongs to it with a seniority which we cannot overtake. In that sense we may call it an 'old' tongue: old in this island. It had become already virtually 'indigenous' when English first came to disturb its possession.

Changes in a language are largely conditioned by its own patterns of sound and function. Even after loosening or loss of former contacts, it may continue to change according to trends already in evidence before migration. So 'Celts' in their new situations in Britain, no doubt, continued for some time to change their language along the same lines as their kinsmen on the Continent. But separation from them, even if not complete, would tend to halt some changes already initiated, and to hasten others; while the adoption of Celtic by aliens might set up new and unprecedented movements. Celtic dialects in this island, as compared with their nearest kin overseas, would slowly become British and peculiar. How far and in what ways that was true in the days of the coming of the English we can only guess, in the absence of records from this side and of connected texts of known meaning in any Celtic dialect of the Continent. The pre-Roman languages of Gaul have for all practical purposes disastrously perished. We may, however, compare the Welsh treatment of the numerous Latin words that it adopted with the Gallo-Roman treatment of the same words on their way to French. Or the Gallo-Roman and French treatment of Celtic words and names may be compared with their treatment in Britain. Such comparisons certainly indicate that British was divergent and in some respects conservative.

The Latin reflected by the Welsh loan-words is one that remains far closer to classical Latin than to the spoken Latin of the Continent, especially that of Gaul. For example: in the preservation of *c* and *g* as stops before all vowels; of *v* (*u̯*) as distinct from medial *b* (*ƀ*); or of quantitative distinctions in vowels, so that Latin *ă, i* are in Welsh treated quite differently from *ā, ę̄*.[10] This conservatism of the Latin element may of course be, at least in part, due to the fact that we are looking at words that were early removed from a Latin context to a British, so that certain features later altered in spoken Latin were fossilized in the British dialects of the West. Since the spoken Latin of southern Britain perished and did not have time to develop into a Romance language, we do not know how it would have continued to develop. The probability is, however, that it would have been very different from that of Gaul.

In a similar way the early English loan-words from French preserve, for instance in *ch* and *ge* (as in *change*), consonantal values of Old French since altered in France. Spoken French also eventually died out in England, and we do not know how it would have developed down to the present day, if it had survived as an independent dialect; though the probability is that it would have shown many of the features revealed in the English loan-words.

In the treatment of Celtic material there was, in any case, wide divergence between Gaul and Britain. For example the Gallo-Roman *Rotomagus*, on its way to *Rouen*, is represented in late Old English as *Roðem*; but in Old Welsh it would have been written **Rotmag*, and later **Rodva*, **Rhodfa*.

English was well set in its own, and in many respects (from a general Germanic point of view) divergent, directions of change at the time of its arrival, and it has changed greatly since. Yet in some points it has remained conservative. It has preserved, for instance, the Germanic consonants *þ* (now written *th*) and *w*. No other Germanic dialect preserves them both, and *þ* is in fact otherwise preserved only in Icelandic. It may at least be noted that Welsh also makes abundant use of these two sounds.[11] It is a natural question to ask: how did these two languages, the long-settled British and the new-come English, affect one another, if at all; and what at any rate were their relations?

It is necessary to distinguish, as far as that is possible, between languages as such and their speakers. Languages are not hostile one to another. They are, in the contrast of any pair, only similar

or dissimilar, alien or akin. In this, actual historical relationship
may be and commonly is involved. But it is not inevitably so.
Latin and British appear to have been similar to one another,
in their phonetic and morphological structure, to a degree
unusual between languages sufficiently far separated in history
to belong to two different branches of western Indo-European
language. Yet Goidelic Celtic must have seemed at least as alien
to the British as the language of the Romans.

English and British were far sundered in history and in structure,
if less so in the department of phonetics than in morphology.
Borrowing words between the two would have presented in
many cases small difficulty; but learning the other speech as a
language would mean adventuring into an alien country with
few familiar paths. As it still does.[12]

Between the speakers of British and English there was naturally
hostility (especially on the British side); and when men are
hostile the language of their enemies may share their hatred.
On the defending side, to the hatred of cruel invaders and robbers
was added, no doubt, contempt for barbarians from beyond the
pale of Rome, and detestation of heathens unbaptized. The
Saxons were a scourge of God, devils allowed to torment the
Britons for their sins. Sentiments hardly less hostile were felt by
the later baptized English for the heathen Danes. The invective
of Wulfstan of York against the new scourge is much like that of
Gildas against the Saxons: naturally, since Wulfstan had read
Gildas and cites him.

But such sentiments, especially those expressed by preachers
primarily concerned with the correction of their own flock, do
not govern all the actions of men in such situations. Invasion has
as first objectives wealth and land; and those who are successful
leaders in such enterprises are eager rather for territory and
subjects than for the propagation of their native tongue, whether
they are called Julius or Hengest or William. On the other side
leaders will seek to hold what they can, and will treat with the
invaders for their own advantage. So it was in the days of the
Roman invasions; and small mercy did the Romans show to
those who called themselves their friends.

Of course in the first turmoils the defenders will not try to
learn the language of the barbarian invaders, and if, as the story

goes in the case of the English-speaking adventurers, these are in part revolted mercenaries, there will be no need. Neither do successful land-grabbers in the first flush of loot and slaughter bother much about 'the lingo of the natives'. But that situation will not last long. There will come a pause, or pauses – in the history of the spread of English there were many – in which the leaders will look ahead from their small conquests to lands still beyond their grasp, and sideways to their rivals. They will need information; in rare cases they may even display intelligent curiosity.[13] Even as Gildas accuses the surviving British princes of warring with one another rather than with the enemy, so the kings of small English realms at once began to do the same. In such circumstances sentiments of language against language, Roman against barbarian, or Christendom against heathendom will not outweigh the need for communication.

How was such communication carried on? Indeed for that matter how were the many surviving British place-names borrowed, once we move farther in and leave the ports and coastal regions that pirates in the Channel might long have known? We are not told. We are left to an estimate of probabilities, and to the difficult analysis of the evidence of words and place-names.

It is, of course, impossible to go into details concerning the problems that these present. Many of them are familiar in any case to English philologists, to whom the Latin loan-words in Old English, for instance, have long been of interest. Though it is probably fair to say that in this matter the importance of the Welsh evidence is not yet fully recognized.

According to probability, apart from direct evidence or linguistic deductions, Latin of a kind is likely to have been a medium of communication at an early stage. Though *medium* gives a false impression, suggesting a language belonging to neither side. Latin must have been the spoken language of many if not most of the defenders in the south-east; while some sort of command of Latin is likely to have been acquired by many 'Saxons'. They had been operating in the Channel and its approaches for a long time, and had gained precarious footholds in lands of which Latin was the official tongue.[14]

Later British and English must have come face to face. But

there was certainly never any iron-curtain line, with everything English on the one side, and British on the other. Communication certainly went on. But communications imply persons, on one side or both, who have at least some command of the two languages.

In this connexion the word *wealhstod* is interesting; and I may perhaps pause to consider it, since it has not (as far as I am aware) received the attention that it deserves. It is the Anglo-Saxon word for an 'interpreter'. It is peculiar to Old English; and for that reason, besides the fact that it contains the element *wealh*, *walh* (on which I will say more in a moment), it is a fair conclusion that it arose in Britain. The etymology of its second element *stod* is uncertain, but the word as a whole must have meant for the English a man who could understand the language of a *Walh*, the word they most commonly applied to the British. But the word does not seem necessarily to have implied that the *wealhstod* was himself a 'native'. He was an intermediary between those who spoke English and those who spoke a *wælisc* tongue, however he had acquired a knowledge of both languages. Thus Ælfric says of King Oswald that he acted as St Aidan's *wealhstod*, since the king knew *scyttisc* (sc. Gaelic) well, but Aidan *ne mihte gebigan his spraece to Norðhymbriscum swa hraþe þa git*.[15]

That the *Walas* or Britons got to know of this word would not be surprising. That they did seems to be shown by the mention among the great company of Arthur in the hunting of the Twrch Trwyth (*Kulhwch and Olwen*) of a man who knew all languages; his name is given as Gwrhyr Gwalstawt Ieithoed, that is Gwrhyr Interpreter of Tongues.

Incidentally it is curious to find a bishop named *Uualchstod* mentioned in Bede's History, belonging to the early eighth century (about A.D. 730); for he was 'bishop of those beyond Severn', that is of Hereford. Such a name could not become used as a baptismal name until it had become first used as a 'nickname' or occupational name, and that would not be likely to occur except in a time and region of communications between peoples of different language.

It would certainly seem that eventually at any rate the English made some efforts to understand Welsh, even if this remained a professional task for gifted linguists. Of what the English in general thought about British or Welsh we know little, and that only from later times, two or three centuries after the first invasions. In Felix of Crowland's life of St Guthlac (referring to the beginning of the eighth century) British is made the language of devils.[16] The attribution of the British language to devils and its description as cacophonous are of little importance. Cacophony is an accusation commonly made, especially by those of small linguistic experience, against any unfamiliar form of speech. More interesting is it that the ability of some English people to understand 'British' is assumed. British was, no doubt, chosen as the language of the devils mainly as the one alien vernacular at that time likely to be known to an Englishman, or at least recognized by him.

In this story we find the term 'British' used. In the Anglo-Saxon version of the Life the expression *Bryttisc sprecende* appears. This no doubt is partly due to the Latin. But *Brettas* and the adjective *brittisc, bryttisc* continued to be used throughout the Old English period as equivalents of *Wealas* (*Walas*) and *wielisc* (*waelisc*), that is of modern *Welsh*, though it also included Cornish. Sometimes the two terms were combined in *Bretwalas* and *bretwielisc*.

In modern England the usage has become disastrously confused by the maleficent interference of the Government with the usual object of governments: uniformity. The misuse of British begins after the union of the crowns of England and Scotland, when in a quite unnecessary desire for a common name the English were officially deprived of their Englishry and the Welsh of their claim to be the chief inheritors of the title British.

'Fy fa fum, I smell the blood of an Englishman', wrote Nashe in 1595 (*Have with you to Saffron Walden*).

> Child Rowland to the dark tower came,
> His word was stil: Fie, foh, and fum,
> I smell the blood of a British man,

Edgar says, or is made to say, in *King Lear* (III. iv).

The modern Englishman finds this very confusing. He has long read of British prowess in battle, and especially of British stubbornness in defeat in many imperial wars; so when he hears of Britons stubbornly (as is to be expected) opposing the landing of Julius Caesar or of Aulus Plautius, he is apt to suppose that the English (who meekly put themselves down as British in hotel-registers) were already there, facing the first of their long series of glorious defeats. A supposition far from uncommon even among those who offer themselves for 'honours' in the School of English.

But in early times there was no such confusion. The Brettas and the Walas were the same. The use of the latter term, which was applied by the English, is thus of considerable importance in estimating the linguistic situation of the early period.

It seems clear that the word *walh, wealh* which the English brought with them was a common Germanic name for a man of what we should call Celtic speech.[17] But in all the recorded Germanic languages in which it appears it was also applied to the speakers of Latin. That may be due, as is usually assumed, to the fact that Latin eventually occupied most of the areas of Celtic speech within the knowledge of Germanic peoples. But it is, I think, also in part a linguistic judgement, reflecting that very similarity in style of Latin and Gallo-Brittonic that I have already mentioned. It did not occur to anyone to call a Goth a *walh* even if he was long settled in Italy or in Gaul. Though 'foreigner' is often given as the first gloss on *wealh* in Anglo-Saxon dictionaries this is misleading. The word was not applied to foreigners of Germanic speech, nor to those of alien tongues, Lapps, Finns, Esthonians, Lithuanians, Slavs, or Huns, with whom the Germanic-speaking peoples came into contact in early times. (But borrowed in Old Slavonic in the form *vlachŭ* it was applied to the Roumanians.) It was, therefore, basically a word of linguistic import; and in itself implied in its users more linguistic curiosity and discrimination than the simple stupidity of the Greek *barbaros*.

Its special association by the English with the Britons was a product of their invasion of Britain. It contained a linguistic judgement, but it did not discriminate between the speakers of Latin and the speakers of British. But with the perishing of the spoken Latin of the island, and the concentration of English interests in Britain, *walh* and its derivatives became synonymous with *Brett* and *brittisc*, and in the event replaced them.[18]

In the same way the use of *wealh* for slave is also due solely to the situation in Britain. But again the gloss 'slave' is probably misleading. Though the word *slave* itself shows that a national name can become generalized in this sense, I doubt if this was true of *wealh*. The Old English word for 'slave' in general remained *þeow*, which was used of slaves in other countries or of other origin. The use of *wealh*, apart from the legal status to which surviving elements of the conquered population were no doubt often reduced, must always have implied recognition of British origin. Such elements, though incorporated in the domain of an English or Saxon lord, must long have remained 'not English', and with this difference preservation in a measure of their British speech may have endured longer than is supposed.

This is a controversial point, and I do not deal with the question of place-names, such as Walton, Walcot, and Walworth, that may be supposed to contain this old word *walh*.[19] But the incorporation in the domains conquered by the English-speaking invaders of relatively large numbers of the previous inhabitants is not denied; and their linguistic absorption must have steadily proceeded, except in special circumstances.

What effect would that have, did that have, on English? It had none that is visible for a long time. Not that we should expect it. The records of Old English are mainly learned or aristocratic; we have no transcripts of village-talk. For any glimpse of what was going on beneath the cultivated surface we must wait until the Old English period of letters is over.

Unheeded language without pride or sense of ancestry may change quickly in new circumstances. But the English did not know that they were 'barbarians', and the language that they brought with them had an ancient cultivation, at any rate in its tradition of verse. It is thus to the appearance of linguistic class distinctions that we should look for evidence of the effects of conquest and the linguistic absorption of people of other language, largely into the lowest social strata.

I know of only one passage that seems to hint at something of the kind. It refers to a surprisingly early date, A.D. 679. In that year the Battle of the Trent was fought between the Mercians and Northumbrians. Bede relates how a Northumbrian noble called Imma was captured by the Mercians and pretended to be a man of poor or servile class. But he was eventually recognized as a noble by his captors, as Bede reports, not only by his bearing but *by his speech*.

The question of the survival in 'England' of British population and still more of British forms of speech is, of course, a matter of debate, differing in the evidence and the terms of the debate from region to region. For instance, Devonshire, in spite of its British name, has been said on the evidence collected by the Place-names Survey to appear as one of the most English of the counties (onomastically). But William of Malmesbury in his *Gesta Regum* says that Exeter was divided between the English and the Welsh as late as the reign of Athelstan.

Well known, and much used in debate and in the dating of sound-changes, are the Welsh place-names given in Asser's *Life of Alfred*: such as *Guilou* and *Uisc* for the rivers Wiley and Exe, or *Cairuuis* for Exeter. Since Asser was a native of South Wales (as we should now call it), Welsh was presumably his native language, though he may eventually have learned as much English, shall we say, as his friend the king learned of Latin. These names in Asser have been used (e.g. by Stevenson) as evidence for the survival of Welsh speech even as far east as Wiltshire as late as the end of the ninth century.

With the mention of Asser I will return, before I close, to the point that I mentioned when I began: the interests and uses of Welsh and its philology to students of English. I do not enter into the controversy concerning the genuineness of Asser's *Life of Alfred*, whether it is a document belonging approximately to A.D. 900, as it purports to be, or is in fact a composition of a much later date. But it is clear that in this debate we have a prime example of the contact of the two schools of learning: Welsh historical and philological scholarship and English. Arguments for and against the genuineness of this document are based on the forms of the Welsh names in it, and an estimate of their cogency requires at least some acquaintance with the problems attending the history of Welsh. Yet the document is a life of one of the most remarkable and interesting Englishmen, and no English scholar can be indifferent to the debate.

To many, perhaps to most people outside the small company of the great scholars, past and present, 'Celtic' of any sort is, nonetheless, a magic bag, into which anything may be put, and out of which almost anything may come. Thus I read recently a review of a book by Sir Gavin de Beer, and, in what appeared to be a citation from the original,[20] I noted the following opinion on the river-name *Arar* (Livy) and *Araros* (Polybius): 'Now Arar derives from the Celtic root meaning running water which occurs also in many English river-names like Avon.' It is a strange world in which *Avon* and *Araros* can have the same 'root' (a vegetable analogy still much loved by the non-philological when being wise about words). Catching the lunatic infection, one's mind runs on to the River Arrow, and even to arrowroot, to Ararat, and the descent into Avernus. Anything is possible in the fabulous Celtic twilight, which is not so much a twilight of the gods as of the reason.

That was perhaps, in this time and place, an unnecessary aside. I am addressing those of rational mind and philological learning; but especially those who in spite of these qualifications have not yet for themselves discovered the interests and the uses of Welsh and its philology.

I have already glanced at the interest of this study to Romance philology, or the later history of spoken Latin, and of the special importance that it has for Anglo-Saxon. But the student of English as a Germanic tongue will find many things that throw new light on his familiar material; and some curious similarities interesting to note, even if they are dismissed as parallels produced by chance.

It would not be my place to treat them extensively, even if I had the time. I will only refer to two points in illustration. A traveller should at least produce some samples.

As an example of a curious parallelism I will mention a peculiar feature of the Old English substantive verb, the modern 'be'. This had two distinct forms of the 'present': A, used only of the actual present, and B, used only as a future or consuetudinal. The B functions were expressed by forms beginning with *b-*, which did not appear in the true present: thus, *bīo, bist, bið*; pl. *bīoð*. The meaning of *bið* was 'is (naturally, always, or habitually)' or 'will be'.

Now this system is peculiar to Old English. It is not found

in any other Germanic language, not even in those most closely related to English. The association with the *b*-forms of two different functions that have no necessary logical connexion is also notable. But I mention this feature of Old English morphology here only because the same distinction of functions is associated with similar phonetic forms in Welsh.

In Welsh one finds a true present without *b*-forms, and a tense with a *b*-stem used both as a future and a consuetudinal.[21] The 3 sg. of the latter tense is *bydd* from earlier **bið*.[22] The resemblance between this and the OE form is perhaps made more remarkable if we observe that the short vowel of OE is difficult to explain and cannot be a regular development from earlier Germanic, whereas in Welsh it is regularly derived.

This similarity may be dismissed as accidental. The peculiarity of OE may be held to depend simply on preservation in the English dialect of a feature later lost in others; the anomalous short vowel of *bist* and *bið* may be explained as analogical.[23] The OE verb is in any case peculiar in other ways not paralleled by Welsh (the 2 sg. of the true present *earð*, later *eart*, is not found outside English). It will still remain notable, none the less, that this preservation occurred in Britain and in a point in which the usage of the native language agreed. It will be a morphological parallel to the phonetic agreement, noted above, seen in the English preservation of *þ* and *w*.

But this is not the full story. The Northumbrian dialect of Old English uses as the plural of tense B the form *biðun, bioðun*. Now this must be an innovation developed on British soil. Its invention was strictly unnecessary (since the older plural remained sufficiently distinct from the singular), and its method of formation was, from the point of view of English morphology, wholly anomalous.[24] Its similarity (especially in apparent relation to the 3 sg.) to Welsh *byddant* is obvious. (The still closer Welsh 1 pl. *byddwn* would not have had, probably, this inflexion in Old Welsh.)

In my second example I return to a matter of phonology, but one of the highest importance. One of the principal phonetic developments in Old English, which eventually changed its whole vocalic system and had profound effect upon its morphology, was that group of changes usually called by us *umlaut* or 'mutation'. These changes are, however, closely paralleled by the changes which in Welsh grammar are usually called 'affection', thus disguising their fundamental similarity, though in detail and in chronology there may be considerable differences between the processes in the two languages.

The most important branch of these changes is *i*-mutation or *i*-affection. The problems attending their explanation in English and in Welsh are similar (for instance, the question of the varying parts played by anticipation or 'vowel harmony' and by epenthesis), and the study of them together throws light on both. Also, since the phonology of the place-names borrowed by the English in Britain is of great importance for the dating of *i*-mutation in their language, it is not only desirable but necessary for the English philologist to acquaint himself with the evidence and the theories on both sides. The English process is also important to the Welsh philologist for similar reasons.

The north-west of Europe, in spite of its underlying differences of linguistic heritage – Goidelic, Brittonic, Gallic; its varieties of Germanic; and the powerful intrusion of spoken Latin – is as it were a single philological province, a region so interconnected in race, culture, history, and linguistic fusions that its departmental philologies cannot flourish in isolation. I have cited the processes of *i*-mutation/*i*-affection as a striking example of this fact. And we who live in this island may reflect that it was on this same soil that both were accomplished.[25] There are, of course, many other features of Welsh that should have a special interest for students of English. I will briefly mention one before I conclude. Welsh is full of loan-words from or through English. This long series, beginning in Anglo-Saxon times and continuing down to the present day, offers to any philologist interesting illustrations of the processes of borrowing by ear and spoken word,[26] besides providing some curious features of its own. The historian of English, so often engaged in investigating the loan-words in his own too hospitable tongue, should find its study of special interest; though in fact it has been mainly left to Welsh scholars.

The earlier loans are perhaps of chief interest, since they sometimes preserve words, or forms, or meanings that have long ceased to exist in English. For instance *hongian* 'hang, dangle', *cusan* 'a kiss', *bettws* 'chapel (subordinate church)' and also 'a secluded spot', derived from OE *hongian*, *cyssan*, (*ge*)*bedhūs*. The

Englishman will note that the long-lost -*an* and -*ian* of Old English infinitives once struck the ears of Welshmen long ago; but he will be surprised perhaps to find that -*ian* became a loan-element in itself, and was added to various other verbs, even developing a special form -*ial*.[27] He cannot therefore, alas, at once assume that such words as *tincian* 'tinkle' or *mwmlian* 'mumble' are evidence for the existence in Old English (*tincian, *mumelian) of words first actually recorded in Middle English.

Even the basest and most recent loans have, however, their interest. In their exaggerated reflection of the corruptions and reductions of careless speech, they remind one of the divergence between Latin and the 'Vulgar' or 'Spoken Latin' that we deduce from Welsh or French. *Potatoes* has produced *tatws*; and in recent loans *submit* > *smit-io*, and *cement* > *sment*. But this is a large subject with numerous problems, and I am not competent to do more than point out to the English that it is one worthy of their attention. For myself, as a West-Midlander, the constant reflection, in the Welsh borrowings of older date, of the forms of West-Midland English is an added attraction.

But no language is justly studied merely as an aid to other purposes. It will in fact better serve other purposes, philological or historical, when it is studied for love, for itself.

It is recorded in the tale of *Lludd a Llefelys* that King Lludd had the island measured in its length and its breadth, and in Oxford (very justly) he found the point of centre. But none the less the centre of the study of Welsh for its own sake is now in Wales; though it should flourish here, where we have not only a chair of Celtic graced by its occupant, but in Jesus College a society of Welsh connexions by foundation and tradition, the possessor among other things of one of the treasures of Medieval Welsh: The Red Book of Hergest.[28] For myself I would say that more than the interest and uses of the study of Welsh as an adminicle of English philology, more than the practical linguist's desire to acquire a knowledge of Welsh for the enlargement of his experience, more even than the interest and worth of the literature, older and newer, that is preserved in it, these two things seem important: Welsh is of this soil, this island, the senior language of the men of Britain; and Welsh is beautiful.

I will not attempt to say now what I mean by calling a language as a whole 'beautiful', nor in what ways Welsh seems to me beautiful; for the mere recording of a personal and if you will subjective perception of strong aesthetic pleasure in contact with Welsh, heard or read,[29] is sufficient for my conclusion.

The basic pleasure in the phonetic elements of a language and in the style of their patterns, and then in a higher dimension, pleasure in the association of these word-forms with meanings, is of fundamental importance. This pleasure is quite distinct from the practical knowledge of a language, and not the same as an analytic understanding of its structure. It is simpler, deeper-rooted, and yet more immediate than the enjoyment of literature. Though it may be allied to some of the elements in the appreciation of verse, it does not need any poets, other than the nameless artists who composed the language. It can be strongly felt in the simple contemplation of a vocabulary, or even in a string of names.

If I were to say 'Language is related to our total psycho-physical make-up', I might seem to announce a truism in a priggish modern jargon. I will at any rate say that language – and more so as expression than as communication – is a natural product of our humanity. But it is therefore also a product of our individuality. We each have our own personal linguistic potential: we each have a *native language*. But that is not the language that we speak, our cradle-tongue, the first-learned. Linguistically we all wear ready-made clothes, and our native language comes seldom to expression, save perhaps by pulling at the ready-made till it sits a little easier. But though it may be buried, it is never wholly extinguished, and contact with other languages may stir it deeply.

My chief point here is to emphasize the difference between the first-learned language, the language of custom, and an individual's native language, his inherent linguistic predilections: not to deny that he will share many of these with others of his community. He will share them, no doubt, in proportion as he shares other elements in his make-up.[30]

Most English-speaking people, for instance, will admit that *cellar door* is 'beautiful', especially if dissociated from its sense (and from its spelling). More beautiful than, say, *sky*, and far more beautiful than *beautiful*. Well then, in Welsh for me *cellar doors* are extraordinarily frequent, and moving to the higher dimension, the words in which there is pleasure in the contemplation of the association of form and sense are abundant.

The nature of this *pleasure* is difficult, perhaps impossible, to analyse. It cannot, of course, be discovered by structural analysis. No analysis will make one either like or dislike a language, even if it makes more precise some of the features of style that are pleasing or distasteful. The pleasure is possibly felt most strongly in the study of a 'foreign' or second-learned language; but if so that may be attributed to two things: the learner meets in the other language *desirable* features that his own or first-learned speech has denied to him; and in any case he escapes from the dulling of usage, especially inattentive usage.

But these predilections are not the product of second-learned languages; though they may be modified by them: experience must affect the practice or appreciation of any art. My cradle-tongue was English (with a dash of Afrikaans). French and Latin together were my first experience of second-learned language. Latin – to express now sensations that are still vivid in memory though inexpressible when received – seemed so *normal* that pleasure or distaste was equally inapplicable. French[31] has given to me less of this pleasure than any other language with which I have sufficient acquaintance for this judgement. The fluidity of Greek, punctuated by hardness, and with its surface glitter, captivated me, even when I met it first only in Greek names, of history or mythology, and I tried to invent a language that would embody the Greekness of Greek (so far as it came through that garbled form); but part of the attraction was antiquity and alien remoteness (from me): it did not touch home. Spanish came my way by chance and greatly attracted me. It gave me strong pleasure, and still does – far more than any other Romance language. But incipient 'philology' was, I think, an adulterant: the preservation in spite of change of so great a measure of the linguistic feeling and style of Latin was certainly an ingredient in my pleasure, an historical and not purely aesthetic element.

Gothic was the first to take me by storm, to move my heart. It was the first of the old Germanic languages that I ever met. I have since mourned the loss of Gothic literature. I did not then.

The contemplation of the vocabulary in *A Primer of the Gothic Language* was enough: a sensation at least as full of delight as first looking into Chapman's *Homer*. Though I did not write a sonnet about it. I tried to invent Gothic words.

I have, in this peculiar sense, studied ('tasted' would be better) other languages since. Of all save one among them the most overwhelming pleasure was provided by Finnish, and I have never quite got over it.

But all the time there had been another call – bound to win in the end, though long baulked by sheer lack of opportunity. I heard it coming out of the west. It struck at me in the names on coal-trucks; and drawing nearer, it flickered past on station-signs, a flash of strange spelling and a hint of a language old and yet alive; even in an *adeiladwyd 1887*, ill-cut on a stone-slab, it pierced my linguistic heart. 'Late Modern Welsh' (bad Welsh to some). Nothing more than an 'it was built', though it marked the end of a long story from daub and wattle in some archaic village to a sombre chapel under the dark hills. Not that I knew that then. It was easier to find books to instruct one in any far alien tongue of Africa or India than in the language that still clung to the western mountains and the shores that look out to Iwerddon. Easier at any rate for an English boy being drilled in the study of languages that (whatever Joseph Wright may have thought of Celtic) offered more hope of profit.

But it was different in Oxford. There one can find books, and not only those one's tutor recommends. My college, I know, and the shade of Walter Skeat, I surmise, was shocked when the only prize I ever won (there was only one other competitor), the Skeat Prize for English at Exeter College, was spent on Welsh.

Under severe pressure to enlarge my apprentice knowledge of Latin and Greek, I studied the old Germanic languages; when generously allowed to use for this barbaric purpose emoluments intended for the classics, I turned at last to Medieval Welsh. It would not be of much use if I tried to illustrate by examples the pleasure that I got there. For, of course, the pleasure is not solely concerned with any word, any 'sound-pattern + meaning', by itself, but with its fitness also to a whole style. Even single notes of a large music may please in their place, but one cannot illustrate this pleasure (not even to those who have once heard the music) by repeating them in isolation. It is true that language differs from any 'large music' in that its whole is never heard, or at any rate is not heard through in a single period of concentration, but is apprehended from excerpts and examples. But to those who know Welsh at all a selection of words would seem random and absurd; to those who do not it would be inadequate under the lecturer's limitations, and if printed unnecessary.

Perhaps I might say just this – for it is not an analysis of Welsh, or of myself, that I am attempting, but an assertion of a feeling of pleasure, and of satisfaction (as of a want fulfilled) – it is the ordinary words for ordinary things that in Welsh I find so pleasing. *Nef* may be no better than *heaven*, but *wybren* is more pleasing than *sky*. Beyond that what can one do? For a passage of good Welsh, even if read by a Welshman, is for this purpose useless. Those who understand him must already have experienced this pleasure, or have missed it for ever. Those who do not cannot yet receive it. A translation is of no avail. For this pleasure is felt most immediately and acutely in the moment of association: that is in the reception (or imagination) of a word-form which is felt to have a certain style, and the attribution to it of a meaning which is not received through it. I could only speak, or better write and speak and translate, a long list: *adar, alarch, eryr*; *tân, dwfr, awel, gwynt, niwl, glaw*; *haul, lloer, sêr*; *arglwydd, gwas, morwyn, dyn*; *cadarn, gwan, caled, meddal, garw, llyfn, llym, swrth*; *glas, melyn, brith*,[32] and so on – and yet fail to communicate the pleasure. But even the more long-winded and bookish words are commonly in the same style, if a little diluted. In Welsh there is not as a rule the discrepancy that there is so often in English between words of this sort and the words of full aesthetic life, the flesh and bone of the language. Welsh *annealladwy, dideimladrwydd, amhechadurus, atgyfodiad*, and the like are far more Welsh, not only as being analysable, but in style, than *incomprehensible, insensibility, impeccable*, or *resurrection* are English.

If I were pressed to give any example of a feature of this style, not only as an observable feature but as a source of pleasure to myself, I should mention the fondness for nasal consonants, especially the much-favoured *n*, and the frequency with which word-patterns are made with the soft and less sonorous *w* and

the voiced spirants *f* and *dd* contrasted with the nasals: *nant,
meddiant, afon, llawenydd, cenfigen, gwanwyn, gwenyn, crafanc,* to set
down a few at random. A very characteristic word is *gogoniant*
'glory':

> *Gogoniant i'r Tad ac i'r Mab ac i'r Ysbryd Glân,
> megis yr oedd yn y dechrau, y mae'r awr hon, ac y
> bydd yn wastad, yn oes oesoedd. Amen.*

As I have said, these tastes and predilections which are revealed
to us in contact with languages not learned in infancy – *O felix
peccatum Babel!* – are certainly significant: an aspect in linguistic
terms of our individual natures. And since these are largely
historical products, the predilections must be so too. My pleasure
in the Welsh linguistic style, though it may have an individual
colouring, would not, therefore, be expected to be peculiar to
myself among the English. It is not. It is present in many of them.
It lies dormant, I believe, in many more of those who today
live in Lloegr and speak Saesneg. It may be shown only in
uneasy jokes about Welsh spelling and place-names; it may be
stirred by contacts no nearer than the names in Arthurian
romance that echo faintly the Celtic patterns of their origin; or
it may with more opportunity become vividly aware.[33]

Modern Welsh is not, of course, identical with the predilections
of such people. It is not identical with mine. But it remains
probably closer to them than any other living language. For
many of us it rings a bell, or rather it stirs deep harp-strings in
our linguistic nature. In other words: for satisfaction and therefore
for delight – and not for imperial policy – we are still 'British' at
heart. It is the native language to which in unexplored desire
we would still go home.

So, hoping that with such words I may appease the shade of
Charles James O'Donnell, I will end – echoing in rejoinder the
envoi of Salesbury's Preface:[34]

> Dysgwn y llon Frythoneg!
> Doeth yw ei dysg, da iaith deg.

NOTES

1 Some of his work is contained in B.M. MS. Add. 31922, together with composi-
tions by Henry and his friends.

2 The names from which *Cerdic* and *Ceadwalla* were derived may be assumed to have
had some such late British form as *Car[a]dīc* and *Cadwallŏn*. In the West-Saxon
forms the accent was shifted back to accord with the normal Germanic initial
stress. In *Ceadwalla*, and probably in *Cerdic*, the initial *c* had been fronted, and the
pronunciation intended was probably nearer modern English *ch* than *k*. The genealogy begins with *Cerdic* in the sense that this name is given to the ancestor of the
later kings who first landed in Britain in A.D. 495 (according to the Chronicle) at a
place called *Cerdices ora*. The relation of this account to real events is debatable.
The borrowing of names must at least indicate close contacts. If *Cerdic* actually
existed, the family to which he belonged can hardly have come first to Britain
in his time. But when we come to *Cadda* in the fourth generation after *Cerdic*,
and *Ceadwalla* in the sixth (in the late seventh century), the situation is quite
different.

3 After the Battle of Thetford in 1004: *hi naefre wyrsan handplegan on Angelcynne ne
gemetton þonne Ulfcytel him to brohte* (Chronicle C and D).

4 Scotland presents different problems, which do not concern us, except as afford-
ing a glimpse of the fact that the celticizing in language of this island was at least
as complicated a process as that which eventually produced 'English'. Of the
survival of a pre-Celtic and non-Indo-European language in 'Pictland' the most
recent discussion is that of Professor Jackson in ch. vi of *The Problem of the Picts*
(ed. F. Wainwright, 1955).

5 Jackson, op. cit., p. 156.

6 The 'Belgic' invasion did not resemble the Scandinavian invasions in routes or
points of impact. Actually in these respects it strikingly resembled the invasion of
those elements in the 'Anglo-Saxon' immigration to whom the debatable name of
'Jutes' is given.

7 In the days of Ulphilas the language of Scandinavia must have been in many
respects far more archaic.

8 Especially aesthetically. In Gothic we are afforded specimens of a real language,
and though unfortunately these do not represent its free and natural use, we can
perceive in them a language of beautiful and well-ordered word-form, well
fitted for the liturgical use to which it was at one time put.

9 The shifts of language naturally do not present sharp boundaries between 'periods',
but this second or 'middle' period of English ended in the thirteenth century; after
which the third period began. Though this is not the division usually made.

10 These features are exemplified in *ciwdod* (*cīuitāt-em*), *ciwed* (*cīuitās*), *gem* (*gemma*);
pader (*Pāter noster*) beside *yscawl*, *ysgol* (*scăla*); *ffydd* (*fīdes*) beside *swydd* (*sēdēs*).

11 Whereas the remigrant British, the Breton of Armorica, has changed *þ* (*th*) to *s*
and later *z*.

12 Though it may be noted that many of the things that strike the modern Saxon as
insuperably odd and difficult about Welsh have no importance for the days of the
first contacts of British and English speech. Chief among these are, I suppose, the
alteration of the initial consonants of words (which revolts his Germanic feeling
for the initial sound of a word as a prime feature of its identity); and the sounds of
ll (voiceless *l*) and *ch* (voiceless back spirant). But the consonant-alterations are due
to a grammatical use of the results of a phonetic process (soft mutation or lenition)
that was probably only just beginning in the days of Vortigern. Old English
possessed both a voiceless *l* and the voiceless back spirant *ch*.

13 Alfred was no doubt an exceptional person. But we see in him a case that shows
how even bitter war may not wholly destroy the desire to know. He was engaged in a desperate conflict with an enemy that came very near to robbing him

of all his patrimony, yet he reports his conversations with a Norseman, Ohthere, about the geography and economics of Norway, a land that he certainly did not intend to invade; and it is clear from Ohthere's account that the king also asked some questions about languages.

14   This may seem probable enough; but it does not promise easy evidence to the historical philologist. He will be faced with Latin incorporated in Welsh, and in English (each with its own phonetic history), and with different kinds of Latin on either side of the Channel.

15   We here see the word applied to a tongue that was though Celtic not British. *Wealhstod* became the ordinary word in Old English for either an interpreter or a translator; but that was at a much later date. It seems never, however, to have been applied to communications with the 'Danes'.

16   Latin Life, ch. xxxiv. 'What follows occurred in the days of Coenred, king of the Mercians [704–9], when the pestiferous British foes of the Saxons were embroiling the English in piratical raids and organized devastation. One night at time of cock-crow, when according to his custom the hero Guthlac of blessed memory began his vigils, suddenly as if he were lost in a trance he seemed to hear the roaring of a tumultuous crowd. At that he started up from his light sleep and rushed from the cell where he sat. Standing with ears cocked he recognized words and the native mode of speech of British soldiers coming from the roof; for when in former times he had been isolated among them on his various expeditions he had learned to understand their cacophonous manner of speaking. Just as he had made sure that it came through the thatch of the roof, at that moment his whole settlement seemed to burst into flames.' The devils then caught Guthlac with their spears.

17   Its origin is not of importance in this context. It is commonly supposed to be the same as that of the Celtic tribal name represented in Latin sources as *Volcae*: that is derived from it at a time sufficiently early to allow it to be germanicized in form.

18   Traces remain of the sense 'Romans'. *Widsith*, which contains many memories of pre-migration days, has an archaic form *mid Rumwalum*, and mentions *Wala rice* as the realm ruled by *Casere* (Caesar); *weala sunderriht* and *reht Romwala* are found in two glosses on *ius Quiritum*. But these are not normal uses. Later applications to Gaul (France) are probably not derived from English tradition.

The men who established themselves at Richard's castle in Hereford in 1052 were called *Normanni* and *þa Frencyscan*, but in the Laud Chronicle *þa welisce* (*waelisce*) men. And when Edward the Confessor returned from abroad the same Chronicle says that he came *of Weal-lande*, meaning Normandy. But these are not natural English uses and are in fact simply items of the influence of Norse upon the English of the late period. In Norse *valskr* and *Valland* had continued to be applied specifically to Gaul. There is other evidence of the influence of Norse in the same part of the same Chronicle: *woldon raedan on hi* (always mistranslated 'plot against') is an anglicization of Norse *ráða á* 'to go for, to attack'.

19   They were generally supposed to do so; but it has been shown that in fact many contain either *weall* 'wall' or *weald* 'forest'. But scepticism has in reaction probably swung too far. In any case a number of these names must still be allowed to contain *walh*, among them several in the east far from Wales: Surrey, Hertfordshire, Norfolk, and Suffolk. When these names were first made they must have referred to groups of people who were not regarded as English, but were recognized as British; and language must have been the principal characteristic by which this was judged. But how long that situation lasted is another matter.

20   For my purpose it does not matter at all whether Sir Gavin or his reviewer was the author of the remark: both were posing as scholars.

21   The association of these two dissimilar functions is again notable. Old Irish uses *b*-forms in these two functions, but distinguishes between future and consuetudinal in inflexion. The Welsh tense (*byddaf*, &c.) as a whole blends the two functions, though the older language had also a form of the 3 sg. *bid* (*bit*) limited to consuetudinal use. The difference of function is not yet fully realized by Anglo-Saxon

scholars. The older dictionaries and grammars ignore it, and even in recent grammars it is not clearly stated; the consuetudinal is usually overlooked, though traces of it survive in English as late as the language of Chaucer (in *beth* as consuetudinal sg. and pl.).

22 The Irish, Welsh, and English forms relate to older *bī, biį-* (cf. Latin *fīs, fit*, &c.). The development from *biį-* to *bið-* in Welsh is due to a consonantal strengthening of *i* which began far back in British. When *ii* reached the stage *ið* is not known, but a date about A.D. 500 seems probable.

23 The influence of the short *ī* in the forms of the true present might be held responsible. In a pre-English stage these would have been *im, is, ist (is)*.

24 The addition of a plural ending (normally belonging to the past tense) to an inflected form of the 3 sg. In this way *bið̆un* differs from the extended form *sindun* made from the old pl. *sind*. The latter was already pl. and its ending *-nd* could not be recognized as an inflexion, whereas the *ið* of *bið* was the normal ending of the 3 sg.

25 Some philologists (e.g. Förster, in *Der Flussname Thenise*) now hold that the English process belonged to the seventh century and was not completed till the beginning of the eighth; it thus belonged wholly to Britain and did not begin until after the completion of the first stage of British *i*-affection (the 'final *i*-affection'). But no linguistic matters are simple in this region. The beginnings of the process in English must lie back in pre-invasion times, whatever may be true of its results, or of any of its vocalic effects sufficient to be recognized in spellings. For this process is not peculiar to the English dialect of Germanic, transferred from its native soil west to Celtic Britain. Indeed the native soil of English seems to have been a focus of this phonetic disturbance (in its inception one primarily affecting consonants). Northwards it is found attacking the Scandinavian dialects with almost equal severity; though southwards its effects were more limited or later. Certainly moving west, within the area of the disturbance, the process was not retarded in English – what would have happened if it had moved southwards is another matter – and in the event English became the language of *i*-mutation *par excellence* and its results were far more extensive than in any form of British. In British, for instance, long vowels were not affected; but in English nearly all long vowels and diphthongs were mutated.

26 For the most part. The cultivated written language of Wales has naturally, at all times, been less open to invasion. Neither has cultivated English been the chief source of the loans.

27 Probably in origin a dissimilation where the verb stem contained nasals: as in *tincian/tincial* (ME. *tinken*); *mwmial, mwmlian* 'mumble'.

28 It also possesses in MS. Jesus Coll. Oxford 29 a copy of the early Middle English *Owl and Nightingale*, which in its history illustrates in other terms the progress of English words. Written in the south-east, it passed to the West Midlands and there received a western dialectal dress; but it was preserved in Wales, and reached Jesus College in the seventeenth century from Glamorgan.

29 For there is concomitant pleasure of the eye in an orthography that is home-grown with a language, though most spelling-reformers are insensitive to it.

30 A difficult proportion to discover without knowing his ancestral history through indefinite generations. Children of the same two parents may differ markedly in this respect.

31 I refer to Modern French; and I am speaking primarily of word-forms, and those in relation to meaning, especially in basic words. *Incomprehensibility* and its like are only art forms in a diluted degree in any language, hardly at all in English.

32 Each, of course, with immediately following 'sense'.

33 If I may once more refer to my work, *The Lord of the Rings*, in evidence: the names of persons and places in this story were mainly composed on patterns deliberately modelled on those of Welsh (closely similar but not identical). This element in the tale has given perhaps more pleasure to more readers than anything else in it.

34 Dyscwch nes oesswch Saesnec / Doeth yw e dysc da iaith dec.

A SECRET VICE

Some of you may have heard that there was, a year or more ago, a Congress in Oxford, an Esperanto Congress; or you may not have heard. Personally I am a believer in an 'artificial' language, at any rate for Europe – a believer, that is, in its desirability, as the one thing antecedently necessary for uniting Europe, before it is swallowed by non-Europe; as well as for many other good reasons – a believer in its possibility because the history of the world seems to exhibit, as far as I know it, both an increase in human control of (or influence upon) the uncontrollable, and a progressive widening of the range of more or less uniform languages. Also I particularly like Esperanto, not least because it is the creation ultimately of one man, not a philologist, and is therefore something like a 'human language bereft of the inconveniences due to too many successive cooks' – which is as good a description of the ideal artificial language (in a particular sense) as I can give.[1]

No doubt the Esperantist propaganda touched on all these points. I cannot say. But it is not important, because my concern is not with that kind of artificial language at all. You must tolerate the stealthy approach. It is habitual. But in any case my real subject tonight is a stealthy subject. Indeed nothing less embarrassing than the *unveiling* in public of a secret vice. Had I boldly and brazenly begun right on my theme I might have called my paper a plea for a New Art, or a New Game, if occasional and painful confidences had not given me grave cause to suspect that the vice, though secret, is common; and the art (or game), if new at all, has at least been discovered by a good many other people independently.

The practitioners are all so bashful, however, that they hardly ever show their works to one another, so none of them know who are the geniuses at the game, or who are the splendid 'primitives' – whose neglected works, found in old drawers, may possibly be purchased at great price (not from the authors, or their heirs and assigns!) for American museums, in after days when the 'art' has become acknowledged. I won't say 'general'! – it is too arduous and slow: I doubt if any devotee could produce more than one real masterpiece, plus at most a few brilliant sketches and outlines, in a life-time.

I shall never forget a little man – smaller than myself – whose name I have forgotten, revealing himself by accident as a devotee, in a moment of extreme ennui, in a dirty wet marquee filled with trestle tables smelling of stale mutton fat, crowded with (mostly) depressed and wet creatures. We were listening to somebody lecturing on map-reading, or camp-hygiene, or the art of sticking a fellow through without (in defiance of Kipling) bothering who God sent the bill to; rather we were trying to avoid listening, though the Guards' English, and voice, is penetrating. The man next to me said suddenly in a dreamy voice: 'Yes, I think I shall express the accusative case by a prefix!'

A memorable remark! Of course by repeating it I have let the cat, so carefully hidden, out of its bag, or at least revealed the whiskers. But we won't bother about that for a moment. Just consider the splendour of the words! '*I* shall express the accusative case.' Magnificent! Not 'it is expressed', nor even the more shambling 'it is sometimes expressed', nor the grim 'you must learn how it is expressed'. What a pondering of alternatives within one's choice before the final decision in favour of the daring and unusual prefix, so personal, so attractive; the final solution of some element in a design that had hitherto proved refractory. Here were no base considerations of the 'practical', the easiest for the 'modern mind', or for the million – only a question of taste, a satisfaction of a personal pleasure, a private sense of fitness.

As he said his words the little man's smile was full of a great delight, as of a poet or painter seeing suddenly the solution of a hitherto clumsy passage. Yet he proved as close as an oyster. I never gathered any further details of his secret grammar; and military arrangements soon separated us never to meet again (up to now at any rate). But I gathered that this queer creature – ever afterwards a little bashful after inadvertently revealing his secret – cheered and comforted himself in the tedium and squalors of 'training under canvas' by composing a language, a personal system and symphony that no else was to study or to hear. Whether he did this in his head (as only the great masters can), or on paper, I never knew. It is incidentally one of the attractions of this hobby that it needs so little apparatus! How far he ever proceeded in his composition, I never heard. Probably he was blown to bits in the very moment of deciding upon some ravishing method of indicating the subjunctive. Wars are not favourable to delicate pleasures.

But he was not the only one of his kind. I would venture to assert that, even if I did not know it from direct evidence. It is inevitable, if you 'educate' most people, many of them more or less artistic or creative, not solely receptive, by teaching them languages. Few philologists even are devoid of the making instinct – but they often know but one thing well; they must build with the bricks they have. There must be a secret hierarchy of such folk. Where the little man stood in this, I do not know. High, I should guess. What range of accomplishment there is among these hidden craftsmen, I can only surmise – and I surmise the range runs, if one only knew, from the crude chalk-scrawl of the village schoolboy to the heights of palaeolithic or bushman art (or beyond). Its development to perfection must none the less certainly be prevented by its solitariness, the lack of interchange, open rivalry, study or imitation of others' technique.

I have had some glimpses of the lower stages. I knew two people once – *two* is a rare phenomenon – who constructed a language called *Animalic* almost entirely out of English animal, bird, and fish names; and they conversed in it fluently to the dismay of bystanders. I was never fully instructed in it, nor a proper Animalic-speaker; but I remember out of the rag-bag of memory that *dog nightingale woodpecker forty* meant 'you are an ass'. Crude (in some ways) in the extreme. There is here, again a rare phenomenon, a complete absence of phonematic invention which at least in embryo is usually an element in all such constructions. *Donkey* was *40* in the numeral system, whence *forty* acquired a converse meaning.

I had better say at once: 'Don't mistake the cat which is slowly emerging from the bag!' I am not dealing with that curious phenomenon 'nursery-languages', as they are sometimes called –

the people I quote were of course young children and went on to more advanced forms later – some of which languages are as individual and peculiar as this one, while some acquire a wide distribution and pass from nursery to nursery and school to school, even country to country, in a mysterious way without any adult assistance, though new learners usually believe themselves in possession of a secret. Like the insertion type of 'language'. I can still remember my surprise after acquiring with assiduous practice great fluency in one of these 'languages' my horror at over-hearing two entirely strange boys conversing in it. This is a very interesting matter – connected with cant, argot, jargon, and all kinds of human undergrowth, and also with games and many other things. But I am not concerned with it now, even though it has affinities with my topic A purely linguistic element, which is my subject, is found sometimes even in this childish make-believe. The distinction – the test by which one can discriminate between the species I am talking about, from the species I am leaving aside – lies, I think, in this. The argot-group are not primarily concerned at all with relations of sound and sense; they are not (except casually and accidentally like real languages) artistic – if it is possible to be artistic inadvertently. They are 'practical', more severely so even than real languages, actually or in pretence. They satisfy either the need for limiting one's intelligibility within circles whose bounds you can more or less control or estimate, or the fun found in this limitation. They serve the needs of a secret and persecuted society, or the queer instinct for pretending you belong to one. The means being 'practical' are crude – they are usually grabbed randomly by the young or by rude persons without apprenticeship in a difficult art, often with little aptitude for it or interest in it.

That being so, I would not have quoted the 'animalic'-children, if I had not discovered that secrecy was no part of their object. Anyone could learn the tongue who bothered. It was not used deliberately to bewilder or to hoodwink the adult. A new element comes in. The fun must have been found in something else than the secret-society or the initiation business. Where? I imagine in using the linguistic faculty, strong in children and excited by lessons consisting largely of new tongues, purely for amusement and pleasure. There is something attractive in the thought –

indeed I think it gives food for various thoughts, and I hope that, though I shall hardly indicate them, they will occur to my hearers.

The faculty for making visible marks is sufficiently latent in all for them (caught young enough) to learn, more or less, at least one graphic system, with severely practical object. It is more highly developed in others, and may lead not only to heights of illumination and calligraphy for sheer pleasure, but it is doubtless allied in many ways to drawing.

The linguistic faculty – for making so-called articulate noises – is sufficiently latent in all for them (caught young as they always are) to learn, more or less, at least one language with merely or mainly practical object. It is more highly developed in others, and may lead not only to polyglots but to poets; to savourers of linguistic flavours, to learners and users of tongues, who take pleasure in the exercise. And it is allied to a higher art of which I am speaking, and which perhaps I had better now define. An art for which life is not long enough, indeed: the construction of imaginary languages in full or outline for amusement, for the pleasure of the constructor or even conceivably of any critic that might occur. For though I have made much of the secrecy of the practice of this art, it is an inessential, and an accidental product of circumstances. Individualistic as are the makers, seeking a personal expression and satisfaction, they are artists and incomplete without an audience. Though like this or any other society of philologists they may be aware that their goods have not a wide popular appeal or a market, they would not be averse to a competent and unbiassed hearing in camera.

But I have somewhat interrupted my argument, and anticipated the end of my line of development, which was to lead from the cruder beginnings to the highest stages. I have seen glimpses of higher stages than *animalic*. As one proceeds higher in the scale doubtless diverse ramifications begin: 'language' has more than one aspect, which may be specially developed. I can imagine developments I have never met.

A good example of a further stage was provided by one of the Animalic community – the other (notably not the originator) dropped off and became interested in drawing and design. The other developed an idiom called *Nevbosh*, or the 'New Nonsense'. It still made, as these play-languages will, some pretence at being a means of limited communication – that is, in the lower stages the differentiation between the argot-group and the art-group is imperfect. That is where I came in. I was a member of the *Nevbosh*-speaking world.

Though I never confessed it, I was older in secret vice (secret only because apparently bereft of the hope of communication or criticism), if not in years, than the *Nevbosh* originator. Yet, though I shared in the vocabulary, and did something to affect the spelling of this idiom, it remained a usable business, and intended to be. It did become too difficult to talk with Animalic fluency – because games cannot take up all one's time with Latin and mathematics and such things forced upon one's notice, but it was good enough for letters, and even bursts of doggerel song. I believe I could still write down a much bigger vocabulary of *Nevbosh* than Busbecq recorded for Crimean Gothic,[2] though more than 20 years[3] have gone by since it became a dead language. But I can only remember entire one idiotic connected fragment:

> Dar fys ma vel gom co palt 'hoc
> Pys go iskili far maino woc?
> Pro si go fys do roc de
> Do cat ym maino bocte
> De volt fac soc ma taimful gyróc!'

Now this vocabulary, if ever I were foolish enough to write it down, and these fragments, of which the only surviving native can still supply a translation, are crude – not in the extreme, but still crude. I have not sophisticated them. But they already provide quite instructive matter for consideration. It is not yet sufficiently developed to present the points of interest for a learned society which I hope may yet arise; the interest is still chiefly discoverable by the scientific and the philological, and so only a side-line with me tonight. But I will touch on it, because it will, I think, be found not altogether foreign to the present purpose of this absurd paper.

One of the points I see is this: What happens when people try to *invent* 'new words' (groups of sounds) to represent familiar notions. Whether the notion becomes in any way affected or not we will leave aside – it is negligible at any rate in a case like

Nevbosh, which is entirely dominated by an established natural idiom. This 'invention' is probably always going on – to the distraction of 'etymology', which more or less assumes, or used to assume, creation once for all in a distant past. Such a special case as *Nevbosh*, supported by others like it, of which no doubt one could find many examples if one knew where to look, might throw light on this interesting problem, which is really part of a more advanced etymology and semantic. In traditional languages invention is more often seen undeveloped, severely limited by the weight of tradition, or alloyed with other linguistic processes, and finds outlet chiefly in the modification of existing sound-groups to 'fit' the sense ('fit' begs a large question, but never mind), or even modification of sense to 'fit' the sound. In this way, in either case, 'new words' are really made – since a 'word' is a group of sounds temporarily more or less fixed +an associated notion more or less defined and fixed in itself and in its relation to the sound-symbol. Made not created. There is in historic language, traditional or artificial, no pure creation in the void.

In *Nevbosh* we see, of course, no real breaking away from 'English' or the native traditional language. Its notions – their associations with certain sounds, even their inherited and accidental confusions; their range and limits – are preserved. *Do* is 'to', and a prefixed inflexion marking the infinitive. *Pro* is 'for, four' and the conjunction 'for'. And so on. This part is not then of any interest. Only on the phonematic side is there much interest. What directed the choice of non-traditional sound-groups to represent the traditional ones (with their sense-associations) as perfectly equivalent counters?

Clearly 'phonetic predilection' – artistic phonetic expression – played as yet a very small part owing to the domination of the native language, which still kept *Nevbosh* almost in the stage of a 'code'. The native language constantly appears with what at first sight appears casual unsystematic and arbitrary alteration. Yet even here there is a certain interest – little or no phonetic knowledge was possessed by its makers, and yet there appears an unconscious appreciation of certain elementary phonetic relations: alteration is mainly limited to shifting within a defined series of consonants, say for example the dentals: *d, t, þ, ð*, &c. *Dar*/there; *do*/to; *cat*/get; *volt*/would. Or where this is broken, as in *ym*/in, we have recognition of the fact that *m/n*, though technically made at different contact points, have in their nasality and resonance a similarity which overrides the more mechanical distinction – a fact which is reflected, shall we say, both in the case of *m/n* interchange in real languages (such as Greek), or in my inability to feel greatly wounded by *m/n* assonances in a rhyming poem.

The influence of learnt languages – or since all are learnt, better 'lesson-languages' – is unfortunately prominent in this *Nevbosh* example, an influence which weakens its interest in some respects, though it brings in an additional point for consideration. The intricate blending of the native with the later-learnt is, for one thing, curious. The foreign, too, shows the same arbitrary alteration within phonetic limits as the native. So *roc/*'rogo' ask; *go/*'ego' I; *vel/*'vieil, vieux' old; *gom/*'homo' man – the ancient Germanic languages did not contribute;[4] *pys/*can – from French; *si/*if – pure plagiarism; *pal/*'parler' speak, say; *taim/*'timeo' fear; and so on. Blending is seen in: *volt/*'volo, vouloir' + 'will, would'; *fys/*'fui' + 'was', was, were; *co/*'qui' + 'who'; *far/*'fero' + 'bear', carry. And in a curious example: *woc* is both the native word reversed, and connected with *vacca*, *vache* (I happen to remember that this is actually the case); but it bred the beginnings of a code-like system, dependent on English, whereby native *-ow* >-*oc*, a sort of primitive and arbitrary sound-law: *hoc/*how; *gyroc/*row.

Perhaps it was not worth going into so deeply. A code is not an interesting subject. Only those words which have no obvious association in traditional or school-learnt languages would possess a deeper interest – and one would have to possess a very great number of documented examples to learn anything of value from them, more than the arousing of a passing curiosity.

In this connexion *iski-li* 'possibly' is odd. Who can analyse it? I can also remember the word *lint* 'quick, clever, nimble', and it is interesting, because I know it was adopted because the relation between the sounds *lint* and the idea proposed for association with them gave *pleasure*. Here is the beginning of a new and exciting element. Certainly, just as in real languages, the 'word' once thus established, though owing its being to this pleasure, this sense of fitness, quickly became a mere chance symbol dominated by the notion and its circle of association, not by the relation of sound and sense – thus it was soon used for mental quickness, and finally the normal *Nevbosh* idiom for 'learn' was *catlint* (become 'lint'), and for 'teach' *faclint* (make 'lint').

Generally speaking, however, only the incipient pleasure found in *linguistic invention*, in getting free from the necessarily limited scope invention has for any individual within a traditional sphere, makes these rude fragments of interest.

This idea of using the linguistic faculty for amusement is however deeply interesting to me. I may be like an opium-smoker seeking a moral or medical or artistic defence for his habit. I don't think so. The instinct for 'linguistic invention' – the fitting of notion to oral symbol, and *pleasure in contemplating the new relation established*, is rational, and not perverted. In these invented languages the pleasure is more keen than it can be even in learning a new language – keen though it is to some people in that case – because more personal and fresh, more open to experiment of trial and error. And it is capable of developing into an art, with refinement of the construction of the symbol, and with greater nicety in the choice of notional-range.

Certainly it is the *contemplation* of the relation between sound and notion which is a main source of pleasure. We see it in an alloyed form in the peculiar keenness of the delight scholars have in poetry or fine prose in a foreign language, almost before they have mastered that language, and long after they have become reasonably familiar with it. Certainly in the case of dead languages no scholar can ever reach the full position of a native with regard to the purely notional side of the language he studies, nor possess and feel all the undercurrents of connotation from period to period which words possess. His compensation remains a great freshness of perception of the word-form. Thus, even seen darkly through the distorting glass of our ignorance of the details of Greek pronunciation, our appreciation of the splendour of Homeric Greek in word-form is possibly keener, or more conscious, than it was to a Greek, much else of other elements of poetry though we may miss. The same is true of Anglo-Saxon. It is one of the real arguments for devoted study of ancient languages. Nor does it mean self-deception – we need not believe we are feeling something that was not there; we are in a position to see some things better at a distance, others more dimly.

The very word-form itself, of course, even unassociated with notions, is capable of giving pleasure – a perception of beauty, which if of a minor sort is not more foolish and irrational than being sensitive to the line of a hill, light and shade, or colour. Greek, Finnish, Welsh (to name at random languages which have a very characteristic and in their different ways beautiful word-form, readily seizable by the sensitive at first sight) are capable of producing this pleasure. I have heard others independently voice my own feeling that the Welsh names on coal-trucks have stirred a sense of beauty, provided you have the barest knowledge of Welsh spelling sufficient for them to cease to be jumbles of letters.

There is purely artistic pleasure, keen and of a high order, in studying a Gothic dictionary from this point of view; and from it a *part*, one element, of the pleasure which might have been gained from the resplendent 'lost Gothic' poetry may still be recaptured.

It is then in the *refinement of the word-form* that the next progress above the *Nevbosh* stage must consist. Most unfortunately above this second still crude *Nevbosh* stage the development tends to dive underground, and to be difficult to document with examples. Most of the addicts reach their maximum of linguistic playfulness, and their interest is swamped by greater ones, they take to poetry or prose or painting, or else it is overwhelmed by mere pastimes (cricket, meccano, or suchlike footle) or crushed by cares and tasks. A few go on, but they become shy, ashamed of spending the precious commodity of time for their private pleasure, and higher developments are locked in secret places. The obviously unremunerative character of the hobby is against it – it can earn no prizes, win no competitions (as yet) – make no birthday presents for aunts (as a rule) – earn no scholarship, fellowship, or worship. It is also – like poetry – contrary to conscience, and duty; its pursuit is snatched from hours due to self-advancement, or to bread, or to employers.

This must be my excuse for becoming more and more auto-biographical – regretfully, and from no arrogance. I should much prefer the greater objectivity of studying other people's efforts. The crude *Nevbosh* was a 'language' in a fuller sense than things we are coming to. It was intended in theory for speaking, and writing, between one person and another. It was shared. Each element had to be accepted by more than one to become current, to become part of *Nevbosh* at all. It was therefore hampered in 'symmetry', either grammatical or phonetic, as traditional languages are. Only the handing on to a wider group, going on during a long time, could have produced in it some of those effects of partially achieved and overlaid symmetries which mark all the traditional human tongues. *Nevbosh* represented the *highest common linguistic capacity* of a small group, not the best that could be produced by its best member. It remained unfreed from the purely *communicative* aspect of language – the one that seems usually supposed to be the real germ and original impulse of language. But I doubt this exceedingly; as much as one doubts a poet's sole object, even primary one, being to talk in a special way to other people.

The communication factor has been very powerful in directing the development of language; but the more individual and personal factor – pleasure in articulate sound, and in the symbolic use of it, independent of communication though constantly in fact entangled with it – must not be forgotten for a moment.

Naffarin – the next stage of which I have evidence to put before you – shows very clear signs of a development in this direction. It was a purely private production, partly overlapping the last stages of *Nevbosh*, never circulated (though not for lack of the wish). It has long since been foolishly destroyed, but I can remember more than enough, accurately and without sophistication, for my present purpose. One set of individual predilections – governed powerfully as is inevitable by accidents of knowledge, but not made by them – comes to some sort of expression. The phonetic system is limited, and is no longer that of the native language, except that it does not contain elements entirely alien to it; there is a grammar, again a matter of predilection and choice of means. (With regard to phonetic system one may say in an aside that the absence of alien elements is not of first-class importance; a very alien word-form could be constructed out of purely English elements; since it is as much in habitual sequences and combinations as in individual 'phonemes' or sound-units that a language, or a language-maker, achieves individuality. A fact which can be readily appreciated by turning English backwards – phonetically, not by spelling. Such a 'native' word as *scratch* becomes *štærks*,[5] each 'phoneme' being perfectly native, the total entirely foreign owing to the fact that English rarely has the sequence *št* – only when it is clearly analysable as *š* + suffix (*crushed*), and never initially; and never has *ær* + consonant. It is this fact, of course, which gives English scholars' 'Greek' still a Greek phonetic character – a representation of Greek with other counters, as *Nevbosh* was a representation of English on the notional side – in spite of its purely English detail. Such scholars need not, however, be unduly comforted – their usage still misrepresents Greek in vital ways, and might be improved vastly still using only English phonetic detail.)

To return – I will give you a brief sample of *Naffarin*.

> O Naffarínos cutá vu navru cangor
> luttos ca vúna tiéranar,
> dana maga tíer ce vru encá vún' farta
> once ya merúta vúna maxt' amámen.

I don't mean to subject this example to the tedious consideration of origins which I inflicted upon you and *Nevbosh*. Etymologically, as you would see if I bothered to translate, it has no greater interest than *Nevbosh*; *vrú* 'ever' – a curiously predominant association in my languages, which is always pushing its way in (a case of early fixation of individual association, I suppose, which cannot now be got rid of) – is the only word of interest from this point of view. In inventing languages one inevitably develops a style and even mannerisms – even though it is one of the elements of the game to study how a linguistic 'style' is composed.

In *Naffarin* the influences – outside English, and beyond a nascent purely individual element – are Latin and Spanish, in sound-choices and combinations, in general word-form. These influences no longer preclude the expression of personal taste, because French and German and Greek, say, all of which were available, were not used or not much used; phonetic taste in individual phonemes is also present, though chiefly negatively: in the absence of certain sounds familiar in English (*w*, *þ*, *š*, *ž*, &c). Allowing oneself to be influenced by one pattern rather than another is a choice. *Naffarin* is definitely a product of a 'Romance' period. But we need not trouble about this specimen any more.

From here onwards you must forgive pure egotism. Further examples must be drawn solely from isolated private experience. My little man, with his interest in the devices for expression of word-relations, in syntactical devices, is too fleeting a glimpse to use. And I should like to represent to you the interest and delight of this domestic and private art, of many facets, as well as to suggest the points for discussion which it raises (other of course than the question whether practitioners are quite right in their heads).

Practice produces skill here, as in other more useful or more exalted pursuits; but skill need not be expended solely on canvases of 80 square feet; there are smaller experiments and sketches. I will offer some specimens of at least one language that has in the opinion of, or rather to the feeling of, its constructor reached a highish level both of beauty in word-form considered abstractly, and of ingenuity in the relations of symbol and sense, not to mention its elaborate grammatical arrangements, nor its hypothetical historical background (a necessary thing as a constructor finds in the end, both for the satisfactory construction of the word-form, and for the giving of an illusion of coherence and unity to the whole).

Here would be the place, perhaps, before submitting the specimens, to consider what *pleasure* or *instruction* or both the individual maker of a play-language in elaborated form derives from his useless hobby. And then, what points worthy of discussion his efforts may suggest to the observer, or critic. I originally embarked on this odd topic because I somewhat dimly grasped at questions which did seem to me to arise, of interest not only to students of language, but to those considering rather mythology, poetry, art. As one suggestion, I might fling out the view that for perfect construction of an art-language it is found necessary to construct at least in outline a mythology concomitant. Not solely because some pieces of verse will inevitably be part of the (more or less) completed structure, but because the making of language and mythology are related functions;[6] to give your language an individual flavour, it must have woven into it the threads of an individual mythology, individual while working within the scheme of natural human mythopoeia, as your word-form may be individual while working within the hackneyed limits of human, even European, phonetics. The converse indeed is true, your language construction will *breed* a mythology.

If I only toss out, or lightly suggest these points it is due both to the fact of my slender grasp of the things involved, and to the original intention of the paper, which is simply to provoke discussion.

To turn to another aspect of language-construction: I am personally most interested perhaps in word-form in itself, and in word-form in relation to meaning (so-called phonetic fitness) than in any other department. Of great interest to me is the attempt to disentangle – if possible – among the elements in this predilection and in this association (1) the personal from (2) the traditional. The two are doubtless much interwoven – the *personal* being possibly (though it is not proven) linked to the traditional in normal lives by heredity, as well as by the immediate and daily pressure of the traditional upon the personal from earliest childhood. The *personal*, too, is doubtless divisible again into (*a*) what is peculiar to one individual, even when all the weighty influence of his native language and of other languages he has learnt in some degree has been accounted for; and (*b*) what is common to human beings, or to larger or smaller groups of them – both latent in individuals and expressed and operative in his own or any language. The really *peculiar* comes seldom to expression, unless the individual is given a measure of release by the practice of this odd art, beyond perhaps predilections for given words or rhythms or sounds in his own language, or natural liking for this or that language offered for his study rather than for another. Of these well-known facts of experience – including doubtless many of the tricks of style, or individuality in say poetic composition – this *individual linguistic character* of a person is probably at least in part the explanation.

There are of course various other interests in the hobby. There is the purely philological (a necessary part of the completed whole though it may be developed for its own sake): you may, for instance, construct a pseudo-historical background and deduce the form you have actually decided on from an antecedent and different form (conceived in outline); or you can posit certain tendencies of development and see what sort of form this will produce. In the first case you discover what sort of general tendencies of change produce a given character; in the second you discover the character produced by given tendencies. Both are interesting, and their exploration gives one a much greater precision and sureness in construction – in the technique in fact of producing an effect you wish to produce for its own sake.

There is the grammatical and logical – a more purely intellectual pursuit: you can (without perhaps concerning yourself so closely, if at all, with the sound-structure, the coherence of the word-form) consider the categories and the relations of words, and the various neat, effective, or ingenious ways in which these can be expressed. In this case you may often devise new and novel, even admirable and effective machinery – though doubt-less, simply because the experiment has been tried by others, your human ancestors and relatives, over such a large area for so long a time, you are not likely really to light on anything that in nature or in accident has never anywhere before been discovered or contrived; but that need not bother you. In most cases you won't know; and in any case you will have had, *only more consciously and deliberately, and so more keenly,* the same creative experience as that of those many unnamed geniuses who have invented the skilful bits of machinery in our traditional languages, for the use (and too often the misunderstanding and abuse) of their less skilful fellows.

The time has come now, I suppose, when I can no longer postpone the shame-faced revelation of specimens of my own more considered effort, the best I have done in limited leisure, or by occasional thefts of time, in one direction. The beautiful phonologies, thrown away or mouldering in drawers, arduous if pleasant in construction, the source of what little I know in the matter of phonetic construction based on my own individual predilections, will not interest you. I will offer some pieces of verse in the one language which has been expressly designed to give play to my own most normal phonetic taste – one has moods in this as in all other matters of taste, partly due to interior causes, partly to external influences; that is why I say 'normal' – and which has had a long enough history of development to allow of this final fruition: verse. It expresses, and at the same time has fixed, my personal taste. Just as the construction of a mythology expresses at first one's taste, and later conditions one's imagination, and becomes inescapable, so with this language. I can conceive, even sketch, other radically different forms, but always insensibly and inevitably now come back to this one, which must therefore be or have become peculiarly mine.

You must remember that these things were constructed deliberately to be personal, and give private satisfaction – not for scientific experiment, nor yet in expectation of any audience. A consequent weakness is therefore their tendency, too free as they were from cold exterior criticism, to be 'over-pretty', to be *phonetically and semantically* sentimental – while their bare meaning is probably trivial, not full of red blood or the heat of the world such as critics demand. Be kindly. For if there is any virtue in this kind of thing, it is in its intimacy, in its peculiarly shy individualism. I can sympathize with the shrinking of other language-makers, as I experience the pain of giving away myself, which is little lessened by now occurring for a second time.[7]

Oilima Markirya

Man kiluva kirya ninqe
oilima ailinello lúte,
níve qímari ringa ambar
ve maiwin qaine?

Man tiruva kirya ninqe
valkane wilwarindon
lúnelinqe vear
tinwelindon talalínen,
vea falastane,
falma pustane,
rámali tíne,
kalma histane?

Man tenuva súru laustane
taurelasselindon,
ondoli losse karkane
silda-ránar,
minga-ránar,

lanta-ránar,
ve kaivo-kalma;
húro ulmula,
mandu túma?

Man kiluva lómi sangane,
telume lungane
tollalinta ruste,
vea qalume,
mandu yáme,
aira móre ala tinwi
lante no lanta-mindon?

Man tiruva rusta kirya
laiqa ondolissen
nu karne vaiya,
úri nienaite híse
píke assari silde
óresse oilima?

Hui oilima man kiluva,
hui oilimaite?

The Last Ark[8]

Who shall see a white ship
leave the last shore,
the pale phantoms
in her cold bosom
like gulls wailing?

Who shall heed a white ship,
vague as a butterfly,
in the flowing sea
on wings like stars,
the sea surging,
the foam blowing,

the wings shining,
the light fading?

Who shall hear the wind roaring
like leaves of forests;
the white rocks snarling
in the moon gleaming,
in the moon waning,
in the moon falling
a corpse-candle;
the storm mumbling,
the abyss moving?

Who shall see the clouds gather,
the heavens bending
upon crumbling hills,
the sea heaving,
the abyss yawning,
the old darkness
beyond the stars falling
upon fallen towers?

Who shall heed a broken ship
on the green rocks
under red skies,
a bleared sun blinking
on bones gleaming
in the last morning?

Who shall see the last evening?

Nieninque

Norolinde pirukendea
elle tande Nielikkilis,
tanya wende nieninqea
yar i vilya anta miqilis.
I oromandin eller tande

ar wingildin wilwarindeën,
losselie telerinwa,
tálin paptalasselindeën.

This of course has an air or tune to it. The bare literal meaning is intended to be: 'Tripping lightly, whirling lightly, thither came little Niéle, that maiden like a snowdrop (Nieninqe), to whom the air gives kisses. The wood-spirits came thither, and the foam-fays like butterflies, the white people of the shores of Elfland, with feet like the music of falling leaves.'[9]

Or one may have a strict and quantitative metre:

Earendel

San ninqeruvisse lútier
kiryasse Earendil or vea,
ar laiqali linqi falmari
langon veakiryo kírier;
wingildin o silqelosseën
alkantaméren úrio
kalmainen; i lunte linganer,
tyulmin talalínen aiqalin
kautáron, i súru laustaner.

'Then upon a white horse sailed Earendel, upon a ship upon the sea, and the green wet waves the throat of the sea-ship clove. The foam-maidens with blossom-white hair made it shine in the lights of the sun; the boat hummed like a harp-string; the tall masts bent with the sails; the wind 'lausted' (not 'roared' or 'rushed' but made a windy noise).'

Earendel at the Helm[10]

A white horse in the sun shining,
A white ship in the sea gliding,
  Earendel at the helm;
Green waves in the sea moving,

White froth at the prow spuming
  Glistening in the sun;
Foam-riders with hair like blossom
And pale arms on the sea's bosom
  Chanting wild songs;
Taut ropes like harps tingling,
From far shores a faint singing
  On islands in the deep;
The bent sails in the wind billowing,
The loud wind in the sails bellowing,
  The road going on for ever,
    Earendel at the helm,
  His eyes shining, the sea gliding,
    To havens in the West.

Or one can have a fragment from the same mythology, but a totally different if related language:

Dir avosaith a gwaew hinar
engluid eryd argenaid,
dir Tumledin hin Nebrachar
Yrch methail maethon magradhaid.
Damrod dir hanach dalath benn
ven Sirion gar meilien,
gail Luithien heb Eglavar
dir avosaith han Nebrachar.

'Like a wind, dark through gloomy places the Stonefaces searched the mountains, over Tumledin (the Smooth Valley) from Nebrachar, orcs snuffling smelt out footsteps. Damrod (a hunter) through the vale, down mountain slopes, towards (the river) Sirion went laughing. Lúthien he saw, as a star from Elfland shining over the gloomy places, above Nebrachar.'[11]

By way of epilogue, I may say that such fragments, nor even a constructed whole, do not satisfy all the instincts that go to make poetry. It is no part of this paper to plead that such inventions do so; but that they abstract certain of the pleasures of poetic composition (as far as I understand it), and sharpen them by making them more conscious. It is an attenuated emotion, but may be very piercing – this construction of sounds to give pleasure. The human phonetic system is a small-ranged instrument (compared with music as it has now become); yet it is an instrument, and a delicate one.

And with the phonetic pleasure we have blended the more elusive delight of establishing novel relations between symbol and significance, and in contemplating them.

In poetry (of our day – when the use of significant language is so habitual that the word-form is seldom consciously marked, and the associated notions have it almost all their own way) it is the interplay and pattern of the notions adhering to each word that is uppermost. The word-music, according to the nature of the tongue and the skill or ear (conscious or artless) of the poet, runs on heard, but seldom coming to awareness. At rare moments we pause to wonder why a line or couplet produces an effect beyond its significance; we call it the 'authentic magic' of the poet, or some such meaningless expression. So little do we ponder word-form and sound-music, beyond a few hasty observations of its crudest manifestations in rhyme and alliteration, that we are unaware often that the answer is simply that by luck or skill the poet has struck out an air which illuminates the line as a sound of music half-attended to may deepen the significance of some unrelated thing thought or read, while the music ran.

And in a living language this is all the more poignant because the language is not constructed to do this, and only by rare felicity will it say what we wish it to, significantly, and at the same time sing carelessly.

For us departed are the unsophisticated days, when even Homer could pervert a word to suit sound-music; or such merry freedom as one sees in the *Kalevala*, when a line can be adorned by phonetic trills – as in *Enkä lähe Inkerelle, Penkerelle, pänkerelle* (Kal. xi.55), or *Ihveniä ahvenia, tuimenia, taimenia* (Kal. xlviii.100), where *pänkerelle, ihveniä, taimenia* are 'non-significant', mere notes in a phonetic tune struck to harmonize with *penkerelle*, or *tuimenia* which do 'mean' something.

Of course, if you construct your art-language on chosen

principles, and in so far as you fix it, and courageously abide by
your own rules, resisting the temptation of the supreme despot to
alter them for the assistance of this or that technical object on any
given occasion, so far you may write poetry of a sort. Of a sort,
I would maintain, no further, or very little further, removed
from real poetry in full, than is your appreciation of ancient
poetry (especially of a fragmentarily recorded poetry such as
that of Iceland or ancient England), or your writing of 'verse'
in such a foreign idiom. For in these exercises the subtleties of
connotation cannot be there: though you give your words
meanings, they have not had a real experience of the world in
which to acquire the normal richness of human words. Yet in
such cases as I have quoted (say Old English or Old Norse), this
richness is also absent, equally absent or nearly so. In Latin and
Greek even it seems to me that this is more often true than many
realize.

But, none the less, as soon as you have fixed even a vague
general sense for your words, many of the less subtle but most
moving and permanently important of the strokes of poetry are
open to you. For you are the heir of the ages. You have not to
grope after the dazzling brilliance of invention of the free adjective,
to which all human language has not yet fully attained. You may
say

> *green sun*
> or *dead life*

and set the imagination leaping.

Language has both strengthened imagination and been freed
by it. Who shall say whether the free adjective has created images
bizarre and beautiful, or the adjective been freed by strange and
beautiful pictures in the mind?

NOTES

(All notes to this essay are editorial except note 6)

1   In what was either a draft for the opening passage of this essay or (more probably)
    a draft for its rewriting, my father wrote that he was 'no longer so sure that [an
    artificial language] would be a good thing', and said that 'at present I think we
    should be likely to get an *inhumane* language without any cooks at all – their place
    being taken by nutrition experts and dehydraters'.

2 Busbecq was a Fleming who recorded some words of 'Crimean Gothic', an Eastern Germanic language still spoken in the Crimea in the sixteenth century.

3 'more than 20 years' was the original reading of the manuscript, changed in pencil to 'almost 40 years'; see the Foreword.

4 The reference is to the word in the Germanic languages that appears in Old English as *guma*, 'man'.

5 The phonetic sign ʒ = 'sh' of English spelling; the sign *æ* = 'a' in 'scratch'.

6 Coeval and congenital, not related as disease to health, or as by-product to main manufacture. [Author's note.]

7 The concluding phrase is part of the original text; see note 3.

8 This version in English is not part of the manuscript text, but a typescript inserted into the essay at this point. As typed, the title was 'The Last Ship'; 'Ship' was changed to 'Ark' later, and at the same time *Oilima Markirya* was written above the English title. In another text of this English version 'green rocks' and 'red skies' in the last verse were emended later to 'dark rocks' and 'ruined skies'. – Other versions of the poem in both languages are given at the end of these notes.

9 The maiden *Nieliq(u)i*, *Nielikki* appears (only) in the earliest form of the mythology, *The Book of Lost Tales*, where she is the daughter of the Valar Oromë and Vána; there also appear 'the Oarni and the Falmaríni and the long-tressed *Wingildi*, spirits of the foam and the surf of ocean'.

10 This poem is a typescript inserted in the manuscript at this point. In another text of the poem there are later emendations: 'Chanting wild songs' > 'Speeding the ship', and 'The loud wind' > 'The east wind'.

11 The name *Nebrachar* occurs nowhere else, and whatever story may be glimpsed in this poem cannot be identified in any form of the mythology that is extant. The poem and its translations are found also in a preliminary draft: in the poem *Luithien* appears in this as *Lúthien*, and in the translation the 'Stonefaces' are explained to be 'Orcs', and *Nebrachar* 'a place of [?goblins]'.

Other Versions of *Oilima Markirya*

Another version of *Oilima Markirya*, with translation, was placed with this essay. The title of both is 'The Last Ark', not 'The Last Ship'; but a note to the 'Elvish' text calls this the 'first version' of the poem (see note 8).

Oilima Markirya

'The Last Ark'

Kildo kirya ninqe
pinilya wilwarindon
veasse lúnelinqe
talainen tinwelindon.

Vean falastanéro
lótefalmarínen,
kirya kalliére
kulukalmalínen.

Súru laustanéro
taurelasselindon;
ondolin ninqanéron
Silmeráno tindon.

Kaivo i sapsanta
Rána númetar,
mandulómi anta
móri Ambalar;
telumen tollanta
naiko lunganar.

Kaire laiqa'ondoisen
kirya; karnevaite
úri kilde hísen
níe nienaite,
ailissen oilimaisen
ala fuin oilimaite,
alkarissen oilimain;
ala fuin oilimaite
ailinisse alkarain.

The Last Ark

A white ship one saw, small like a butterfly,
upon the blue streams of the sea with
wings like stars.

The sea was loud with surf, with waves
crowned with flowers. The ship shone with
golden lights.

The wind rushed with noise like leaves of forests,
the rocks lay white shining in the silver moon.

As a corpse into the grave the moon went down
in the West; the East raised black shadows out of
Hell. The vault of heaven sagged upon the
tops of the hills.

The white ship lay upon the rocks; amid red
skies the Sun with wet eyes dropped tears of
mist, upon the last beaches after the last night
in the last rays of light – after the last night
upon the shining shore.

A greatly changed version of the poem comes from a much later time – I would judge, from the last decade of my father's life. This is extant in two texts, clearly more or less contemporaneous; the earlier of the two has a glossarial commentary. I give here the second text, with variants from the former in footnotes, and follow it with the commentary.

Men kenuva fáne kirya
métima hrestallo kíra,
i fairi néke

ringa súmaryasse
5   ve maiwi yaimië?

Man tiruva fána kirya,
wilwarin wilwa,
ëar-kelumessen
rámainen elvië,
10   ëar falastala,
winga hlápula
rámar sisílala,
kále fifírula?

Man hlaruva rávëa súre
15   ve tauri lillassië,
ninqui karkar yarra
isilme ilkalasse,
isilme píkalasse,
isilme lantalasse
20   ve loikolíkuma;
raumo nurrula,
undume rúmala?

Man kenuva lumbor na-hosta
Menel na-kúna
25   ruxal' ambonnar,
ëar amortala,
undume hákala,
enwina lúme
elenillor pella
30   talta-taltala
atalantië mindoninnar?

Man tiruva rákina kirya
ondolisse morne
nu fanyare rúkina,
35   anar púrëa tihta
axor ilkalannar
métim' auresse?
Man kenuva métim' andúne?

Variant readings from the other text: 3 *i néka fairi*; 16 *ninqui ondor yarra*; 31 *atalantëa*; 35 *tihtala*; 37 *métima amaurëasse*; 38 *andúnie*.

A few changes were made subsequently to the second text : 21 *nurrula* > *nurrua*; 22 *rúmala* > *rúma*; 23 *na-hosta* > *ahosta*; 24 *na-kúna* > *akúna*; 31 *atalantië* > *atalantëa*; 31 *mindoninnar* > *mindonnar*.

The glossarial commentary to the first text is as follows:

1   *ken-* 'see, behold'   *fáne* 'white'
2   *métima* 'ultimate, final'   *hresta* 'beach'

3 *fairë* 'phantom; disembodied spirit, when seen as a pale shape'   *néka*
   'vague, faint, dim to see'
4 *súma* 'hollow cavity, bosom'
5 *yaime* 'wailing', noun, *yaimëa* adjective
7 *wilwa* 'fluttering to and fro'   *wilwarin* 'butterfly'
8 *kelume* 'flowing, flood (tide), stream'
9 *elvëa* 'starlike'
10 *falasta-* 'to foam'
11 *winga* 'foam, spray'   *hlapu-* 'fly or stream in the wind'
12 *sisíla-* frequentative of *sil-* 'shine (white)'
13 *kále* 'light', noun   *fifíru-* from *fir-* 'die, fade': 'slowly fade away'
14 *rávëa* < *ráve* 'roaring noise'
15 *lillassië* plural of *lillassëa* 'having many leaves'
16 *yarra-* 'growl, snarl'
17 *isilme* 'moonlight'   *ilkala* participle of *ilka* 'gleam (white)'
18 *píka-* 'lessen, dwindle'
20 *loiko* 'corpse, dead body'   *líkuma* 'taper, candle' < *líko* 'wax'
21 *raumo* '(noise of a) storm'   *nurru-* 'murmur, grumble'
22 *rúma-* 'shift, move, heave (of large and heavy things)'
23 *hosta-* 'gather, collect, assemble'. When the bare stem of the verb is used
   (as after 'see' or 'hear') as infinitive *na-* is prefixed if the noun is the object
   not the subject. So *na-kúna* 24 < *kúna-* derivative verb < *kúna* 'bent,
   curved'
30 *talta-* 'slip, slide down, collapse'
31 *atalante* noun 'collapse, downfall', *atalantëa* 'ruinous, downfallen'
32 *rákina* past participle of *rak-* 'break'
34 *fanyare* 'the skies – not heaven or firmament – the upper airs and clouds'
   rúkina 'confused, shattered, disordered'
35 *púrëa* 'smeared, discoloured'   *tihta-* 'blink, peer'
36 *axo* 'bone'
37 *amaurëa* poetic word for 'dawn, early day'

It will be seen that while the vocabulary of this version is radically different
from that given in the essay, the meaning is precisely the same (with the changes
to 'dark rocks' and 'ruined skies' mentioned in note 7).

VALEDICTORY ADDRESS TO THE UNIVERSITY OF OXFORD

It might be held characteristic that, though I have occupied two
chairs (or sat uneasily on the edge of two chairs) in this university,
I have not yet delivered an inaugural lecture: I am now about
34 years behind. At the time of my first election I was too
astonished (a feeling that has never quite left me) to gather my
wits, until I had already given many ordinary lectures as required
by statute, and it seemed to me that an inaugural that would not
inaugurate was a ceremony better omitted. On the second
occasion, my ineffectiveness as a lecturer was already well known,
and well-wishers had made sure (by letter or otherwise) that I
should know it too; so I thought it unnecessary to give a special
exhibition of this unfortunate defect. And, though twenty years
had then gone by, during which this matter of the overdue
inaugural had been much on my mind, I had not yet discovered
anything special to say.

Fourteen more years have now passed, and I still have nothing
special to say. Nothing, that is, of the kind proper to inaugurals –
as far as I can judge by those that I have read: the products of
minds more sanguine, or more efficient and magisterial than
mine. The diagnosis of what is wrong, and the confident prescription of the cure; the wide view, the masterly survey; plans
and prophecies: these have never been in my line. I would always
rather try to wring the juice out of a single sentence, or explore
the implications of one word than try to sum up a period in a
lecture, or pot a poet in a paragraph. And I am afraid that what
I would rather do is what I have usually done.

For I suppose that, at any rate since the golden days long past
when English studies were unorganized, a hobby and not a
trade, few more amateurish persons can 'by a set of curious
circumstances' have been put in a professional position. For
thirty-four years my heart has gone out to poor Koko, taken

from a county jail; though I had one advantage over him. He was appointed to cut off heads, and did not really like it. Philology was part of my job, and I enjoyed it. I have always found it amusing. But I have never had strong views about it. I do not think it necessary to salvation. I do not think it should be thrust down the throats of the young, as a pill, the more efficacious the nastier it tastes.

But if the ranks of Tuscany should feel inclined to cheer, let me hasten to assure them that I do not think their wares are necessary to salvation either; much of what they offer is peddler's stuff. I have indeed become more, not less, bigoted as a result of experience in the little world of academic English studies.

'Bigoted' is for the Tuscans. Speaking to the Romans, defending the city and the ashes of their fathers, I would say 'convinced'. Convinced of what? Convinced that Philology is never nasty: except to those deformed in youth or suffering from some congenital deficiency. I do not think that it should be thrust down throats as a pill, because I think that if such a process seems needed, the sufferers should not be here, at least not studying or teaching English letters. Philology is the foundation of humane letters; 'misology' is a disqualifying defect or disease.

It is not, in my experience, a defect or disease found in those whose literary learning, wisdom, and critical acumen place them in the highest rank – to which so many in the Oxford School have in various ways attained. But there are other voices, epigonal rather than ancestral. I must confess that at times in the last thirty odd years I have been aggrieved by them; by those, afflicted in some degree by misology, who have decried what they usually call *language*. Not because they, poor creatures, have evidently lacked the imagination required for its enjoyment, or the knowledge needed for an opinion about it. Dullness is to be pitied. Or so I hope, being myself dull at many points. But dullness should be confessed with humility; and I have therefore felt it a grievance that certain professional persons should suppose their dullness and ignorance to be a human norm, the measure of what is good; and anger when they have sought to impose the limitation of their minds upon younger minds, dissuading those with philological curiosity from their bent, encouraging those without this interest to believe that their lack marked them as minds of a superior order.

But I am, as I say, an amateur. And if that means that I have neglected parts of my large field, devoting myself mainly to those things that I personally *like*, it does also mean that I have tried to awake *liking*, to communicate delight in those things that I find enjoyable. And that without suggesting that they were the only proper source of profit, or pleasure, for students of English.

I have heard sneers at certain elementary kinds of linguistic 'research' as mere spelling-counting. Let the phonologist and the orthographer have their swink to them reserved! Of course. And the same to the bibliographer and typographer – still further removed from the living speech of men which is the beginning of all literature. Contemplating the workings of the B.Litt. sausage-machine, I have at times dared to think that some of the *botuli*, or *farcimina*, turned out were hardly either tasty or nourishing, even when claimed to be 'literary'. But, to use a perhaps more apt simile, the twin peaks of Parnassus are approached through some very dim valleys. If scrambling in these, without any climbing, is sometimes rewarded with a degree, one must hope that one of the peaks at least has been glimpsed from afar.

However, that is not a matter which I wish to explore deeply: that is, 'research' and 'research degrees' in relation to the ordinary courses of learning – the so-called 'postgraduate' activities, which have in recent years shown such rapid growth, forming what one might call our 'hydroponic' department. A term which, I fear, I only know from science-fiction, in which it seems to refer to the cultivation of plants without soil in enclosed vehicles far removed from this world.

But all fields of study and enquiry, all great Schools, demand human sacrifice. For their primary object is not culture, and their academic uses are not limited to education. Their roots are in the desire for knowledge, and their life is maintained by those who pursue some love or curiosity for its own sake, without reference even to personal improvement. If this individual love and curiosity fails, their tradition becomes sclerotic.

There is no need, therefore, to despise, no need even to feel pity for months or years of life sacrificed in some minimal enquiry: say, the study of some uninspired medieval text and its fumbling dialect; or of some miserable 'modern' poetaster and his life (nasty, dreary, and fortunately short) – NOT IF the sacrifice is voluntary, and IF it is inspired by a genuine curiosity, spontaneous or personally felt.

But that being granted, one must feel grave disquiet, when the legitimate inspiration is not there; when the subject or topic of 'research' is imposed, or is 'found' for a candidate out of some one else's bag of curiosities, or is thought by a committee to be a sufficient exercise for a degree. Whatever may have been found useful in other spheres, there is a distinction between accepting the willing labour of many humble persons in building an English house and the erection of a pyramid with the sweat of degree-slaves.

But the matter is not, of course, as simple as all that. It is not just a question of the degeneration of real curiosity and enthusiasm into a 'planned economy', under which so much research time is stuffed into more or less standard skins and turned out in sausages of a size and shape approved by our own little printed cookery book. Even if that were a sufficient description of the system, I should hesitate to accuse anyone of planning it with foresight, or of approving it wholeheartedly now that we have got it. It has grown, partly by accident, partly by the accumulation of temporary expedients. Much thought has gone into it, and much devoted and little remunerated labour has been spent in administering it and in mitigating its evils.

It is an attempt to treat an old trouble and a real need with the wrong tool. The old trouble is the loss of the M.A. as a genuine degree. The real need is the desire for knowledge. The wrong tool is a 'research' degree, the proper scope of which is much more limited, and which functions much better when it is limited.

But the M.A. has become a reward for a small 'postgraduate' subscription to the university and to a college, and is untouchable. Meanwhile many of the better students – I mean those who have studied English for love, or at least with love as one of their mixed motives – wish to spend *more time* in a university: more time in *learning* things, in a place where that process is (or should be) approved and given facilities. What is more, such students are still at a time of life, soon to pass, and the sooner the less the faculty is exercised, when the acquisition of knowledge is easier, and what is acquired is more permanent, more thoroughly digested and more formative. It is a pity that so often the last of the growing, feeding, years are spent in the premature attempt to add to knowledge, while the vast existing storehouses remain unvisited. Or if they are visited, too often this is done after the manner of research-mice running off with little bits nibbled out of unexplored sacks to build up a little thesis. But alas! those with the more eager minds are not necessarily those who possess more money. The powers that hold the purse-strings require a degree; and those who allot places in an overcrowded university require one too. And we have only a so-called research degree to offer them. This is, or can be, better than nothing. Many would-be learners do well enough at minor research. Some take the chance of using much of their time in reading what they wish, with little reference to their supposed task: that is, in doing on the side, hampered and left-handed, what they should be doing openly and unhindered. But the system cannot be praised for this accidental good that may in spite of it occur within it. It is not necessarily the swifter or wider mind that it is easiest to 'find a subject' for, or to bring down to brass tacks and business to the satisfaction of the Applications Committee. The ability to tackle competently and within approved limits a small subject is, in the early twenties, as likely to belong to a small and limited mind as to a future scholar with the hunger of youth.

If the reform that I always had at heart, if the B.Litt. regulations could have been altered (as I once hoped) to allow an alternative approach by examination, to reward reading and learning at least equally with minor research, I should have left the English School more happily. If even now the School could embrace the newer B.Phil. (an unnecessary and inappropriate additional degree-title), I should regard it as a far greater advance than any remodelling or 'new look' given to the Honour syllabus.

As far as my personal experience goes, if I had been allowed to guide the further reading and study of those for whom the Honour School had opened vistas and awakened curiosity, I could have done more good in *less time* than in the so-called supervision of research, done by candidates who had essential territories yet to explore, and who, in the breathless march from

Prelim. to Final Schools, had also left much country in rear, only raided and not occupied.

There are always exceptions. I have met some. I have had the good fortune to be associated (the right word) with some able researching graduates, more of them than my small aptitude for the task of supervisor has merited. Some of them took to research like otters to swimming. But they were the apparent exceptions that prove the thesis. They were the natural researchers (the existence of whom I have never denied). They knew what they wanted to do, and the regions that they desired to explore. They acquired new knowledge and organized it quickly, because it was knowledge that they desired to have anyway: it and the particular enquiry were all of one piece; there was no mere mugging up.

I said that I did not wish to explore the matter of the organization of research deeply; but I have nonetheless spoken (for such an occasion) too long about it. Before I stand down finally, I must say something about our main business: the Final Honour School. Not that the topics are unconnected. I think that the possibility of taking a higher, or at least a further, degree for learning things, for acquiring more of the essential parts of the English field, or for digging deeper in some of them, might well have good effects on the Honour School. In brief: if the abler students, the future scholars, commonly took a *third* public examination, it might no longer be felt necessary to arrange in the *second* public examination a four-year syllabus for the reading-time of two years and a bit.[1]

It is in any case, I suppose, obvious that our Honour syllabus is over-crowded, and that the changes that come into force next year have not done much to cure this. The reasons are various. For one thing, related to the situation of the M.A., three years is supposed, in this land, to be quite long enough to play with books in a university, and four years is extravagant. But while the academic *vita* is shortened, the *ars* gets longer. We now have on our hands *one thousand and two hundred years* of recorded English letters, a long unbroken line, indivisible, no part of which can without loss be ignored. The claims of the great nineteenth century will soon be succeeded by the clamour of the twentieth. What is more, to the honour of English but not to the convenience of syllabus-planners, some of the earliest writings show vitality and talent that makes them worthy of study in themselves, quite apart from the special interest of their earliness. So-called Anglo-Saxon cannot be regarded merely as a root, it is already in flower. But it is a root, for it exhibits qualities and characteristics that have remained ever since a steadfast ingredient in English; and it demands therefore at least some first-hand acquaintance from every serious student of English speech and English letters. This demand the Oxford School has up to now always recognized, and has tried to meet.

In such a range divergence of interests, or at any rate of expertise, is inevitable. But the difficulties have not been helped, indeed they have been bedevilled, by the emergence of two legendary figures, the bogeys *Lang* and *Lit*. So I prefer to call them, since the words *language* and *literature*, though commonly misused among us, should not be thus degraded. Popular mythology seems to believe that *Lang* came from a cuckoo-egg laid in the nest, in which he takes up too much room and usurps the worms of the *Lit* chicken. Some believe that *Lit* was the cuckoo, bent on extruding her nest-fellow or sitting on him; and they have more support from the actual history of our School. But neither tale is well-founded.

In a Bestiary more nearly reflecting the truth *Lang* and *Lit* would appear as Siamese Twins, Jekyll-Hyde and Hyde-Jekyll, indissolubly joined from birth, with two heads, but only one heart, the health of both being much better when they do not quarrel. This allegory at least resembles more closely our older statute: *Every candidate will be expected to show a competent knowledge of both sides of the subject, and equal weight in the examination will be attached to each.*

What the 'sides' were was to be deduced from the title of the School which we still bear: *The Honour School of English Language and Literature*. Though this becomes in the running headline of the Examination Statutes: *English Language, etc.* And that I have always thought a more just title; not that we require the *etc.* The full title was, I think, a mistake; and it has in any case had some unfortunate results. *Language* and *Literature* appear as 'sides' of one subject. That was harmless enough, and indeed true enough, as long as 'sides' meant, as it should, aspects and emphases, which since they were of 'equal weight' in the subject as a whole, were neither of them normally exclusive, neither the sole property of this or that scholar, nor the sole object of any one course of study.

But alas! 'sides' suggested 'parties', and too many then took sides. And thus there entered in *Lang* and *Lit*, the uneasy nest-fellows, each trying to grab more of the candidates' time, whatever the candidates might think.

I first joined the School in 1912 – by the generosity of Exeter College to one who had been up to then an unprofitable exhibitioner; if he learned anything at all, he learned it at the wrong time: I did most of my undergraduate work on the Germanic languages before Honour Moderations; when English and its kindred became my job, I turned to other tongues, even to Latin and Greek; and I took a liking to *Lit* as soon as I had joined the side of *Lang*. Certainly I joined the side of *Lang*, and I found the party-breach already wide; and unless my recollections are mistaken, it went on widening for some time. When I came back from Leeds in 1925, WE no longer meant students of English, it meant adherents of *Lang* or of *Lit*. THEY meant all those on the other side: people of infinite guile, who needed constant watching, lest THEY should down US. And, the rascals, so they did!

For if you have Sides with labels, you will have Partisans. Faction fights, of course, are often fun, especially to the bellicose; but it is not clear that they do any good, any more good in Oxford than in Verona. Things may to some have seemed duller in the long period during which the hostility was damped; and to such they may seem livelier if the smoulder breaks out again. I hope not. It would have been better if it had never been kindled.

Removal of the misunderstanding of words may sometimes produce amity. So though the time left is short, I will now consider the misuse of *language* and *literature* in our School. I think the initial mistake was made when *The School of English Language and Literature* was first adopted as our title. Those who love it call it the *School of English* or the *English School* – in which, if I may intrude a *Lang* remark, the word *English* is not an adjective, but a noun in loose composition. This simple title, *School of English*, is sufficient. And if any should say 'English what?', I would answer: 'For a thousand recorded years *English* as a noun has meant only one thing: the English Language.'

If the title then is made explicit, it should be *The School of English Language*. The parallel formula is held good enough for our peers, for French and Italian and others. But lest it be thought that this is a partisan choice, let me say that actually, for reasons that I will give, I should be well content with *Literature* – if *Letters* is now too archaic.

We hold, I suppose, that the study of *Letters* in all languages that possess them is 'humane', but that Latin and Greek are 'more humane'. It may, however, be observed that the first part of the School of Humaner Letters is stated to be 'The Greek and Latin Languages'; and that this is defined as including 'the minute critical study of authors ... the history of Ancient Literature' (that is *Lit*) 'and Comparative Philology as illustrating the Greek and Latin Languages' (that is *Lang*).

But of course it can be objected that English, in an English-speaking university, is in a different position from other Letters. The English language is assumed to be, and usually is, the native language of the students (if not always in a Standard form that would have been approved by my predecessor). They do not have to learn it. As a venerable professor of Chemistry once said to me – I hasten to add that he is dead, and did not belong to Oxford – 'I do not know why you want a department of English Language; I know English, but I also know some chemistry.'

Nonetheless I think that it was a mistake to intrude *Language* into our title in order to mark this difference, or to warn those who are ignorant of their own ignorance. Not least because *Language* is thus given, as indeed I suspect was intended, an artificially limited and pseudo-technical sense which separates this technical thing from *Literature*. This separation is false, and this use of the word 'language' is false.

The right and natural sense of Language includes Literature, just as Literature includes the study of the language of literary works. *Litteratura*, proceeding from the elementary sense 'a collection of letters; an alphabet', was used as an equivalent of Greek *grammatike* and *philologia*: that is, the study of grammar and idiom, and the critical study of authors (largely concerned with their language). Those things it should always still include.

But even if some now wish to use the word 'literature' more narrowly, to mean the study of writings that have artistic purpose or form, with as little reference as possible to *grammatike* or *philologia*, this 'literature' of theirs remains an operation of Language. Literature is, maybe, the highest operation or function of Language, but it is none the less Language. We may except only certain subsidiaries and adminicles: such as those enquiries concerned with the physical forms in which writings have been preserved or propagated, epigraphy, palaeography, printing, and publishing. These may be, and often are, carried on without close reference to content or meaning, and as such are neither Language nor Literature; though they may furnish evidence to both.

Only *one* of these words, *Language* and *Literature*, is therefore needed in a reasonable title. *Language* as the larger term is a natural choice. To choose *Literature* would be to indicate, rightly as I think, that the *central* (central if not sole) business of Philology in the Oxford School is the study of the language of *literary* texts, or of those that illuminate the history of the English literary language. We do not include some important parts of linguistic study. We do not teach directly 'the language as it is spoken and written at the present day', as is done in Schools concerned with modern languages other than English. Nor are our students expected to compose verses or to write proses in the archaic idioms that they are supposed to learn, as are students of the Greek and Latin languages.

But whatever may be thought or done about the title of our School, I wish fervently that this abuse in local slang and of the word *language* might be for ever abandoned! It suggests, and is used to suggest, that certain kinds of knowledge concerning authors and their medium of expression is unnecessary and 'unliterary', the interest only of cranks, not of cultured or sensitive minds. And even so it is misapplied in time. In local parlance it is used to cover everything, within our historical range, that is medieval or older. Old and Middle English literature, whatever its intrinsic merit or historical importance, becomes just 'language'. Except of course Chaucer. His merits as a major poet are too obvious to be obscured; though it was in fact Language, or Philology, that demonstrated, as only Language could, two things of first-rate literary importance: that he was not a fumbling beginner, but a master of metrical technique; and that he was an inheritor, a middle point, and not a 'father'. Not to mention the labours of Language in rescuing much of his vocabulary and idiom from ignorance or misunderstanding. It is, however, in the backward dark of 'Anglo-Saxon' and 'Semi-Saxon' that Language, now reduced to the bogey *Lang*, is supposed to have his lair. Though alas! he may come down like Grendel from the moors to raid the 'literary' fields. He has (for instance) theories about puns and rhymes!

But this popular picture is of course absurd. It is the product of ignorance and muddled thinking. It confuses three things, quite different. Two of them are confined to no period and to neither 'Side'; and one though it may attract and need specialist attention (as do other departments of English studies) is also confined to no period, is neither dark, nor medieval, nor modern, but universal.

We have *first*: the linguistic effort and attention required for the reading of all texts with intelligence, even those in so-called modern English. Of course this effort increases as we go back in time, as does the effort (with which it goes hand in hand) to appreciate the art, the thought and feeling, or the allusions of an author. Both reach their climax in 'Anglo-Saxon', which has become almost a foreign language. But this learning of an idiom and its implications, in order to understand and enjoy literary or historical texts, is no more *Lang*, as an enemy of literature, than the attempt to read, say, Virgil or Dante in their own tongues. And it is at least arguable that *some* exercise of that kind of effort and attention is specially needed in a School in which so much of the literature read seems (to the careless and insensitive) to be sufficiently interpreted by the current colloquial speech.

We have *second*: actual technical philology, and linguistic history. But this is confined to no period, and is concerned with all aspects of written or living speech at any time: with the barbarous forms of English that may be met today as much as with the refined forms that may be found a thousand years ago. It may be 'technical', as are all departments of our studies, but it is not incompatible with a love of literature, nor is the acquisition of its technique fatal to the sensibility either of critics or of authors. If it seems too much concerned with 'sounds', with the audible structure of words, it shares this interest with the poets. In any case this aspect of language and of the study of language is basic: one must know sounds before one can talk; one must know one's letters before one can read. And if philology seems most exercised in the older periods, that is because any historical enquiry must begin with the earliest available evidence. But there is also another reason, which leads to the *third* thing.

The *third* thing is the use of the findings of a special enquiry, not specially 'literary', for other and more literary purposes. Technical philology can serve the purposes of textual and literary criticism at all times. If it seems most exercised in the older periods, if the scholars who deal with them make most use of philology, that is because Philology rescued the surviving documents from oblivion and ignorance, and presented to lovers of poetry and history fragments of a noble past that without it would have remained for ever dead and dark. But it can also rescue many things that it is valuable to know from a past nearer than the Old English period. It seems strange that the use of it seems by some to be regarded as less 'literary' than the use of the evidence provided by other studies not directly concerned with literature or literary criticism; not only major matters such as the history of art and thought and religion, but even minor matters such as bibliography. Which is nearer akin to a poem, its metre or the paper on which it is printed? Which will bring more to life poetry, rhetoric, dramatic speech or even plain prose: some knowledge of the language, even of the pronunciation, of its period, or the typographical details of its printed form?

Medieval spelling remains just a dull department of *Lang*. Milton's spelling seems now to have become part of *Lit*. Almost the whole of the introduction in the *Everyman* edition of his poems, which is recommended to the students for our Preliminary, is devoted to it. But even if not all of those who deal with this facet of Milton criticism show an expert grasp of the history of English sounds and spelling, enquiry into his orthography and its relation to his metre remains just *Lang*, though it may be employed in the service of criticism.

Some divisions in our School are inevitable, because the very length of the history of English letters makes mastery all along the line difficult even to the widest sympathy and taste and a long life. These divisions should not be by *Lang* and *Lit* (one excluding the other); they should be primarily by period. All scholars should be to an adequate degree, within any period to which they are devoted, both *Lang* and *Lit*, that is both philologists and critics. We say in our Regulations that all candidates taking papers in English Literature (from *Beowulf* to A.D. 1900) 'will be expected to show such knowledge of the history of England as is necessary for the profitable study of the authors and periods which they offer'. And if the candidates, the teachers too, one may suppose. But if the history of England, which though profitable is more remote, why not the history of English?

No doubt this point of view is more widely understood than it once was, on both sides. But minds are still confused. Let us glance again at Chaucer, that old poet out in the No-man's land of debate. There was knifework, axe-work, out there between the barbed wire of *Lang* and *Lit* in days not so far back. When I was a young and enthusiastic examiner, to relieve the burden of my literary colleagues (at which they loudly groaned), I offered to set the Chaucer paper, or to help in reading the scripts. I was astonished at the heat and hostility with which I was refused. My fingers were dirty: I was *Lang*.

That hostility has now happily died down; there is some fraternization between the barbed wire. But it was that hostility which, in the reformed syllabus of the early thirties (still in essentials surviving), made necessary the prescription of *two* papers dealing with Chaucer and his chief contemporaries. *Lit* would not allow the greedy hands of *Lang* to soil the poet. *Lang* could not accept the flimsy and superficial papers set by *Lit*. But now, with the latest reform, or mild modification, that comes into force next year, once more Chaucer is presented in one common paper. Rightly, I should have said. But alas! What do we see? 'Candidates for Courses I and II[2] may be required to answer questions on language'!

Here we have hallowed in print this pernicious slang misuse. Not 'his language', or 'their language', or even 'the language of the period'; just 'language'. What in the name of scholarship, or poetry, or reason, can that here mean? It *should* mean, in English fit to appear in documents of the University of Oxford, that certain candidates may be asked questions of general linguistic import, without limitation of time or place, on a paper testing knowledge of the great poetry of the Fourteenth Century, under the general heading 'English Literature'. But since that is lunatic, one must suppose that something else is meant.

What kind of question can it mean which no candidate of Course III need ever touch? Is it wicked to enquire, in paper or *viva voce*, what here or there Chaucer really meant, by word or form, or idiom? Is metre and verse-technique of no concern to sensitive literary minds? Must nothing in any way related to Chaucer's medium of expression be ever allowed to disturb the cotton wool of poor Course III? Then why not add that only Course I and II may be required to answer questions that refer to history or politics, to astronomy, or to religion?

The logical result of this attitude, indeed its only rational expression, would be this direction: 'Courses I and II may be expected to show knowledge of Chaucer in the original; Course III will use a translation into contemporary English'. *But*, if this translation, as may well happen, should at any point be erroneous, this may *not* be mentioned. That would be 'language'.

I have once or twice, not so long ago, been asked to explain or defend this *language*: to say (I suppose) how it can possibly be profitable or enjoyable. As if I were some curious wizard with arcane knowledge, with a secret recipe that I was unwilling to divulge. To compare the less with the greater, is not that rather like asking an astronomer what he finds in mathematics? Or a theologian what is the interest of the textual criticism of Scripture? As in Andrew Lang's fable a missionary turned on a critic with the words: 'Did Paul know Greek?' Some members of our School would probably have said: 'Did Paul know language?'

I did not accept the challenge. I did not answer, for I knew no answer that would not appear uncivil. But I might have said: 'If you do not know any *language*, learn some – or try to. You should have done so long ago. The knowledge is not hidden. Grammar is for all (intelligent persons), though not all may rise to star-spangled grammar.[3] If you cannot learn, or find the stuff distasteful, then keep humbly quiet. You are a deaf man at a concert. Carry on with your biography of the composer, and do not bother about the noises that he makes!'

I have said enough, perhaps more than enough for this occasion. I must now get out of the chair and finally stand down. I have not made any effective *apologia pro consulatu meo*, for none is really possible. Probably my best act in it is the leaving of it – especially in handing it on to its elected occupant, Norman Davis. Already one of the chair-borne, he will know that in the cosy cushions, which legend furnishes for professorial seats, many thorns lurk among the stuffing. He can have those too, with my blessing.

If we consider what Merton College and what the Oxford School of English owes to the Antipodes, to the Southern Hemisphere, especially to scholars born in Australia and New Zealand, it may well be felt that it is only just that one of them should now ascend an Oxford chair of English. Indeed it may be thought that justice has been delayed since 1925. There are of course other lands under the Southern Cross. I was born in one; though I do not claim to be the most learned of those who have come hither from the far end of the Dark Continent. But I have the hatred of *apartheid* in my bones; and most of all I detest the segregation or separation of Language and Literature. I do not care which of them you think White.

But even as I step off – not quite the condemned criminal, I hope, that the phrase suggests – I cannot help recalling some of the salient moments in my academic past. The vastness of Joe Wright's dining-room table (when I sat alone at one end learning the elements of Greek philology from glinting glasses in the further gloom). The kindness of William Craigie to a jobless soldier in 1918. The privilege of knowing even the sunset of the days of Henry Bradley. My first glimpse of the unique and dominant figure of Charles Talbut Onions, darkly surveying me, a fledgling prentice in the Dictionary Room (fiddling with the slips for WAG and WALRUS and WAMPUM). Serving under the generous captaincy of George Gordon in Leeds. Seeing Henry Cecil Wyld wreck a table in the Cadena Café with the vigour of his representation of Finnish minstrels chanting the *Kalevala*. And of course many other moments, not forgotten if not mentioned; and many other men and women of the Studium Anglicanum: some dead, some venerable, some retired, some translated elsewhither, some yet young and very much with us still; but all (or nearly all – I cannot say fairer than that and remain honest) nearly all dear to my heart.

If then with understanding I contemplate this venerable foundation, I now myself *fród in ferðe*[4] am moved to exclaim:

> *Hwǽr cwóm mearh, hwǽr cwóm mago? Hwǽr cwóm*
> *máððumgyfa?*
> *Hwǽr cwóm symbla gesetu? Hwǽr sindon seledréamas?*
> *Éalá, beorht bune! Éalá, byrnwiga!*
> *Éalá, þéodnes þrym! Hú seo þrág gewát,*
> *genáp under niht-helm, swá heo nó wǽre!*

(Where is the horse gone, where the young rider? Where now the giver of gifts? Where are the seats at the feasting gone? Where are the merry sounds in the hall? Alas, the bright goblet! Alas, the knight and his hauberk! Alas, the glory of the king! How that hour has departed, dark under the shadow of night, as had it never been!)

But that is 'Language'.

> *Ai! laurië lantar lassi súrinen!*
> *Yéni únótimë ve rámar aldaron!*
> *Yéni ve lintë yuldar vánier –*[5]
> *Sí man i yulma nin enquantuva?*

(Alas! as gold fall the leaves in the wind!
Years innumerable as the wings of trees!
Years like swift draughts of wine have passed away –
Who now will fill again the cup for me?)

But that is 'Nonsense'.

In 1925, when I was untimely elevated to the *stól* of Anglo-Saxon, I was inclined to add:

> *Nearon nú cyningas ne cáseras*
> *ne goldgiefan swylce iú wǽron!*[6]

(There are not now any kings or emperors, nor any patrons giving gifts of gold, such as once there were!)

But now when I survey with eye or mind those who may be called my pupils (though rather in the sense 'the apples of my eyes'): those who have taught me much (not least *trawþe*, that is fidelity), who have gone on to a learning to which I have not attained; or when I see how many scholars could more than worthily have succeeded me; then I perceive with gladness that the *duguð* has not yet fallen by the wall, and the *dréam* is not yet silenced.[7]

NOTES

1 An alternative would be the provision, beside the ordinary Preliminary, of an English Honour Moderations, which would enable the abler or more ambitious to spend four years in reading. It would, I think, be less useful in the English School, the variety and scope of which is little exhibited or understood at earlier stages. Our need is rather to provide for those who first at a university discover what there is to know and do, and what are their true bents and talents. [The suggestion is that in addition to the Preliminary Examination (at that time taken after two terms' work) there should be, as an option, a sterner examination ('Honour Moderations', in which candidates would be classed) taken after two years: the whole course for such candidates thus taking four years. In the event, the ingenious decision was that all students reading English should take an examination called 'Honour Moderations' after *one* year, the whole course taking three years as before. – Ed.]

2 Courses I and II: options in the English School at Oxford allowing the student to concentrate on earlier periods. These courses, taken by relatively few, are largely *Lang*; while Course III, taken by the great majority, is very largely *Lit*. [Ed.]

3 'star-spangled grammar': the reference is to enquiry into the forms of words before the earliest records; in those studies the conventional practice is to place an asterisk before hypothetical, deduced forms. [Ed.]

4 *fród in ferðe*: having at heart the wisdom of experience.

5 *vánier* was the reading of the text of *Namárië* (Galadriel's lament in Lórien) in the first edition of *The Lord of the Rings*; it was changed to *avánier* for the second edition (1966). [Ed.]

6 These lines are from *The Seafarer*; the other Anglo-Saxon verses and references are from *The Wanderer*. [Ed.]

7 *duguð*: the noble company (in a king's hall). *dréam*: the sound of their glad voices and the music of their feasts.

GLEN COVE PUBLIC LIBRARY

3 1571 00065 0443

410 T
Tolkien, J. R. R   C.1
The monsters and the
  critics, and other
  essays

Glen Cove Public Library
Glen Cove, New York
Phone: OR 6-2130

230